THIS TRANSCENDING GOD

The Prayer and the Prologue of *The Cloud of Unknowing*,
MS. Harleian 674.

(Reproduced by courtesy of The British Museum)

THIS TRANSCENDING GOD

The Teaching of The Author of
"The Cloud of Unknowing"
by

CONSTANTINO SARMIENTO NIEVA

A.B., LL.B., S.T.D.
MEMBER, PHILIPPINE BAR

WITH FOREWORDS BY
BISHOP CHRISTOPHER BUTLER, O.S.B.
THE REV. GERVAIS DUMEIGE, S.J.
AND
PROFESSOR DAVID KNOWLES, O.S.B.

THE MITRE PRESS · LONDON
52 LINCOLN'S INN FIELDS, W.C.2.

TO MY LORD BISHOP
MONSIGNOR ALFREDO MA. OBVIAR, D.D.
BY WHOSE LEAVE THIS STUDY WAS
UNDERTAKEN

and

TO THE WHITE FATHERS OF AFRICA
UNDER WHOSE KINDLY ENGLISH ROOFS
"THIS WORK" WAS STARTED AND FINISHED

DIOCESE OF LUCENA
Lucena City, Philippines
3rd of May, 1969

Dear Father Nieva,
I wish to tell you how much I appreciate that you have dedicated to me your thesis "The Cloud of Unknowing".

Its publication is not only the reward for your long study, but I consider it also as an honour for our diocese. I feel very happy and proud, indeed, that one of our too few priests has had the courage to devote himself to the difficult task of studying a subject which has been neglected in the past. Through your efforts you have contributed to make known what was unknown and to put into light what was in darkness. You have revived the mystical doctrine of the "Cloud of Unknowing" and although the original book itself was written in the 14th century, you have shown that its teaching is still up to date in our time. The author's mysticism was based on the slogan of modern Theology "Back to the Bible", because his love for God consisted in meeting Him at the example of Moses' encounter with Yahweh who told him: "I am the God of your father, the God of Abraham, the God of Isaac and the God of Jacob" (Exodus 3:6).

Now that you have finished your difficult and painstaking work, I hope and pray that your book will be stimulating for many readers and that it will be an inspiration for them.

With my blessing, please accept, dear Father Nieva, the expression of my appreciation for the great work you have done.

Sincerely yours in Christ,

Alfredo Ma. Obviar, D.D.
Bishop of Lucena

v

TABLE OF CONTENTS

vii

CONTENTS (Cont.)

CONTENTS (Cont.)

CHAPTER V

The Cloud of Forgetting

CHAPTER VI

The Cloud of Unknowing

FOREWORD

By

His Lordship, B. C. BUTLER, O.S.B.

BISHOP OF NOVA BARBARA, AUXILIARY BISHOP OF WESTMINSTER

At a time when Christians, concerned to make the gospel effective in the life of the world to which Christ was sent, and to which he sent his Church, find themselves more and more involved in external activity, it is good that we should be recalled to the truth of the abiding necessity of the life of prayer not only for the salvation and sanctification of individual believers, but as the inspiration also of the Church's work in and for the world.

The writings of the anonymous author of *The Cloud of Unknowing* are classics of Christian religious literature. Directed mainly to a person or persons living the "contemplative life", they have much to teach those whose calling from God involves them in the turmoil of a more "active" existence. If this study of the great mediaeval teacher's thought serves to encourage the reading of his works and the practice of interior prayer, it will amply reward the devotion of the Philippine scholar-priest to whose industry we are indebted for it. The theological issues which it raises may in some cases be controversial, and Father Nieva is commendably humble in offering his own solutions. But the general reader will, perhaps, be less interested in these matters than in the teaching of the mediaeval author himself, and in the inspiration to be derived from his beautifully expressed instructions and reflections. These have helped many Christians in the centuries since they were first written down. May they continue to do so in our changed circumstances; for the truth of God is not subject to the vicissitudes of evolving history.

FOREWORD

By

THE REV. GERVAIS DUMEIGE, s.j.

DEAN, INSTITUTE OF SPIRITUALITY
PONTIFICAL GREGORIAN UNIVERSITY, ROME

Certain works have a curious history, among them *The Cloud of Unknowing,* one of the masterpieces of English mediaeval spirituality, which after six centuries still keeps both its secret and its fascination. It has been the object of several publications and studies in its country of origin, it was critically edited twenty-five years ago and more recently it tempted a Philippino to work patiently on it during the time of his studies in Europe. I am happy to present the results of this research, the work of Father Constantine Nieva, Doctor of Theology of the Gregorian University.

Theology nowadays gives rise to a certain anxiety. Some people are asking, "How can man talk to God if he cannot even talk about God?". Father Nieva's study shows that negative theology can yield a positive result, that the purification of language — accompanied by a purification of heart — can allow an encounter with God Whose nearness reveals itself as transcendence.

Who wrote *The Cloud of Unknowing?* The work remains anonymous, perhaps through the author's skill in concealment, or, I am inclined to think, because of his humility and detachment. Here Father Nieva gives his reasons for thinking Walter Hilton the most likely candidate for authorship. Although we have no name to go on, both *The Cloud* and the works which are incontestably linked with it present the spiritual portrait of a writer who thought it of small importance to say who he was when writing about Him Who is.

The Cloud of Unknowing presents a sufficient number of characteristic expressions, "this work", "the naked Being of God", "a deep ghostly sorrow" and others, to allow its teaching to be studied on a basis of strict vocabulary analysis. Here language-study sheds light on spirituality. In *The Cloud,* where

xiii

the affective prevails over the intellectual, the writer falls back on two fundamental categories of Christian existence, "God" and "sin". His spiritual path which involves so much stripping away brings him to find in all its purity Yahweh's mysterious affirmation about Himself, "I am who am".

Father Nieva's aim is to keep close to the work he has been studying and he has judged that the reality expressed in *The Cloud* would be best presented by letting the work speak for itself and refraining from a more modern version which would distort. Comparisons made with other spiritual masters who valued its symbolism are designed merely to give *The Cloud* its place in the line of mystical tradition. The result of this scrupulous approach is that a work designed for the spiritual progress of a mediaeval recluse opens even to our contemporary man an approach to God which is all the surer for respecting His mystery.

FOREWORD

By

PROFESSOR DAVID KNOWLES, o.s.b.

FORMER REGIUS PROFESSOR OF HISTORY, CAMBRIDGE

The spiritual writers known as the English medieval mystics have in the present century emerged from the neglect with which their countrymen had previously treated them. As a group they are unrivalled by any similar succession of writers in what was an epoch of mystical profusion, save for the line of the Rhineland tradition that ran from Eckhardt through Tauler to Ruysbroeck. They are four in number: Richard Rolle, the unknown author of *The Cloud of Unknowing*, Walter Hilton, and Dame Julian of Norwich. Of the four the most noteworthy, in the opinion of many, is the author of *The Cloud*. He is concerned with recording, guiding and analyzing the approach of the soul to contemplative or mystical prayer, that is, the ground covered by the prayer of loving attention and the prayer of supernatural recollection in the *Way of Perfection* of St. Teresa of Avila, and the third and fourth Mansions of the same saint's *Interior Castle*, both of which cover the transition from "meditation" to "contemplation" in the scheme of St. John of the Cross. *The Cloud* provides also instructions for "beginners" and a few glimpses of the life that is fully mystical. The reader cannot fail to be impressed by the clarity of thought, the theological firmness of outline, and the forceful and eloquent language which undoubtedly reflect a mind of distinction and a compelling personality, veiled in an anonymity which has resisted all attempts to penetrate its secret. Even after the revival of interest in these works, they were familiar only to devout readers and to scholars interested in Middle English literature, but some ten years ago an Italian theologian, Fr. Paul Molinari, S.J., published a penetrating study of Dame Julian. The writer of the present book, Fr. Constantino S. Nieva, a priest from the Philippine Republic, when seeking a subject for a doctoral thesis at the Gregorian University, was directed towards *The Cloud* by Fr. Molinari, and his dissertation, on which this

XV

book is based, was a study of the theological outlook of the unknown author.

While concerned principally with spiritual theology, he recognizes the psychological and human factors in the spiritual life. Moreover, he has studied the findings of such distinguished scholars as Evelyn Underhill, Dame Helen Gardner and Professor Phyllis Hodgson, who have discussed the language and background of *The Cloud*. But it is primarily a theological work, and the mystical life, and the life of grace of which the mystical life is part, cut across some of the most celebrated debates in the history of theology and the practice of spiritual direction. The author deals with these according to his judgment, with which not all will be in agreement. Similarly the dating of *The Cloud* and its relationship to *The Scale* of Hilton are matters of debate. It has even been suggested that Hilton was the author of *The Cloud,* and the author seems attracted by this opinion, which I myself do not favour. It is clearly both of interest and value that a scholar and a theologian from a culture of such different traditions to ours should, from a Roman college, look out upon an English mystic and the medieval scene of six hundred years ago. He may well notice some things and challenge others that have passed us by as familiar and commonplace.

ACKNOWLEDGMENTS

The author acknowledges with gratitude the permissions granted by the following publishers, authors, and editors, to quote from copyrighted material:

Bruce Publishing Company for the extracts from
J. Plastaras, *The God of Exodus,* © 1966.

Burns & Oates Ltd., for the extracts from
D. Jones, *The Minor Works of Walter Hilton.*
St. Thomas, *Summa Theologica.*
D. Knowles, *The English Mystical Tradition.*
J. McCann, *The Cloud of Unknowing,* 1947 edition.
J. McCann, *The Cloud of Unknowing,* The Golden Library Edition, 1964.
E. Allison-Peers, *The Complete Works of St. John of The Cross,* Three Volumes in one, 1964.

The Rev. Adrian Carey, for the information on the B.B.C. Programme on "The Cloud of Unknowing".

Geoffrey Chapman Ltd., for the extracts from *The Documents of Vatican II.*

Chatto & Windus, Ltd. for the extracts from
E. G. Gardner, *The Cell of Self-Knowledge.*

The Clarendon Press, Oxford, for the extracts from
H. Gardner, "Walter Hilton and the English Mystical Tradition", in *Essays and Studies,* Vol. XXII, 1937.
H. Gardner, "Walter Hilton and The Authorship of The Cloud", in *Review of English Studies,* 1933.

Constable & Co. Ltd., for the extracts from
C. Butler, *Western Mysticism.*

Darton, Longman & Todd, Ltd. for the extracts from
The Jerusalem Bible, © 1966, Darton, Longman & Todd and Doubleday & Company, Inc.
H. Farmer, *The Monk of Farne.*

Desclee Co. Inc. for the extracts from
W. Johnston, *The Mysticism of The Cloud of Unknowing.*

The Early English Text Society, Oxford, for the extracts from
P. Hodgson, *The Cloud of Unknowing*, 1958.
P. Hodgson, *Deonise Hid Diuinite*, 1958.

The Epworth Press, for the extracts from
T. W. Coleman, *English Mystics of the Fourteenth Century*.

Faber & Faber, Ltd. for the extracts from
"Richard of St. Victor", translated by C. Kirchberger.
The Goad of Love, Edited by C. Kirchberger.

H. Farmer, for the extracts from his work
The Monk of Farne, published in *Studia Anselmiana*.

Dame Helen Gardner, for a special permission to quote from her published works.

The Rev. Fr. Thomas Gilby, O.P. Director of Blackfriars Publications, for the extracts from
C. Pepler, *The English Religious Heritage*.
D. Callus, *The Condemnation of St. Thomas at Oxford*.

The Gregorian University Press, for the extracts from
A. Hughes, *Walter Hilton's Direction to Contemplatives*.

Harper & Row, Publishers, Inc., for the extracts from
C. Butler, *Western Mysticism*.

Professor Phyllis Hodgson, for a special permission to quote from her published works.

The Rev. Fr. Pascal Lefébure, O.P., Editor, for the extracts from
M. Noetingeer, "The Authorship of The Cloud", *Blackfriars*, April, 1924.
E. Colledge, "Recent Work on Walter Hilton", *Blackfriars*, June, 1956.

Longmans, Green & Co. Ltd. for the extract from
P. Molinari, *Julian of Norwich*.

Professor J. A. W. Bennett, Editor of *Medium Aevum*, for the extracts from
H. Gardner, "The Cloud of Unknowing", XVI, 1947.
H. Gardner, "The Text of The Scale". V, 1936.

Dr. F. J. Stopp, Editor, for the copyright material published in *The Modern Language Review*:
P. Hodgson, "Walter Hilton and The Cloud".

John Murray, for the extracts from
E. Colledge, *The Mediaeval Mystics of England*.

The Rev. Dom Daniel Rees, O.S.B. for the material published in *The Downside Review*:
D. Knowles, "The Excellence of The Cloud," January, 1931.
G. Sitwell, "Contemplation in The Scale", Summer, 1949.

Routledge & Kegan Paul, Ltd. for the extracts from
A. Poulain, *The Graces of Interior Prayer*.

The Society for Promoting Christian Knowledge, for the extracts from
Dionysius The Areopagite on The Divine Names and The Mystical Theology, edited by C. E. Rolt.
F. D. S. Darwin, *The English Mediaeval Recluse*.

The S. C. M. Press, for extracts from
M. Noth, *Exodus*.

The Editor of *Scripture,* for the extracts from
C.R.A. Cunliffe, "The Divine Names of Jahweh".
W. O'Rourke, "Moses and the Prophetic Vocation".

The Rev. Dom Alberic Stacpoole, O.S.B., Editor, for the copyright material published in *The Ampleforth Journal*:
J. McCann, "The Cloud of Unknowing".

Vincent Stuart and John M. Watkins, Ltd., for the extracts from
E. Underhill, *The Cloud of Unknowing*.
E. Underhill, *The Scale of Perfection*.

PREFACE

I made my first acquaintance with the English Mystics in a rather round-about way. When searching for a suitable subject for a dissertation, I had asked counsel of a Passionist Priest friend, Rev. Sylvan Rouse, C.P. I had been attracted to his own dissertation on the *Spirit of Understanding,* and I thought that perhaps a thesis on some aspect of the Third Person of the Blessed Trinity might prove a useful field of study. Fr. Sylvan suggested that the writings of some monastic author of the 12th or 13th century on the Holy Spirit could be an interesting and profitable endeavour. With this idea in mind I approached Rev. Fr. Paul Molinari, S.J., who was then one of the professors in our graduate courses. It was during this interview that Fr. Molinari asked me if I knew the English Mystics. I confessed to a complete ignorance of their existence or their writings.

While the possibility of doing my thesis on mystical writers proved daunting in the beginning, I thought it would be a good idea to read something about them. The fascination of this group of English spiritual writers grew as I came to know more about them through their writings. As the subject of the dissertation started to crystallize I became more and more impressed by Walter Hilton. Towards the end of the year, I decided to do my thesis on the work of Walter Hilton. At the same time I ruled out the possibility of a thesis on *The Cloud of Unknowing* because of the difficulties already apparent, even at so early a time. But what was originally intended did not materialize. Rev. Fr. Alfred C. Hughes had just successfully defended and published his thesis, *Walter Hilton's Direction to Contemplatives.* On the other hand, the prospect of using another year just to look for a subject for a thesis was not attractive. It was then that I decided to write my dissertation on *The Cloud of Unknowing.* However, the careful reading of *The Scale of Perfection* of Walter Hilton was not without value.

Now that "This Work" is completed I should like to proffer my thanks to the many people who contributed to this dissertation.

To my Mother, Sra. Elvira S. de Nieva, and my brother and sisters from half a world away in Boac, Marinduque, Philippines: Mr. and Mrs. Bernardo Jambalos, Jr.; Atty and Mrs. Guillermo S. Nieva; Mrs. Rosario N. Carrion; Mrs. Ester N. Seño; Mr. and Mrs. Conrado L. Luarca; Mr. and Mrs. Romulo Sto. Domingo; Dr. and Mrs. Rafael S. Ocampo.

Sincere thanks are likewise due to Reverend Fathers Patrick Fitzgerald, W.F., José Oñate, S.J.; The Most Honoured Brother Charles Henry, F.S.C.; Reverend Father Reginald Arliss, C.P.,* and Staff of the *Pontificio Colegio Filipino in Rome;* to Reverend Fathers Malcolm La Velle, C.P., James P. Moran, S.J., Sylvan Rouse, C.P., Bartley McFadden, C.S.C., Bernard Duffy, W.F., Tom Conway, W.F., David Cullen, W.F., and the Staff and Students of St. Edward's College, Broome Hall, and Rutherglen. Grateful thanks are also due to Mrs. Kathleen Fitzgerald, Miss Modesta Leonor and Mrs. Margaret McFadden.

I wish to acknowledge with sincere thanks the assistance of the following scholars who were very generous in sharing their knowledge in the field of the 14th-century spiritual writers: Rev. Fathers Paul Molinari, S.J., Conrad Pepler, O.P., Dom Gerard Sitwell, O.S.B., James Walsh, S.J., Edmund Colledge, O.S.A., Dr. Hugh Farmer, Rev. Peter Jolliffe, Professor Phyllis Hodgson, Dame Helen Gardner, Dr. Roger Lovatt, Dr. Joy Russell-Smith, Dr. Stanley Hussey. This list will not be complete without a mention of Rev. Fr. Kees van den Bosch, W.F., Rev. Fr. John Bernard, O.D.C., Mr. Thomas Gallivan, and the Staff of the British Museum, where it is a joy to work.

Most especially, very grateful thanks are due to Rev. Fr. Gervais Dumeige, S.J., who never wavered in the faith that "This Work" was possible, whose wisdom and vast learning steered the study through many a difficult way, and whose unfailing kindliness always inspired me to go on with the dissertation.

There are a host of other kind friends who made my stay in Europe a most enriching experience. The fact that they are not mentioned by name does not mean they are less important.

May *This Transcending God* "unto whom all hearts be open, and unto whom no privy thing is hid" be their blessing and reward.

C.S.N.

*Consecrated Bishop of Marbel, Cotabato, Philippines on February 24, 1970.

AUTHOR'S NOTE

For purposes of brevity, the treatises will be referred to in the course of this study simply as: *The Cloud, Privy Counsel, Epistle of Prayer, Discretion of Stirrings, Knowing of Spirits, Study of Wisdom, Denis Hid Divinity.* Professor Phyllis Hodgson has made a critical edition of all these writings. *The Cloud of Unknowing,* (E.E.T.S., 1958), contains *The Cloud* and *Privy Counsel. Deonise Hid Diuinite* (E.E.T.S., 1958) contains all the rest. For purposes of the dissertation, all references to the critical editions will be simply done in this manner: Hodgson, 138: 28, which means page 138 of the corresponding critical edition, line 28. All quotations will have cross-references to the corresponding texts of the critical edition of Professor Hodgson.

Quotations for *The Cloud* are taken from the Sixth Edition of Evelyn Underhill, John M. Watkins, 1956, and will be cited as *Underhill;* those for *Privy Counsel* are taken from the edition of Abbot Justin McCann, Golden Library Edition, 1964, and will be referred to as *McCann.* Quotations for *Denis Hid Divinity* are taken from the edition of Abbot McCann, *The Cloud of Unknowing,* Fifth Edition, 1947. Quotations for *Epistle of Prayer, Discretion of Stirrings, Knowing of Spirits, Study of Wisdom* are taken from the Anthology entitled *The Cell of Self-Knowledge,* edited by Edmund G. Gardner, 1910, and will be referred to as *Gardner.*

Quotations from Walter Hilton's *Scale of Perfection* are taken from the edition of Evelyn Underhill, 1948, and will be cited as *Scale I* or *II, Underhill.* Quotations from the other writings of Walter Hilton are taken from the *Minor Works of Walter Hilton,* edited by D. Jones, 1929, and will be referred to as *Jones.*

Quotations from Scripture are taken from the *Jerusalem Bible,* London, 1966. All quotations from A. Poulain *The Graces of Interior Prayer,* are taken from the 1957 edition, translated from the Sixth Edition by Leonora L. Yorke Smith and corrected to accord with the Tenth French Edition with an Introduction by J. V. Bainvel. All quotations from the works of St. John of the Cross are taken from the edition of E. Allison-Peers, Three-Vols.-In-One, 1964, and will be cited as

Allison-Peers. When a quotation from the works of St. John of the Cross or St. Teresa of Avila is taken from A. Poulain, *The Graces of Interior Prayer*, it will be expressly indicated. Quotations from C. Butler, *Western Mysticism*, are taken from The Grey Arrow Edition, 1960.

It is the opinion of Professor Hodgson that the Underhill translation of *The Cloud* "kept very close indeed to what I felt was the best of the early texts". Dr. Roger Lovatt of Peterhouse, Cambridge, is of the opinion that the "Underhill version is the best of the modern translations".

The present writer hopes that Professor Phyllis Hodgson would consider putting out an edition in modern English of all the treatises in *The Cloud* group based on her critical editions of the same. This hope has already been expressed by Dame Helen Gardner in "The Cloud of Unknowing", *Medium Aevum*, XVI, (1947), p. 42.

CHAPTER I

Introductory Matter

A. REASONS FOR THE PRESENT STUDY

The choice of title may bring a smile to those who read this work for is not God the *Alpha* and the *Omega*, the inspirer, sustainer and finisher of all our good works? That God Himself is the unifying factor of any dissertation perhaps need not be said, for is not God the principle of all being, the ruler of life and death and of all this world contains, both material and spiritual?

God is the unifying principle and pervading theme of this dissertation, but in one particular aspect—that of a way, an ascent to Him, and a final union in love—and this in the particular experience and teaching of a 14th-century English writer whose identity has so far resisted solution[1].

This particular way and ascent to God as taught by the author will be subjected to a theological scrutiny and appraisal. We shall examine whether, in the light of the traditional teaching of Holy Mother Church, the teaching of this 14th-century English writer can stand the test of the 20th century. For instead of looking forward to the future we have to go back some 600 years to examine the works of an author who chose to remain exceedingly obscure. *Cui bono*?

The need for such a theological appraisal has been felt and voiced by an eminent authority on the 14th-century English spiritual writers.

"On the personal and philological aspects of their writings much careful scholarship has been expended by a series of the ablest students of Middle English literature, but hitherto, save for the notable work of Father Molinari, s.j., on Julian of Norwich, the doctrinal and ascetical side of the English mystics has been left for treatment to those who have prepared editions of their works for the devout reader"[2].

This learned volume includes not only the unknown writer

---

1 H. Gardner, "Walter Hilton and the Authorship of The Cloud" *The Review of English Studies*, April 1933, p. 129.
2 D. Knowles, *The English Mystical Tradition*, p. viii; see also T. Merton, Introduction to W. Johnston, *The Mysticism of The Cloud of Unknowing*, pp. xii-xiii; C. Pepler, *The English Religious Heritage*, pp. 3-4.

1

we are considering in this dissertation but all the commonly known and described "English Mystics" of the 14th century. They are Richard Rolle, Walter Hilton, Julian of Norwich, Margery Kempe. Father Augustine Baker, who actually belongs to the 17th century, is also included. While a work with such a broad base and extent has given a profound insight into the works and the authors included in the study, there is the limitation that is understandably connected with a broadly-based work, namely, a not too detailed examination of the teaching of any one of them. The author is aware of this limitation and emphasizes that his work is intended as a guide for present day readers[3].

It is interesting to note the large number of books published these days on mysticism, at one time the patrimony of only a handful of contemplatives in monasteries. Mystical Theology is always difficult reading, and this awakening of interest in these quiet books could be indicative of a stirring of the profounder depths of the human spirit in this restless age of great scientific achievements.

Of more particular interest in this dissertation is the fact that *The Cloud* which is the most difficult of the spiritual writings in the 14th century, has gone through several editions in English and other languages. This is further incentive for undertaking a more thorough theological study of *The Cloud* and its attendant treatises[4]. No definitive stand has been taken on problems regarding *The Cloud*, and they are not few or irrelevant. For one *The Cloud* has been judged differently. One writer has placed the book in the category of "The Perfection of Christian Life" and the author has been described as "a master of the way of union"[5]. As regards the more particular theological interest and purpose of this dissertation, we shall show in the course of this study that *The Cloud* and *Privy Counsel* are writings of a mystical character, in the tradition of the *Mystics of the Divine Essence*. A basic des-

---

[3] D. Knowles, *The English Mystical Tradition*, p. viii.
[4] The continuing interest on *The Cloud* is likewise shown by a radio broadcast over BBC's Home Service on Sunday, August 29, 1965, from 8-8.30 p.m. Written by a Quaker, Jack Shepherd, it took the form of questions addressed by Mr. Shepherd to the anonymous author who purported to reply (always in words from the book itself).
[5] C. Pepler, *The English Religious Heritage*, p. 218.

cription of this tradition may be seen in the following statement of Fr. Poulain:

"The characteristic of the states of the *first group* consists in this, that it is *God Himself*, and God alone, who manifests Himself. We call them the *mystic union*, or, again, *mystical* (or infused) *contemplation* of the Divinity"[6].

The present writer prefers the phrase *contemplative penetration of the Divinity*. As regards the author of *The Cloud* we say that he was a mystic, a chosen soul whom God had touched with His Mystic Grace.

Then, too, how easy it is for anyone to find in any spiritual writing, and even in mystical writings, very close similarities to their particular experiences at certain times in the spiritual life. It would need little stretch of the imagination for people to believe that they had been touched by the mystic grace, simply because they found in certain writings a correspondence with their inner experience.

This fact is recognized by the author of *The Cloud*, and he is aware that there could be souls who would find consolation and comfort from reading *The Cloud*[7]. But he is most insistent that his teaching is not meant for everyone, but must be limited to the disciple, and to anyone whom the disciple thought had the kindred disposition, gifts and qualifications to profit from the message of *The Cloud*[8]. Twice he makes this point. This may be seen as a mere convention on the part of the author. However, it is not the case for the teachings are open to misunderstanding[9], and from the tone and insistence on the prohibition against circulation, we can see that

6 A. Poulain, *The Graces of Interior Prayer*, p. 52. This is distinguished fundamentally from the states of the *second group* which deal with such created objects as the Humanity of Christ, the Blessed Virgin, etc. The tradition of the *Mystics of the Divine Essence* is revealed in the writings of the continental mystics of the 13th and 14th centuries, and in particular in the writings of Eckhart. (Cf. F. Vandenbroucke, *The Spirituality of the Middle Ages*, 1968, pp. 362, 376 - 377, 384 - 386, 390, 392). Others do not rate *The Cloud* so highly. Cf. D. Knowles, *The English Mystical Tradition*, pp. 92, 191-192; also *English Mystics*, 1927, p. 102; J. Walsh, "The Cloud" in *The Month*, December 1963, p. 325; "The Cloud of Unknowing" in *Pre-Reformation English Spirituality*, p. 176; *A Letter of Private Direction*, p. 9.
7 *The Cloud*, Prologue, Underhill, p. 41; Hodgson, 3: 1-8.
8 Ibid. Prologue, Underhill, p. 39; Hodgson, 1: 14, 2: 1-8; Ch. 74, Underhill, p. 265; Hodgson, 130: 3-6.
9 P. Hodgson, *The Cloud of Unknowing* (E.E.T.S., 1958), Introduction, p. lii.

the author intended his admonition to be taken seriously. In *Privy Counsel*, he repeats and insists on the exclusiveness of his teaching.

"Ghostly friend in God: as touching thine inward occupation as me thinketh thee disposed, I speak at this time in special to thyself, and not to all those that this writing shall hear in general. For if I should write unto all, then must I write a thing that were according to all generally. But since at this time I shall write to thee in special, therefore I write none other thing but such as methinketh is most speedful and according to thy disposition only"[10].

The author makes it clear that the danger of misunderstanding is greater the nearer one approaches God.

"Beware of error here, I pray thee; for ever, the nearer men touch the truth, more wary men behoveth to be of error. I mean but well: if thou canst not conceive it, lay it by thy side till God come and teach thee. Do then so, and hurt thee not"[11].

If by outlining and discussing the nature and teaching of *The Cloud*, the tests by which one may know the presence of a special grace to make the teaching operative in his life, a reader could have some clear judgment of the workings of the Spirit in his case, then the labour put in this study will be more than rewarded. It is not intended by this study to discourage those for whom the particular teaching of *The Cloud* is not meant from going on with their reading if they find comfort and consolation for their spiritual life. The danger is that such a reader may think that he is called to a more special work through a feeling of affinity with the teachings.

These then are the controlling motives for undertaking this study, and it is not proposed to pass judgment on whatever has been written so far on *The Cloud* and other treatises.

B.   THE SCOPE AND EXTENT OF THE PRESENT STUDY

This dissertation will include all the works commonly attributed to the author of *The Cloud*. These are: *The Cloud of Unknowing, The Book of Privy Counselling, The Epistle of Prayer, The Epistle of Discretion of Stirrings, Of Knowing of Spirits, The Study of Wisdom, Denis Hid Divinity*.

A very learned and scholarly study of the phonology,

---

10 *Privy Counsel*, Prologue, McCann, p. 105; Hodgson, 135: 1-7.
11 *The Cloud*, Ch. 34, Underhill, p. 154; Hodgson, 69: 17-20.

grammar and vocabulary of the seven treatises has shown
the homogeneity of the seven works[12]. This critical edition of
all seven treatises is the last word on the matter of texts, and
on the textual level it leaves nothing to be desired.

1. THEOLOGICAL UNITY OF THE SEVEN TREATISES

In addition to the arguments for the homogeneity of the
seven treatises based on philological grounds, the present
dissertation calls attention to the theological unity of the
writings. In *Privy Counsel* the author specifically mentions his
three other works, which makes it certain that four treatises
are by the same author[13], namely, *The Cloud, Epistle of
Prayer, Denis Hid Divinity*. And when he treats of Benjamin
and his mother Rachel, regarding the primacy of the will and
love over the intellect in the act of contemplation, he is referring to *The Study of Wisdom*, which is a free paraphrase of
Benjamin Minor of Richard of St. Victor[14]. *Discretion of
Stirrings* has a lovely description of God which brings down
the heavily metaphysical God of *The Cloud* to the level of
practical spiritual exercises. *Knowing of Spirits* describes the
state of soul of the disciple very similar to that of the travail
in *The Cloud* and *Privy Counsel*, which in turn is very reminiscent of *The Four Degrees of Passionate Love* of Richard
of St. Victor. There is likewise the lengthy discussion of the
Sacrament of Penance which is a personal addition of the
author to the Sermons of St. Bernard. It is tempting to think
that it is in this section that the author expounds in detail on
the note of Confession as regards "This Work".

The present writer sees in this theological unity a suggestion
that *The Cloud* and *Privy Counsel* were written at approxi-
mately the same time. Regarding *Privy Counsel*, it has been
observed that ". . . This epistle is undoubtedly the work of a
man 'consummatus' in age as well as in wisdom. The style
has no longer the alertness which makes *The Cloud* so lively,
and the thought itself seems sometimes to be growing dim,
with a tendency to repetition"[15]. Professor Knowles acknow-

---

12 P. Hodgson, *Deonise Hid Diuinite* (E.E.T.S. 1958), p. lvii; E. Underhill,
   The Cloud, pp. 6, 9, 29.
13 *Privy Counsel*, McCann, p. 124; Hodgson, 154: 13-18.
14 Ibid. McCann, p. 120; Hodgson, 150: 10-23.
15 M. Noetinger, "The Authorship of The Cloud", *Blackfriars*, March
   1924, p. 1458.

ledges and admits the continuity of doctrine between *The Cloud* and *Privy Counsel* with this qualification, however.

> "Of the original works the *Book of Privy Counselling* is a continuation and companion of *The Cloud*, written considerably later and containing, both in style and matter, some of the writer's most mature and admirable work, while the *Epistles* are shorter pieces bearing on the same themes and using the same ideas and expressions"[16].

We disagree with the observations of these important scholars and submit that *The Cloud* and *Privy Counsel* are letters of spiritual direction on a very specialized matter of the spiritual life, which would brook no delay. *The Cloud* author is telling his disciple just what to do, to follow a definite course of action and a pattern of life, not just something literary to be examined and commented upon for intellectual delight. The author cautions his disciple that the teaching is open to misunderstanding. The whole tone of the *Privy Counsel* gives the impression that the disciple had already seen the difficulties in *The Cloud* teaching for which he asks some clarification. The author explicitly invites his disciple to write and make inquiry if there should be need.

> "And if thee think that there be any matter therein that thou wouldest have more opened than it is, let me wit which it is, and thy conceit thereupon; and at my simple cunning it shall be amended if I can"[17].

The burden of the message of *Privy Counsel* is on the translation of the teaching of *The Cloud* to the practical level of prayer life, as well as on the seeming downgrading of the intellect in *The Cloud*. Right at the start of *Privy Counsel* we have a synthesis of the prayer of *The Cloud*, as well as the *naked intent* in the consideration of God only as IS.

> "And look that nothing remain in thy working mind but a naked intent stretching unto God, not clothed in any special thought

---

[16] D. Knowles, *The English Mystical Tradition*, p. 67. Professor Hodgson is content to say this: "It is reasonable to suppose that *The Cloud* is the earliest of the extant works, that the translation followed soon after in date, and *The Book of Privy Counselling* is the latest." (*The Cloud of Unknowing*, E.E.T.S., 1958, Introduction, p. lxxviii). She is therefore noncommittal as to the lapse of time intervening between *The Cloud* and *Privy Counsel*.

[17] *The Cloud*, Ch. 74, Underhill, pp. 265-266; Hodgson, 130: 14-17.

of God, in himself, how he is in himself, or in any of his works, but only that he is as he is"[18].

This development continues in great detail in *Privy Counsel* till what was before in the order of speculation or theory in *The Cloud* is now translated into the prayer life of the disciple as an *offering*.

"Look up then lightly and say to thy Lord, either with mouth or meaning of heart: 'That that I am, Lord, offer unto Thee; for Thou it art'. And think nakedly, plainly, and boisterously, that thou art as thou art, without any manner of curiosity"[19].

We see in the above passage an intimation of the "being of man" which is a definite progression in the treatment of *The Cloud* exercise, and which will be the major concern of *Privy Counsel*. In insisting that the intellect is not downgraded in *The Cloud* the tone of the author is one of impatience, which cannot be present if *Privy Counsel* were written at a much later date than *The Cloud*.

"How oft have ye read and heard, and of how many both holy, wise, and true, that as soon as Benjamin was born his mother Rachel died? . . . And if ye believe it, how dare ye then ransack and seek within your reason in the words and the deeds of Benjamin?"[20].

The main ideas of *The Cloud* are developed more fully in *Privy Counsel*. More concrete instruction is given as to how to stand firmly in the *travail* that must be undergone, and this *travail* is further described in the sense of actual pain with reference to intensity. The tests whereby one may know the presence of special grace are made more descriptive and specific. This continuity of message and teaching will be seen in greater clarity when the texts of *Privy Counsel* are compared with *The Cloud*.

This writer is of the opinion that the author could not have been a young person when he wrote *The Cloud*, for the disciple was already twenty-four years old[21]. We are also of the opinion that *Privy Counsel* was written soon after *The Cloud*. This being so, the objection based on the supposition that *Privy*

---

[18] *Privy Counsel*, McCann, p. 105; Hodgson, 135: 19-22.
[19] Ibid. McCann, p. 107; Hodgson, 136: 30, 137: 1-3.
[20] Ibid. McCann, p. 120; Hodgson, 150: 10-19.
[21] *The Cloud*, Ch. 4, Underhill, p. 69; Hodgson, 20: 19.

Counsel was written much later than *The Cloud* does not seem insuperable.

> "If we suppose that Hilton wrote *The Cloud* and this *Epistle*, then we are bound to conclude that he wrote the *Scale of Perfection*, the *Song of Angels*, etc., later on, that is, in extreme old age. And this does not seem very credible"[22].

This difficulty based on chronology has also been noted. ". . . and I feel, as I felt then, the difficulty of a satisfactory chronology, if we accept Hilton's claim"[23]. But if *Privy Counsel* were written soon after *The Cloud*, when the author was relatively young, there can be no difficulty in the known works of Hilton coming after *Privy Counsel*. At this stage, we wish to call attention to the opinion of Professor Gardner bearing on this point.

> "*The Cloud* is a work of genius; *The Scale*, though beautiful, is not. But might not the change in tone and temper be a parallel to the change of mind which led Hilton from a solitary's cell to the unheroic life of an Austin Canon? The unoriginality of *The Scale* compared with *The Cloud* might be a consequence of such a withdrawal from 'Singular Living' "[24].

2. *THE POPULARITY OF* THE CLOUD OF UNKNOWING

The reawakening of interest in the spiritual writings of the 14th century on such a specialized subject as the higher reaches of the spiritual life brings to mind the question of their popularity when they first appeared. This study is limited to the question of *The Cloud*. It has been said that copies of *The Cloud* "walked up and down at deer rates"[25]. This observation seems borne out by the number of extant manuscripts and "judging from their distant relationship to each other, the seventeen extant manuscripts must represent only a very small proportion of the total number of transcriptions"[26]. But not everyone agrees.

22 M. Noetinger, "The Authorship of The Cloud", *Blackfriars*, March 1924, p. 1459.
23 H. Gardner, "The Cloud of Unknowing", *Medium Aevum*, XVI (1947) p. 41.
24 Ibid. See also "Walter Hilton and the Mystical Tradition in England", *Essays and Studies* XXII (1937), pp. 108-110.
25 D. McIntyre, "The Cloud of Unknowing", *Expositor*, 7th Series, October 1907, p. 373.
26 H. Gardner, quoting Professor Hodgson in "The Cloud of Unknowing", *Medium Aevum*, XVI (1947), p. 37.

"I have never felt any confidence in this 'old writer', who has been quoted again and again by writers on *The Cloud*, and feel that, until the source of Mr. M'Intyre's quotation is discovered, his picturesque but cryptic remark had better be ignored[27].

As regards the arguments drawn from the number of extant manuscripts, we hear the same dissenting voice.

"This is not a safe argument in view of the constant modernization, interpolation, and contamination which Dr. Hodgson herself has described. No doubt a good many manuscripts have been lost, but the number extant is so markedly fewer than in the case of comparable works, that we may suspect that *The Cloud* did not have the immediate popularity or wide distribution of Hilton's *Scale of Perfection*, or of the most popular works of Rolle"[28].

The popularity or otherwise of *The Cloud* is irrelevant to the teaching for the author himself insisted on the exclusiveness of the teaching and gave serious injunction against its free circulation. That the writing actually received a wide circulation despite these strong prohibitions is a tribute to the value of *The Cloud*, for lesser stuff could not have stood the test of time. We are therefore inclined to the view that *The Cloud*, when it did finally circulate freely, was popular among religious circles[29].

3. *THE ORDERLY TREATMENT OF THE TEACHING OF*
    THE CLOUD.

Even at this early stage, one gets an idea that the area within which *The Cloud* matter moves is in the higher reaches of the spiritual life. A very common characteristic of writings of this kind is the seeming lack of order in the exposition and treatment of the matter. One not conversant with literature of this kind can easily get the impression that the writer is running all over the field, that he has many after-thoughts and second thoughts. Perhaps the difficulty stems more from the

27 Ibid.
28 Ibid. "I believe that discussion of the authorship should begin with the recognition that *The Cloud* was written for a special kind of person, and that the author's warning in the prologue, repeated emphatically in the last chapter, that the work should be kept close, was very seriously meant. The points made above all suggest that the warning was seriously taken and that the distribution of *The Cloud* was restricted." (Ibid. p. 38.)
29 D. Knowles, "The Excellence of The Cloud", *Downside Review*, January 1934, p. 71.

fact that a few readings do not suffice to give a clear understanding of works such as these, so that what we see as a lack
of order in the writings could be better described as a difficulty in understanding on our part. That this is so in *The
Cloud* is made explicit by the author. Repeated readings are
necessary and one must not jump to hurried conclusions. This
is a source of misunderstandings and deceits.

> "And therefore read over twice or thrice; and ever the ofter the
> better, and the more thou shalt conceive thereof. Insomuch, per-
> adventure, that some sentence that was full hard to thee at the
> first or the second reading, soon after thou shalt think it
> easy. . . . And if thou shalt let any such men see it, then I pray
> thee that thou bid them take them time to look it all over. For
> peradventure there is some matter therein in the beginning, or in
> the midst, the which is hanging and not fully declared there as
> it standeth. But if it be not there, it is soon after, or else in the
> end. And thus if a man saw one part and not another, peradven-
> ture he should lightly be led into error: and therefore I pray thee
> to work as I say thee"[30].

The present writer is of the opinion that *The Cloud* author
has a definite pattern of development. The texts reveal a
certain scheme that the author maintains. We notice right at
the Prologue the main themes which *The Cloud* will treat of,
namely, the part of God, the part of the soul, the difficulties
and the travail involved, and the state of life wherein the particular exercise can be performed. The author intimates the
nature of the exercise by using the expression "ghostly", which
will be developed at great length in the text. In the Prologue,
too, the author gives a broad sweep of the whole treatise by
citing the number of chapters and saying that the last chapter
deals with the tests by which the presence of special grace
can be known and verified.

We see the development of *The Cloud* in three successive
waves. The main themes have been enunciated in the Prologue,
and these are developed in some detail in Chapters 1 and 2 till
a height is reached in Chapter 4 with the figure of the "sparkle
from the coal"[31]. The rate of development drops, and subsidiary ideas closely connected with the matter of *The Cloud*
are developed. This continues in detail till the development

---

[30] *The Cloud*, Ch. 74, Underhill, pp. 264-265; Hodgson 129: 18-25, 130:
1-13.
[31] Ibid. Ch. 4, Underhill, p. 71.

reaches another height in Chapter 26 with the figure of "piercing this cloud of unknowing"[32]. Then, starting with Chapter 27, *The Cloud* enunciates explicitly that certain matters will be discussed [33]. These main ideas are developed in the succeeding chapters together with new details as regards the leading themes already introduced in the previous chapters. This development reaches a new height in Chapter 69 with the figure of the "cloud of unknowing" now being identified with the "nought" of the exercise[34]. The "cloud of unknowing" is the end and term of the teaching. The succeeding chapters till the end are developments of themes already connected with "the cloud" theme, but the rate has already dropped.

The author follows still another line of development that is quite logical and easy to follow. He has a predilection for ending chapters with a particular subject which he follows up in the next chapter. This is continued for several chapters if the matter needs further elucidation. Chapter 62, for example, ends with a note on the powers of the soul. Chapter 63 immediately follows with the analysis of the powers of the soul, and this continues on till Chapter 67.

The present writer is of the opinion that *The Cloud* clearly demonstrates an order of development as well as a unity of message that is remarkably clear and concise. There is, too, that economy of description, with an accompanying precision and accuracy, which is the hall mark of an experience faithfully narrated.

4. *THE GENUS LITTERARIUM OF* THE CLOUD *GROUP*

It helps very much to know the mind of a writer, as this gives us some idea as to the intent and purpose of his writings. In this we can be aided by seeing exactly to what class of writings they belong. This we intend to do in this section so that we may have a clearer grasp of the mind of *The Cloud* author.

The Cloud of Unknowing is called by the author "A Book of Contemplation". It is really a treatise in spiritual theology, although it is written in the form of a letter addressed to a

---

[32] Ibid. Ch. 26, Underhill, p. 140.
[33] Ibid. Ch. 27, Underhill, p. 141.
[34] Ibid. Ch. 69, Underhill, p. 253.

particular "ghostly friend". *The Book of Privy Counselling* is
a letter addressed to a "ghostly friend" with the purpose of
making clear some specialized ideas of *The Cloud*. We are
of the opinion that the addressee of this letter is the same as
that of *The Cloud*. *The Epistle of Prayer* is another letter on
matters "touching thine asking of me, how thou shalt rule
thine heart in the time of thy prayer . . ."[35]. *The Epistle of
Discretion of Stirrings* is also a letter addressed to a "ghostly
friend in God" on matters relative to some spiritual exercises.
Knowing of Spirits is called by the author "A Devout Treatise
of Discerning of Spirits, Very Necessary for Ghostly Livers"[36].
While it does not have the personal tone of the other letters,
it nevertheless treats of a particular point of the spiritual life
which further explains teachings already mentioned in *The
Cloud* and *Privy Counsel*. *The Study of Wisdom* is a free and
running paraphrase of the *Benjamin Minor* of Richard of St.
Victor, done with a set purpose and with a completion and a
finish of an original tract. *Denis Hid Divinity* is a close paraphrase of the Pseudo-Dionysius' *Mystica Theologia*. In this
paraphrase the author says he is following the version of
Thomas Gallus, Abbot of Vercelli. As the texts reveal, the
version of Sarracenus was also used[37]. With the exception of
The Study of Wisdom and *Denis Hid Divinity,* all the other
five writings have the tone of letters, despite their being
differently entitled.

It is interesting to note that this particular director of souls
should carry on his spiritual direction by letter, when the more
usual way was to conduct them by oral communication. When
we consider the very specialized subject matter of *The Cloud*
and *Privy Counsel,* and the ease with which it can be misunderstood, this fact of writing letters of spiritual direction
acquires important proportions. Could it be that the author
and his disciple were unable to meet? We know that Margery
Kempe visited Mother Julian of Norwich in her anchorhold,
and that she also visited her director, a Dominican anchorite.
Another spiritual director who conducted spiritual direction by
letter was Walter Hilton.

35 *Epistle of Prayer,* Gardner, p. 77; Hodgson, 48 : 1-2.
36 *Knowing of Spirits,* Gardner, p. 119. See Hodgson *Deonise Hid
   Diuinite* (E.E.T.S. 1958), p. 80, note 1.
37 J. McCann, *The Cloud of Unknowing* (1947), pp. 130-149.

5. THE CLOUD *AS THE FOCAL POINT OF THIS STUDY*

Of the seven tracts we are considering *The Cloud* will be the focal point of inquiry. It is in reference to *The Cloud* that the other writings will revolve as satellites. Needless to say, of the seven writings *The Cloud* is the major one. A recent study on *The Cloud* and other writings makes *Privy Counsel* the more central point of discussion, and the passages which are considered mystical are those of *Privy Counsel*[38]. *The Cloud* presents a particular method of attaining union with God in this life. It alone presents a doctrine seen as a cohesive whole, fully developed in the way that the author knew and experienced. The other writings supplement and explain, though they are not really necessary for the completion of doctrine and teaching of *The Cloud*. It alone is sufficient, and on the strength of it the disciple could have had enough initiation and guidance to carry out the behests of the teaching. The disciple could continue from the teaching, and God could teach him the rest much better than the author himself could hope to do. The guide-posts in *The Cloud* are clear and precise enough. But the same cannot be said of *Privy Counsel* and the other treatises. The passages considered mystical in these other writings take on their particular meaning and shade only in the light shed on them by *The Cloud*. It is by their association with the dominant themes of *The Cloud* that their meanings are heightened and particularized. Without this association they could well be snatches from essays on the higher reaches of the spiritual life, without being exactly mystical. Another difficulty also stands in the way. It has not been proven yet that all the four letters were written to the same disciple. This is significant since the author stresses the fact of a *special grace* and a *call* from God to do "This Work". The author says that he and the disciple possess this *special grace*. To stress the mystical element of passages in these other writings independently of *The Cloud* would be to multiply the disciples who were the recipients of this *special grace*. Needless to say the passages in these other writings considered as mystical are neither numerous nor comprehensive enough to stand a searching scrutiny. To recapitulate, *The Cloud of*

[38] W. Johnston, *The Mysticism of The Cloud of Unknowing*, pp. 249-255

Unknowing can stand on its own independently of the other writings. This cannot be said of the other writings.

C.   METHOD OF APPROACH TO THE TEACHINGS OF
THE CLOUD

It is the teaching of this 14th-century English author that we present to our readers in this study. There is a variety of ways of doing this. There is the possibility of digesting and synthesizing the teachings under study, and the content of the writings becomes, as it were, refracted through the mind of the expositor. This has the advantage of ease in understanding, for the expositor should have already subjected the text to close scrutiny and study. This particular approach would be useful in producing a relatively short work. The other possibility would be to cite the texts and let the author speak for himself, with the expositor keeping his interpretation down to a minimum. This could result in a work that would be unduly long and tedious, and many might be deterred from even starting such a tome.

This dissertation hopes to take advantage of the benefits of both methods, and reduce to a minimum their disagreeable features. Hence, the complete assimilation of doctrine and teaching to such a point that the teaching is almost exclusively refracted through the expositor's mind is not used here. Neither will merely a narration of texts be employed. Rather, *The Cloud* author will have to speak for himself, and the commentary will be done in such a way that the doctrine is that of the author, and the understanding of it that which is most supported by the texts themselves. This was the method followed by Abbot Cuthbert Butler in his classical work *Western Mysticism*[39] as well as by Professor David Knowles[40]. This was also the manner of presentation employed by Fr. Poulain which he describes as that of the *descriptive school*[41]. The present writer shares the view that "mystical science is not yet complete and that the time for a definite synthesis has not yet come"[42]. This is the service of the *descriptive*

---

[39] C. Butler, *Western Mysticism*, p. 5
[40] D. Knowles, *The English Mystical Tradition*, p. 77.
[41] A. Poulain, *The Graces of Interior Prayer*, p. xi.
[42] J. V. Bainvel, Introduction to A. Poulain, *The Graces of Interior Prayer*, p. cx.

method that we hope the analysis and synthesis of the teaching of *The Cloud* will perform. This has another advantage. Because of the varying commentaries that have been made on *The Cloud* and other treatises[43], this method will prevent the study becoming polemical. For the main purpose of this dissertation is the exposition precisely of what it is that *The Cloud* and other treatises teach. References to other writings will be kept at a minimum to prevent the study from becoming involved and complicated.

This work does not expect to bring to light all the depth of meaning hidden in the texts of *The Cloud* and other writings. Hence, while brevity of citations is a great virtue, in some places quotations from the texts have been made longer to put them in bolder relief. It is hoped that by this way some future student of *The Cloud* group will find citations in a wider setting of their immediate context.

The Mysticism of The Cloud of Unknowing is a recent book by Fr. William Johnston of the Society of Jesus, and deserves detailed attention. Its principal purpose seems to be a correlation of the Japanese philosophy of Zen Buddhism to the teaching of *The Cloud,* and the present writer is not competent to judge the merits of the book on this ground.

The title of the book presupposes that it is a fact that *The Cloud* is a writing invested with a mystical character. However, this is not a commonly admitted fact as previously pointed out [44]. Fr. Johnston seems to have overlooked the fact that there are two dominant schools of Mystical Theology, represented generally by the Jesuits and the Dominicans. The book says that the mysticism of *The Cloud* is Trinitarian: "Here it is radically different from the mysticism of any other religion; here it is truly Trinitarian"[45]. As proof of this asser-

---

43 H. V. H. Elwin, *Christian Dhyana,* London, 1930. This is a study of *The Cloud* from the viewpoint of Indian Philosophy. I. Progoff, *The Cloud of Unknowing,* London, 1959. This study sees the relation of *The Cloud* to modern psychology as well as to Oriental Philosophies. G. Hort, *Sense and Thought,* London, 1936. This study sees the phenomenon of "the cloud" in a material sense and in relation to modern depth psychology. W. Johnston, *The Mysticism of The Cloud of Unknowing,* New York, 1967. This commentary sees much of the Japanese Philosophy of Zen Buddhism in *The Cloud.* See also: C. Pepler, *The English Religious Heritage,* pp. 226-229.
44 See footnote 6, p.3.
45 W. Johnston, *The Mysticism of The Cloud,* p. 236.

tion, Fr. Johnston writes: "Its specific features are that its 'ground' is faith, its motivation is the blind stirring of love, and its object is the Blessed Trinity: 'God that *made* thee and *bought* thee, and graciously *called* thee to *His* love' "[46]. The present writer is of the opinion that the invocation of the Trinity is not enough to classify a writing as *Trinitarian* mysticism. Against the background of this categorical statement, Fr. Johnston later on vacillates: "While the author claims that his fleshly blabbering tongue can give no details of this experience, all the indications are that his mysticism, if Trinitarian, is not that of the person who looks at a picture from outside; rather is it an experience of the Blessed Trinity from within"[47]. This *Trinitarian* aspect is explained further in the background of the Incarnation and the Redemption[48]. It is the opinion of the present writer that this attempt to see the *Trinitarian* aspect in this light is not sufficient to distinguish the *unitive* offering of which the book speaks from that of the sacrifices and tremendous love of God shown by the Martyrs, Confessors, Virgins, Doctors, Pontiffs, Apostles and other Saints of the Church whose love for God is so intense and so complete as this life would allow it, but whom the Church has not specifically described as "mystics". The present writer also wishes to call attention to the opinion of Fr. L. Reypens on the matter of the *mysticism* of the 14th-century English Spiritual writers:

"Concerning the English mystics of the 14th century, we must say that their experience is limited to the vision through assimilation of love, with the stress on the affective element. A mysticism which is formally Trinitarian does not present itself among them"[49].

Fr. Johnston is of the opinion that the ". . . English writer's doctrine leads to a form of prayer that is no more than an intensification of the ordinary Christian life"[50]. Against this view we have the statement of Fr. Poulain to the effect that "a supernatural state should not be described as mystic if it

---

46 Ibid. p.265.
47 Ibid. p. 249.
48 Ibid. pp. 238-242.
49 L. Reypens, "Connaissance Mystique de Dieu", *Dictionnaire de Spiritualité*, III, Col. 887, last paragraph (free translation).
50 W. Johnston, *The Mysticism of The Cloud*, p. 257; also pp. 259, 28, 88, 93, 110, 113, 140-141, 180, 242.

differs only in *intensity* or in duration from that which anyone can produce at will"[51]. Fr. Johnston is not precise in the meanings which he gives to terms which have already acquired classical meanings in Mystical Theology. Hence his notions of *passivity*[52], *ordinary* and *extraordinary*[53] are not consistent with the accepted meanings of the terms. Rather, the new meanings that he gives to the terms can add to the confusion and misunderstandings already present in such a difficult matter as Mystical Theology.

And as the author of *The Cloud* would say: "But forth of our matter".

D. THE FOURTEENTH CENTURY SPIRITUAL WRITERS IN ENGLAND AND THE CONTINENT

"The wind blows wherever it pleases"[54]. This passage best describes the mysterious ways of the Spirit of God. There was much commerce going on between England and the Netherlands, since the main outlet for the English wool was into the ports of the Low Countries. The region of Norwich is right in the direct route of ships plying between England and Flanders. It is very interesting to note the geographical propinquity of the English and Flemish spiritual writers as well as the Rhineland writers. The question then has been raised as to the possibility of influence on the English spiritual writers by the Flemish and perhaps also by the Rhineland spiritual writers. For all over Europe we see a sudden flowering of these writers[55]. It is this contemporaneous flowering of mystical and spiritual writings, already predominantly in the vernacular, that gave rise to the question of influence on one side of the North Sea by the other. The influence of the

---

51 A. Poulain, *The Graces of Interior Prayer*, p. 2.
52 W. Johnston, *The Mysticism of the Cloud*, pp. 40, 176, 179-180, 192, 236, 248, 259.
53 Ibid. pp. 264-265; see also, pp. 12-13, 93, 176-177, 261-262.
54 John 3: 8.
55 We have the following writers of the 14th century in continental Europe: Guigue de Pont, a Carthusian (died 1297), Angela of Foligno (died 1309), both of whom wrote in Latin; Eckhart (died. c. 1327), who wrote in Latin and German; and the following who wrote in the vernacular: Mechtilde of Hackeborn (died 1298), Jean de Cologne (died c. 1320), Tauler (died 1361), Suso (died 1361), Gerald Appelmans (died c. 1350), Catherine of Siena (died 1327), Jean van Leeuwen (died 1378), Ruysbroek (died 1381). Gerlac Peters (died 1411). See *Dictionnaire de Spiritualité*, III, Cols. 901-910.

continental writers on the English writers has been dealt with by a scholar on the English writers of the 14th century[56].

As regards the general condition of the times in England and the Continent, the 14th century saw the Hundred Years War, The Black Death, the strained relations between the Court of England and the Holy See and, of course, the Great Schism (1378-1420)[57].

But in the midst of the disturbed conditions of the times there were some who led a peaceful and undisturbed life, quietly enjoying their communion with God. In England, the 14th century enclosed the group of four writers in the vernacular, namely, Richard Rolle, Walter Hilton, *The Cloud* author, and Mother Julian.

Richard Rolle is best known for his tender love and devotion to the Holy Name of Jesus. He was born about 1300 at Thornton, a village two and a half miles East of Pickering. He spent a short time at Oxford but soon returned to his home to become a hermit[58].

Walter Hilton is best known for his major work *The Scale*

[56] D. Knowles, *The English Mystical Tradition*, p. 38. Dr. Roger Lovatt of Peterhouse, Cambridge, has very kindly given permission to quote his unpublished opinions on the subject of the relationships of the Continental mystics and the English spiritual writers of the 14th century. "My own work is limited to the mystical writers of northern Europe, as you know, and could be put thus—there is no evidence that the works of Eckhart or Tauler were known in medieval England. Suso's *Horologium Sapientiae* was certainly in England by 1393, and probably arrived c. 1380. The first mention of Suso's *Horologium* in England occurs in a will dated 1393; see T. P. Wadley, *Notes . . . of the Wills . . . contained . . . in the Great Orphan Book and Book of Wills* (Bristol and Gloucs. Archaeological Soc., 1886) pp. 35-6. But this is probably a text of the English version, which would mean that the original Latin version must have entered the country some years previously. Ruysbroek's *De Gheestelike Brulocht* (The *Spiritual Marriage*) was in England, in Groot's Latin translation, by 1419, and possibly c. 1390; his short treatise *Vanden Blinckenden Steen* (*The Shining Stone*) had reached England, also in Latin translation, by c. 1450. The author of the *Cloud could* have read all of these works—I give the dates *by which* they were *certainly* known in England—but there is absolutely no evidence that he did so. I hope you will not think that I am being nihilistic, but there has already been a great deal of speculation about what the author of the *Cloud* might have read, and none of it has got us much further. The problems of date and authorship must be settled first".

[57] M. McKisack, *The Fourteenth Century*, 1307-1399, Oxford, 1963. D. Knowles, *The English Mystical Tradition*, Ch. III. C. Pepler, *The English Religious Heritage*, pp. 29-35. P. Hodgson, *Three Fourteenth-Century English Mystics* p. 7.

[58] C. Horstman, *Yorkshire Writers*, Vol. II, Introduction, pp. v-viii.

of Perfection. He has been included in the Roll of Cambridge Men[59].

Of Mother Julian of Norwich we also have scanty knowledge of her life and circumstances[60].

These writers are always considered together to form the group known as the "English Mystics" of the 14th century. A very scholarly and exhaustive study has also been made of another 14th century writer not commonly included in the ranks of these writers. Perhaps it is because he wrote in Latin that John Whiterig, known as the Monk of Farne, is generally excluded. The work attributed to him is entitled *Meditaciones cuisdam monachi apud Farneland quondam solitarii*, and contains seven meditations in all[61].

This common description of the 14th century English writers as the "English Mystics" provokes the question as to whether they are all "mystics" in the theological acceptance of the word.

The word "mystic" has been described in all sorts of ways, from the divine to the ridiculous[62]. This confusion regarding the estimate of the mystical life can be multiplied easily. But since the mystical life is inseparably linked with the life of faith and grace, in the religious context, the real meaning must be taken from those who have studied mystical states in the context of the religious life of faith and grace. We do not touch here the problem of whether the mystical grace is limited only to those who profess the Catholic Faith, which necessarily removes those who profess another belief from the ambit of the mystical life[63]. Rather, since the object of this study is to scrutinize the works of the particular author under consideration in the light of Catholic Theology, the definition of the mystical life must be taken from the specialists in this

---

59 A. E. Emden, *A Biographical Register of the University of Cambridge to 1500*, pp. 305-306. "No edition of *The Scale of Perfection* has yet been published in its Middle English form, though editions of both *Books I* and *II* are now being prepared for publications by the E.E.T.S." (P. Hodgson, *Three 14th-Century English Mystics*, p. 45).

60 P. Molinari, *Julian of Norwich*, p. 7.

61 H. Farmer, *Studia Anselmiana*, Fasc. 41, pp. 141 ss. Rome, 1957.

62 J. Milosh, *The Scale of Perfection and the English Mystical Tradition*, pp. 20-23. C. Butler, *Western Mysticism*, pp. 65-68. T. W. Coleman, *English Mystics of the Fourteenth Century*, pp. 11-14.

63 This problem has been noted by G. E. Hodgson in *English Mystics*, pp. 2-3; also by T. W. Coleman, *English Mystics of the Fourteenth Century*, pp. 14-28; D. Knowles, *What is Mysticism?* Ch. 13, pp. 122-126.

field of study. The author wrote his treatises when dissent
and discord were but distant rumbles. This is the only way
by which we can be faithful to the mind of the author.

We provide then an accepted definition of *mysticism* in the
framework of Catholic Theology.

> "We apply the word mystic to those supernatural acts or states
> which our own industry is powerless to produce, *even in a low
> degree, even momentarily* . . . it follows that a supernatural
> state should not be described as mystic if it differs only in
> *intensity* or in *duration* from that which anyone can produce
> at will"[64].

In this definition is stressed the element of *passivity* which
has "commonly come nowadays to be taken as the test of
real contemplation"[65]. Despite the divergent views strongly
held by the two dominant schools of *Mystical Theology*, one
represented by Fr. Augustin Poulain and having in its ranks
mostly Jesuit theologians, and the other represented by Abbé
Auguste Saudreau, in whose ranks is no less a theologian than
Fr. Reginald Garrigou-Lagrange, O.P. this definition stresses
an element which is acceptable to all.

> "There is common agreeement that such passivity is the mark
> of the mystical experience in its strictest and fullest accepta-
> tion, so that it receives the name, among others, of 'passive
> union' . . ."[66].

In taking our definition from Fr. Poulain it would seem that
this study is taking sides in a controversy of no little importance. However, this is only an initial impression. Furthermore, in following the enumeration made by Fr. Poulain of
the *fundamental* and *subsidiary marks* of the *mystical life*[67]

---

[64] A. Poulain, *The Graces of Interior Prayer*, pp. 1-2.
[65] C. Butler, *Western Mysticism*, p. 28.
[66] Ibid.
[67] Fr. Poulain enumerates the following as the characteristic marks of the
mystical life. He divides them into *principal* and *subsidiary*. We follow
the numbering made by Fr. Poulain for an easy reference to his classic
work, *The Graces of Interior Prayer*, pp. 64-65, 88, 114.
A. *Principal*:
1. (1) The mystic states which have God for their object attract attention at the outset by the impression of recollection and union
which they cause us to experience. Hence the name of mystic union.
(2) Their real point of difference from the recollection of ordinary
prayer is this: that in the mystic state, God is not satisfied merely
to help us to *think* of Him and to *remind* us of His Presence: He
gives us an experimental, intellectual knowledge of this presence.
In a word, He makes us feel that we really enter into communica-

it is not the intention of this study to make *The Cloud* teaching fit into the descriptions of Fr. Poulain. Rather we shall follow what he terms the method of presentation which "consists in a study of the details, describing one set of special states"[68]. For this, the clear and concise enumeration of Fr. Poulain is very handy and practical. Needless to say, there is no intention at all in this study to discount the opinions of the school led by Abbé Saudreau.

At this juncture, it is good to see *The Cloud* teaching in the light of this controversy, and see how *The Cloud* author stands in relation to them.

A very good summary has been made of this controversy by Fr. J. V. Bainvel[69] and Dom Cuthbert Butler[70]. The reconciling spirit with which Dom Butler handles the discussion on this controversy is indeed worthy of praise.

It would help very much for clarity and understanding to set forth the issues on which *The Cloud* author does not concern himself. Firstly, *The Cloud* does not deal *ex professo* on the theology of Grace in relation to "This Work". What-

> tion with Him. (3) In the lower degrees, however (prayer of quiet), God only does this in a somewhat obscure manner. The manifestation increases in directness as the union becomes of a higher order.
> 2. This "experimental knowledge of the presence of God . . . is the result of an impression, a spiritual *sensation* of a special kind".
> B. *Subsidiary*:
> 3. It does not depend upon our own will;
> 4. The knowledge of God accompanying it is obscure and confused;
> 5. The mode of communication is partially incomprehensible;
> 6. The union is produced neither by reasonings, nor by the consideration of creatures, nor by sensible images;
> 7. It varies incessantly in intensity;
> 8. It demands less effort than meditation;
> 9. It is accompanied by sentiments of love, of repose, of pleasure, and often of suffering;
> 10. It inclines the soul of itself and very efficaciously to the different virtues;
> 11. It acts upon the body and is acted upon in return.
> 12. It impedes to a greater or lesser extent the production of certain interior acts; this is what is called the ligature.
> The list is ponderous. In the course of the dissertation, we note that of these twelve marks of the *mystic state*, ten are verified in *The Cloud* writings. The last two are absent. They have to do with ecstasy with which *The Cloud* does not deal.

68 A. Poulain, *The Graces of Interior Prayer*, p. 64.
69 J. V. Bainvel, in *Introduction* to A. Poulain, *The Graces of Interior Prayer*, pp. lxvii-lxxxvi, xcviii-cxii.
70 C. Butler, in *Afterthoughts* introducing the 1960 edition *of Western Mysticism*, pp. 9-58.

ever he says on this matter must be inferred from his passages which are more practical and scriptural, rather than one that leans towards a particular school of theology. He says that the Source of his teaching is God alone. He does not then attempt to trace "This Work" to the *Gifts* of the Holy Ghost or the *Virtues*. His explicit mention of the Holy Ghost is to the general working of His Inspiration which he calls "the privy teaching of the Spirit of God". The intervention of God is described as that of one Person to another, rather than that involving the fine distinctions of a text in theology. The succeeding discussions will show that there is need for a "special grace" for "This Work", that there is a *break* and a *cleavage* between the state of "the cloud of unknowing" and that of the *breakthrough* and *Personal Intervention* of God, as well as that of the state before the "call" and that after it. This being so, *The Cloud* is principally concerned with the higher reaches of the *mystical life,* the *perfections* of "This Work", and is not affected by the controversy as regards "acquired and infused contemplation". In its historical context the term "acquired contemplation" came into use in the 17th century[71]. And, in passing, the differences of opinion between the Thomist and the Molinist Schools of Theology were, at the time of *The Cloud,* still a distant reality. The divergence has to do with the early stages of the mystical life which St. John of the Cross calls "the prayer of loving attention", or Poulain "the prayer of simplicity". Although almost at the end of *The Cloud* the author speaks of "ravishing"[72] it cannot be said with certainty that he speaks of *ecstasy* as it is commonly understood. It is significant that the last two *subsidiary marks* of the *mystical life* which have to do with ecstasy are noticeably absent from *The Cloud* group of writings. On the other hand, since the study will show that *The Cloud* author belongs to the tradition of the *Mystics of the Divine Essence, ecstasy* is not always to be expected. *The Cloud* author does not state explicitly that there are two unitive ways, one *mystical* the other *non-mystical*. But by the *descriptive method* we could see that at least he means a *difference in kind* be-

---

71 A. Poulain, *The Graces of Interior Prayer*, p. 61.
72 *The Cloud,* Ch. 71, Underhill, pp. 257-259; Hodgson, pp. 125-127.

tween the state before the "call" and the one after and not
merely one of *degree* or *intensity*.

Basically the controversy centres on the fact that for Fr.
Poulain mystical prayer is "no doubt the reward and the
crowning of previous endeavours; but still itself is a thing
in no way 'achieved' but wholly 'given'. Consequently he
ranges the prayer of simplicity, of faith in the category of
'ordinary' and non-mystical prayers, and calls it 'acquired
contemplation', one that can be acquired in some measure by
our own industry and exercisings—of course assisted always
by divine grace. This setting up of two different kinds of contemplation, one acquired and non-mystical, the other infused
and mystical, is vehemently opposed by the other school, by
Saudreau and the Dominicans"[73].

Fr. Poulain, too, has made "the direct perception of God . . .
the essential element of states truly mystical, so that he would
not accord the name to any kind of prayer or any religious
experience from which the perception of God's Being is
absent"[74]. The group of Abbé Saudreau is of course against
this view "maintaining that the experimental perception of
God is not an element of the mystical experience at all; he
holds that the expressions of the mystics that seem to assert
some such thing are to be taken as figures of speech, metaphors, and signify that the Presence of God is not directly
perceived, but only inferred from the effects of love, devotion,
surrender felt in the soul. He seems to make an exception for
St. John of the Cross's substantial touches, placing them apart
as a practically unique experience"[75]. Dom Butler calls this
"direct perception of God" the *Mystic Claim*.

These then are the main points of divergence on which
much writing has been done. There are indeed many ramifica-
tions and shades of distinctions that would not be very useful
in this study.

In concluding this brief discussion on the controversy seen
in relation to *The Cloud* teaching, we make our own the careful and reconciling conclusions of Dom Cuthbert Butler:

"With St. Teresa's prayer of quiet, and still more with the

[73] C. Butler, *Western Mysticism*, p. 16.
[74] Ibid. p. 43.
[75] Ibid. p. 44.

prayer of union, a change comes in, a new element—the element which she designates 'supernatural', in her peculiar sense of the word. This change Père Joret explains theologically by saying that up to this point the prayer is made in virtue of co-operating grace, but afterwards by operating grace. Above this line lie the various manifestations of the mystical experience spoken of by the mystics—passive union, experimental perception of God, substantial divine touches, intellectual vision, transforming love, spiritual marriage. Whether such experiences are to be termed extraordinary or ordinary (in whatever sense), I range myself with those who hold that there is a difference in kind between them and those lowlier contemplations that have so far mostly been occupying our attention"[76].

This observation is noteworthy since it incorporates the opinion of a Dominican writer, who admits that there is a point wherein is verified a "change". *The Cloud* teaching on the *perfections* of "This Work" is surely in an area above this "change", and so is not affected by the dispute.

Dom Butler thinks that Fr. Poulain went too far in maintaining his position, in the same way that Abbé Saudreau went as far in the opposite direction. There is also a need, he thinks, for precision in the use of the terms "ordinary" and "extraordinary", as well as other expressions having to do with mystical theology[77]. The present writer sees a position similar to *The Cloud* wherein "the prayer of faith" is seen as the terminal of the ordinary perfection of prayer, and beyond this prayer becomes extraordinary. Between these two stages Fr. De Besse, Capuchin, gives three tests, which in a way parallel the *break* and the *tests* which *The Cloud* author gives to distinguish the state before the "call" to "This Work" and that after the "call"[78].

As regards the Mystic Claim, Dom Butler has this to say:

". . . the claim of the great mystics is, in one way or another, that in the heights of the mystic experience they have got into immediate conscious contact with the Being of God—be it expressed as experimental perception of His Presence in the soul, or as substantial touch, or as passive union, or as intellectual intuition . . . In order to have clearly before his mind the

---

76 Ibid. pp. 34-35.
77 Ibid. pp. 54, 57-58; also J. V. Bainvel, *Introduction* to A. Poulain, *The Graces of Interior Prayer*, p. lxxxv.
78 C. Butler, *Western Mysticism*, pp. 12-13.

nature of the claim of the mystics, let the reader go over the set of citations in the Prologue and the series of pieces from St. John of the Cross in the Epilogue: he will see that it really is what is set forth above, and that the language cannot reasonably be explained away as figurative or metaphorical. The claim may be unfounded, an illusion; but that is what it is"[79].

The following and concluding passage of this section from Dom Butler can help to clear the air in the matter of the controversy as well as establish the serenity and quiet that is so much the hall mark of the Benedictine PAX.

"Great discussion goes on whether there be two 'unitive ways' or only one. There is much to be said for the view that they are not one nor two, but many, just as there are many mansions in our Father's House"[80].

With this characterization of the mystical life, what can we say about the spiritual writers of the 14th century in England, commonly described as "mystics"?

The highest experience of Richard Rolle has been described by a scholar on Rolle.

"After this preparation—which, as he carefully sums up, lasted 3 years minus 3-4 months—he at last got to the third stage, the 'contemplatio' or 'sight' when 'man sees into heaven with his ghostly eye'; when 'through the open door of heaven with unveiled face the eye of the heart contemplates (sees) the heavenly spirits (superos)'. In this stage he subsequently—the doors of heaven remaining open—experienced the 3 phases which he describes as calor, canor, dulcor. . . . In this warmth he had continued for 9 months, when suddenly he felt the canor. . . . This gift . . . he calls a free gift of Christ accorded to those only who so specially love the name of Jesus that it never recedes from their minds' "[81].

One feels uncomfortable before a claim like this, which suggests, perhaps unwittingly, that he was a mystic. The narration of the experience, the very acute and minute descriptions of it, reveal the fact that the experience took place at the level of sense[82] and not in the depths of which the mystics write. Nor is there that vagueness, that generality of description of the experience, almost to the point of not really knowing

79 Ibid. pp. 44-45.
80 Ibid. p. 43; see also J. V. Bainvel, *Introduction* to A. Poulain, *The Graces of Interior Prayer*, p. lviii.
81 C. Horstman, *Yorkshire Writers*, Vol. II, p. vii.
82 C. Pepler, *The English Religious Heritage*, pp. 212-213.

what it is all about, save the fact that something happened
of which they are aware and which they know for certain was
the presence somehow of the Godhead.

As if such an encounter with the Godhead could be located
in a spiritual thing like the human soul, mystics have nevertheless tried to describe the experience as having taken place
in what they call "apex mentis"[83], or in the phraseology of St.
John of the Cross "in its deepest centre", "in the depth of the
soul", "in the inmost centre of the depth of the soul" and
similar expressions[84]. The author of *The Cloud* describes this
point of encounter as taking place "in the highest and
sovereignest point of the spirit"[85]. The mystics simply mean
that the encounter took place in a level too deep for them to
express, while somehow affirming that an encounter actually
did take place.

As regards Walter Hilton, the experiences that he narrates
somehow partake of the tenor of one writing a treatise in
Spiritual Theology rather than a narration of a personal and
immediate experience of the Godhead. Even from a consideration of the purpose for which *Scale I* and *Scale II* were written,
one cannot expect a narration of a mystical experience. *Scale
I* is addressed to a woman recluse just beginning her solitary
life, quite different from the disciple of *The Cloud*[86]. And
"though *Book II* is written in a personal interrogatory style,
it does not give the same impression of teaching adapted to
the needs of an individual soul"[87] but has a wider range, and
Hilton is seen as "painting on a bigger canvas, and covering
all aspects of the spiritual life . . ."[88]. There are no passages
in Hilton comparable with the passages in *The Cloud* and *Privy*

---

83 Thomas Gallus gives the term, *summus affectionis apex,* called in other
   places *synteresis* or *principalis affectus.* St. Bonaventure describes the
   experience as having taken place *in aliquo affectu interiori,* while
   Eckhart describes it as the "depth of the spirit", and for Eckhart, "the
   supreme union of the depth of the soul to the depth of the Divinity
   remains the central perspective" (from *Dictionnaire de Spiritualité,* III.
   Cols. 887, 895, 896, 902, 903).
84 St. John of the Cross, *The Living Flame,* Allison-Peers, pp. 6, 21, 22,
   23, 24, 25, 26, 28, 35, 37, 40, 43, 44, 85, 86, 90, 94, 97, 100. Also,
   The Spiritual Canticle, p. 65.
85 *The Cloud,* Ch. 37, Underhill, p. 163; Hodgson, 74: 12-13; also Ch.
   51, Underhill, p. 203; Hodgson, 95: 5.
86 H. Gardner, "The Text of the Scale", *Medium Aevum,* V (1936), p. 14.
87 Ibid.
88 G. Sitwell, "Contemplation in The Scale", *Downside Review,* Summer
   1949, p. 289.

Counsel describing the heights reached by the soul in the state of the "cloud of unknowing" as well as that describing the *personal intervention* and *invasion* by God of the soul. The parallel citation of passages between the two groups of writings will show that as *The Cloud* goes higher the parallel passages become fewer in the case of Hilton. It is not quite exact, therefore, to put too much stress on the different usage of words between the two writings, since the stages in the spiritual life that they describe are not the same. It is the opinion of the present writer that Walter Hilton was not a mystic if we have only his writings to go by. There is none of that immediacy, concentration, intensity, economy and precision as well as the dominance and intransigence that characterize mystical writings[89]. The figure of the lights starting to filter through from the city of Jerusalem as the pilgrim nears the end of his journey[90] is not enough to classify the entire *Scale* as mystical, nor is this passage enough of itself to show its mystical character. And where there are passages reminiscent of mystical experiences it is interesting to note that they are quite similar to those described in *The Cloud* and other writings of the unknown author. At no point in *The Scale* does Walter Hilton say that his writings are mystical, as does the author of *The Cloud*.

As regards Mother Julian, we have the following conclusion:

"For my part, I should be inclined to go farther and maintain that the attitude of sincere humility, obedience in faith and prudence, as well as the astounding theological accuracy of this 'woman unlettered', point to the divine origin of the Shewings. By applying, then, the same criteria to Julian's further experiences and lights I should be inclined to assert that the 'lightings and touchings' 'often renewed' during her life came

[89] Fr. Alfred Hughes, in his study on Hilton, does not think that Hilton was a mystic. "Nor does this claim to limitation parallel the passages common in mystical writings wherein the writers profess their own incapability to express the ineffable experiences they have witnessed. It is obvious that these writers are expressing ignorance in how to express mystical experiences, not ignorance of the *nature* of this experience. Hence, this writer admits that Walter Hilton was a deeply spiritual man with definite experience in at least the fundamental degrees of contemplation. But he is inclined to question Hilton's having reached the very heights of mystical union with God . . . at least as revealed in his writings". *Walter Hilton's Direction to Contemplatives*, p. 10.
[90] Walter Hilton, *Scale II*, Ch. 25, Underhill, p. 328.

indeed—as Julian hoped they did—from God, and hence that
she should be ranked among the true mystics of the Church"[91].

It is the opinion of Dr. Hugh Farmer that John Whiterig,
the Monk of Farne, was a mystic.

"The following passage however is worth quoting; it describes
a vision of our Lord at a time when the author was preoccupied about his own salvation:
'It was not sufficient for Thee (to teach me through others),
Thou didst so by Thy own mouth. . . . Glady and with tran-
quil face Thou didst answer; Love, and you shall be saved,
Thou didst say this as it were with a smile.'
"The influence of such an experience on his outlook must have
been profound, and if he later preferred to keep his secret for
himself, should anyone blame him for that, or misinterpret his
silence as lack of spirituality?[92].

Stemming from this consideration of whether all the
14th-century English spiritual writers are "mystics",
one wonders whether there is in fact an "English Mystical
Tradition". This phrase has become quite a favourite expression among writers on this group. We think, however, that
while the expression is not entirely misleading, it is not exact.
We are not aware of the exact beginnings of this expression
and so we cannot say for certain just what the originator of
this expression meant. But we add our own understanding of
the expression. We think that the tradition of English mystical
writing is not entirely English, for indeed it embraces the full
span of time from Gregory of Nyssa and the Pseudo-Dionysius,
through St. Augustine and St. Bernard and Gregory the Great,
to Richard of St. Victor and Thomas Gallus. *The Cloud* author
for one insists that the origin and source of his teaching on
the special message of *The Cloud* is God Himself. While the
mystics use expressions that they have been brought up with,
still the *breakthrough* and *personal intervention* and *invasion*
by God of the soul is distinctly God's own. Every mystic
stands alone before God. We are not aware of a similar
expression describing a "Spanish Mystical Tradition" or an
"Italian Mystical Tradition" though there are mystics comparable with the English among their groups. We think that it

[91] P. Molinari, *Julian of Norwich*, p. 198. See also C. Pepler, *The English
Religious Heritage*, p. 218.
[92] H. Farmer, *Studia Anselmiana*, Fasc. XLI (1957) p. 150.

is more exact to speak of the English Mystics simply as such, as we do of the Spanish Mystics, or the Dutch Mystics.

From all these considerations we move on to the problem of the authorship of *The Cloud* and the allied treatises which has been described as "another of history's teasing tricks"[93].

E. THE PROBLEM OF THE AUTHORSHIP OF *THE CLOUD*

After nearly 600 years the problem "has so far resisted solution"[94]. That a book like *The Cloud,* considered "the most excellent work on contemplative prayer ever written in the English language"[95], should have lost completely any trace of its author, seems most surprising. The question of the authorship was raised in 1924, admitting that ". . . In literal fact nothing at all is known about him, and we have not in his case even so much as the probabilities that we have for the author of the Imitation"[96].

Various candidates have been proposed for the honour of the authorship of *The Cloud.* But right at the start "several may be ruled out at once by a mere consideration of dates. *The Cloud* belongs to the fourteenth century, and a fourteenth century writer must be found for it"[97]. Hence Maurice Chauncey and Blessed William Exmew, both belonging to the 16th century, are removed from the list. A certain Louis of Fountains Abbey has likewise been mentioned but evidence in his case is insufficient[98]. The author has been thought to have been a "cloistered contemplative monk . . . not a Carthusian"[99]. The description of the crown in *Discretion of Stirrings* has been seen to give some indication that the author might have been a Scotsman, since the fleurs-de-lis fitted more the description of either the crown of France or Scotland, and "it is not very likely that an author writing in France would have used the English tongue"[100].

---

[93] T. W. Coleman, *English Mystics of the Fourteenth Century,* p. 84.
[94] H. Gardner, "Walter Hilton and the Authorship of the Cloud", *Review of English Studies,* April 1933 p. 129.
[95] D. Knowles, "The Excellence of The Cloud", *Downside Review,* LII (1934), p. 92.
[96] M. Noetinger, "The Authorship of The Cloud", *Blackfriars,* March 1924, pp. 1457-1458.
[97] Ibid. p. 1458.
[98] Ibid. p. 1459.
[99] Ibid. p. 1459-1460.
[100] Ibid. p. 1461.

1.   *WALTER HILTON AS THE CANDIDATE MOST MENTIONED*

"The Cloud belongs to the fourteenth century, and . . .
such a one is Walter Hilton (died 1396) and many have
supported his authorshop"[101]. From the following quotation
we see the reasons supporting this view, while in the same
breath difficulties which appear insurmountable are at once
given.

"The view would indeed explain how it comes about that the
doctrine of the *Cloud* is so close to that of Hilton: whole
chapters of the *Cloud* are summarized in the *Scale of Perfection*.
But we cannot forget that Hilton does the same for several
other writers, and the connection may be quite well explained if
we suppose that the author of the *Cloud* lived sometime before
Hilton. The style of the two works is different, and the *Scale*
shows a less philosophical mind than does the *Cloud*. Besides,
another argument against the identification may perhaps be
found in the *Epistle of Privy Counsel*"[102].

A Carthusian tradition dating as early as 1500 that Hilton
was the author of *The Cloud* was put forth in support of the
claim. The fact of language, locality and date, as well as
literary background were seen to be in Hilton's favour. This
tradition is traceable to within a century of Hilton's death,
and "a Carthusian living in a community where *Cloud* and
Scale were constantly read from the beginning and where they
were frequently copied, would know all that there was to be
known about either of them"[103]. However, the value of the
ascription made by the Carthusian scribe was impugned on
the strength of a false tradition regarding Hilton originating
from the Carthusian houses of London and Schene, and the
Brigittine house of Syon, all of which had close connections
with one another[104]. The evidence of similarity of background
of scholarship which Dom McCann raised in favour of the
Hilton claim was likewise questioned since this fact can be
explained by common background: "The author of the *Cloud*,
while using the same writers as Hilton, stresses different aspects

---

101 Ibid. p. 1458.
102 Ibid.
103 J. McCann, "The Cloud of Unknowing", *Ampleforth Journal*. Summer
    1924. p. 196.
104 H. Gardner, "Walter Hilton and the Authorship of The Cloud", *Re-
    view of English Studies*, April 1933, pp. 134-135.

of their work"[105]. There are likewise the strong arguments against the Hilton claim based on psychological improbability, as well as the difficulty of fitting *The Cloud* and its epistles into the Hilton canon[106]. Dom McCann noted that the different usage of similar terminology can perhaps be explained by the fact that *The Cloud* author and Hilton had different audiences in mind. This has been described as "the different audience theory", which has been impugned as an improbable hypothesis "in view of Hilton's lack of adaptation of his teaching in his own works"[107].

"The two authors appear, in the present writer's opinion, to present strongly marked and different personalities, which no amount of common background or shared phraseology can disguise. Style, manner, vocabulary and imagery can be borrowed, but personality is inalienable"[108].

These formidable arguments against the Hilton claim would have put an end to the problem of the authorship of *The Cloud* had not the writer herself partially retraced her steps and taken away some force from her arguments. When we consider the strength of the above arguments as well as the finality with which they were presented, we can only say that such a turnabout is possible only with a truly great scholar, who remains ever open to further suggestions. The attention of the writer of the above quotation was called by the Rolle specialist, Miss Hope Emily Allen, to an annotation in MS Douce 262 of James Grenehalgh. Professor Helen Gardner recognized the value of this annotation and admitted that "Grenehalgh cannot be brushed aside as lightly as I dismissed an unknown monk writing a hundred years after Hilton's death"[109]. Another reason for the retraction is the fact that Professor Phyllis Hodgson "has established that the language of her basic text is very consistent, and probably represents fairly well the author's own . . . 'in the north part of the central East Midlands', which is the Thurgarton district"[110].

In summing up her partial retraction Professor Helen

---

[105] Ibid. p. 135.
[106] Ibid. p. 144.
[107] Ibid. p. 147.
[108] Ibid.
[109] H. Gardner, "The Cloud of Unknowing", *Medium Aevum*, XVI (1947), p. 41.
[110] Ibid.

Gardner calls attention to the possible rephrasing of the problem of authorship as regards the Hilton claim.

"Perhaps we ought to put our question the other way round, and ask, not whether Hilton could possibly have written *The Cloud*, but whether the author of *The Cloud* could possibly have written the works of Hilton"[111].

As a sequel to this partial retraction Professor Phyllis Hodgson wrote a very scholarly study, which in the absence of stronger evidence to the contrary must remain, for the present, the last word on the question of the Hilton claim. It is good to remember that this penetrating study is done for the most part from a philological viewpoint[112].

2. *SOME NEW LIGHTS ON AN OLD PROBLEM*

Throughout this study parallel citations between *The Cloud* texts and comparable passages in the published works of Walter Hilton will be made. It is hoped that this will shed light on the authorship of *The Cloud*. In her Introduction to the *Minor Works of Walter Hilton*, Miss Dorothy Jones writes:

"The editor hopes, at a later date, to consider both *Lambeth Ms.* 472 and the writings of Walter Hilton from other points of view that would be out of place in the introduction to this book"[113].

It is the aim of this study to fulfil in some measure this unfulfilled hope of Miss Dorothy Jones. And, in doing so the attitude of Miss H. E. Allen regarding questions concerning Richard Rolle is an inspiration for this further exploration of the Hilton claim.

"An attempt has been made to be explicit in claiming no more certainty than exists, but to suppress working hypotheses altogether would seem to check the lines of future inquiry. These hypotheses may lead the future scholar astray, but the chances are that he is more likely to turn up significant new facts as to Rolle's life with them than without them—provided he does not hold his clues for more than they are worth"[114].

There, too, is another advantage to this noting of parallel

---

111 Ibid. p. 42.
112 P. Hodgson, "Walter Hilton and The Cloud", *Modern Language Review*, October 1955, pp. 395-406.
113 D. Jones, (Ed.) *Minor Works of Walter Hilton*, p. lx.
114 H. E. Allen, (Ed.) *Writings Ascribed to Richard Rolle*, The Modern Language Association of America, Monograph Series, III, p. 2.

and kindred passages between the two groups of writings. Because of the anonymity of the author of *The Cloud* the question of influence has become a real problem. It is hoped that the parallel citations can afford some help, for in places where the body of writings exhibit very close resemblance of doctrine, especially in the more specialized areas, then, indirectly through Walter Hilton, we can have some closer grasp of the writers who influenced the author of *The Cloud*. As the study progresses we shall have an opportunity to notice in which places the parallel citations are heaviest. This might help in understanding and making clear the differences in usage that Walter Hilton makes of similar terms and phrases of *The Cloud* group. This might take some force from the objection raised against the "different audience" theory.

It is true that Professor Helen Gardner has herself taken away much of the rub from her previous statement when she wrote:

"The unoriginality of *The Scale* compared with *The Cloud* might be a consequence of such a withdrawal from 'Singular Living'. Again, if we think of *The Cloud* as kept close, and *The Scale* as widely distributed, is it impossible that the author of *The Cloud* should have schooled himself to 'mind not high things, but condescend to men of low estate'? He might have deliberately avoided the witty brevity of *The Cloud* as well as its difficult doctrine when writing for simpler souls than himself or his chosen disciples"[115].

In this connection it is good to note the different people for whom Hilton wrote.

"What first strikes one is the variety of men he taught. The first book of *The Scale* is written to an anchoress. . . . A Latin epistle, *De Imagine Peccati*, is also addressed to a recluse, this time a man. . . . Another Latin epistle *Epistola Aurea*, is written to a friend, Adam Horseley, an official of the King's Exchequer . . . The beautiful little English tract, *of Angels' Song*, is an answer to a friend who had written to inquire how angels' song and heavenly melody were heard in a man's soul; . . . *Mixed Life*, was written to a worldly lord . . ."[116].

115 H. Gardner, "The Cloud of Unknowing", *Medium Aevum*, XVI (1947), pp. 41-42.
116 H. Gardner, "Walter Hilton and the Mystical Tradition in England", *Essays and Studies*, XXII (1937), pp. 106-107. See also J. D. Russell-Smith, "Walter Hilton", in *Pre-Reformation English Spirituality*, pp. 188-189, 193-194.

The "Different Audience Theory," which is a term given to the adaptation that *The Cloud* author could possibly have made to vary his teachings according to the recipient of the direction, has indeed a relevance and urgency all its own. For it is a common practice with spiritual directors that, in matters where serious obligations are not concerned, direction can be insisted upon with one soul which cannot be done with another for sheer weakness, or other reasons known to the director alone.

It is good to remember that spiritual directors do have in mind the needs of the soul they are directing, and what is acceptable to one soul may not be acceptable to another, simply for the reason that they have different needs or occupy different places in the ladder of the spiritual life. For a spiritual director does not write a treatise on merely theoretical topics, but for a life to be lived which can have repercussions for time and for eternity.

Despite divergences of opinion brought about by the anonymity of the author, there are however some matters on which scholars agree. So, the opinion regarding the origin of *The Cloud* as being located "in the north part of the central East Midlands"[117] is commonly accepted. It is also commonly admitted that the author wrote in the second half of the 14th century[118]. That the author was a priest is generally accepted though the fact cannot be established by the blessing given at the end of *The Cloud,* which is used to support the argument [119]. The blessing reads

"Farewell, ghostly friend, in God's blessing and mine! And I beseech Almighty God, that true peace, holy counsel, and

---

[117] P. Hodgson, *The Cloud of Unknowing* (E.E.T.S., 1958), p. 1. As regards all the writings of *The Cloud* group, Professor Hodgson writes: "The study of the language of all the manuscripts would seem to indicate that *The Cloud* and its attendant treatises were written in a central district of the North-East Midlands", *The Cloud of Unknowing* (E.E.T.S. 1958), p. lxxxiv.

[118] P. Hodgson, *The Cloud of Unknowing* (E.E.T.S., 1958). Introduction, p. lxxxv; *Deonise Hid Diuinite* (E.E.T.S., 1958). Introduction, p. xxiii: *Three 14th-century English Mystics,* p. 21; D. Knowles, *English Mystics,* 1927, p. 90, *The English Mystical Tradition,* p. 70; J. McCann, "The Cloud of Unknowing", *Ampleforth Journal,* Summer, 1924, p. 194.

[119] P. Hodgson, *The Cloud of Unknowing* (E.E.T.S. 1958), p. lxxxii, D. Knowles, *The English Mystical Tradition,* pp. 70-71; C. Pepler, *The English Religious Heritage,* p. 233.

ghostly comfort in God with abundance of grace, evermore be with thee and all God's lovers in earth. Amen"[120].

This blessing alone is not sufficient to establish the author's priestly state. There is no proof that only priests could give a blessing with this formula, something perhaps that is contained in the present day *Rituale Romanum*. On the other hand, the blessing cited may be seen simply as an expression of a desire for the Lord's blessing to be bestowed on a friend. But surely the author was a theologian, and a mystical theologian at that, of no mean degree. His fund of background knowledge in the spiritual life moves in a very specialized area of theology. As regards his literary ability, he may "justifiably be described as a pioneer in his use of words, an 'inventor', who enriched the language by his attempts to express philosophical and theological conceptions . . . a craftsman as attentive to sound as to the shaping of thought"[121].

It is interesting to note that objections to the Hilton claim tend to be answered in the texts of Hilton himself. We have noticed previously that even formidable arguments raised against the Hilton claim have been softened as a result of further study and insight.

For example one writer on *The Cloud* and Walter Hilton has made the observation that while *The Cloud* gives the primacy to the will and its act of love, Walter Hilton does not.

"If we were to accept the theory—and the present writer does not—that *The Cloud* and its allied tracts are the work of the young Hilton, we must accept the hypothetical case of a mystic, totally engrossed by Dionysian theology, and experiencing and teaching a non-cognitive union, who later came to teach that such union is something else, is cognitive. This hypothesis seems essentially improbable"[122].

Again the same writer raised a similar objection in another work.

". . . is it likely, is it possible that Hilton in *The Cloud* and its attendant treatises taught the *via negativa* towards an essentially Dionysian union with God, in which cognition has no part,

---

120 *The Cloud*, Ch. 75, Underhill, p. 270; Hodgson, 133: 4-7.
121 P. Hodgson, *Deonise Hid Diuinite*, (E.E.T.S., 1958), Introduction, pp xxxiii, li.
122 E. Colledge, *The Mediaeval Mystics*, p. 65.

and that then, a few years later, for any reason whatever, he embarked upon the *Scale* and his other acknowledged works, in which similarities of language to that used in *The Cloud* only serve to stress the essentially different, cognitive union which *The Scale* teaches? Is this psychologically possible, is it inherently probable, and, above all, what other mystics can be shown who have done thus or similarly?"[123].

In answer to the above observations we wish to cite passages from Hilton himself.

"Then his love toucheth me nearer than his sight doeth. For when knowing faileth for weakness of reason, then is love mightiest and highest in his working through inspiring of grace. And forasmickle as he desireth so much for to see me as I am —that I am Jesu Saviour, sovereign might, sovereign wisdom and sovereign goodness—and shineth so bright to my sight; therefore I *shall* shew me to him fully in my full bliss and *fulfil his desire*"[124].

And in another place Walter Hilton writes:

"But I may not see thee in thy blessed kind, what thou art in thyself; my sight faileth, my wit and reason wanteth there, though it be lightened through grace. Lord, thus far may I see thee and know thee: and that is, that I may not take thee under my knowing. The better that I see thee through grace, the more unknown art thou to me, and the farther fleest thou from me. But, nevertheless, where knowing faileth, there love hitteth. That that I know not, that love I best. For when my thought is withdrawn through grace from beholding of all creatures and all special works of God, that I see nothing, then love I best the Maker of all things"[125].

In her learned article Professor Gardner notes that "homlynes, stabilnes, sikernes, these are Hilton's favourite words and best sum up the temper of his mind"[126]. It should be noted that *The Cloud* author has revealed a like predilection for the word "sikernes"[127]. The other two words also appear though

[123] E. Colledge, "Recent Work on Walter Hilton", *Blackfriars*, June 1956, p. 270.
[124] Walter Hilton, *Qui Habitat*, Jones, pp. 167-168.
[125] Walter Hilton, *Bonum Est*, Jones, pp. 185-186.
[126] H. Gardner, "Walter Hilton and The Mystical Tradition in England", *Essays and Studies*, XXII (1937), p.123.
[127] *sekyrnes*—once in *The Cloud*.
sekirly—41 times in *The Cloud*; 4 times in *Privy Counsel*.
sikerly—twice in *The Cloud*.
sekir—4 times in *The Cloud*; twice in *Privy Counsel*; twice in *Epistle*

not with the same frequency[128].

Dom Gerard Sitwell, in his penetrating analysis of the higher reaches of the contemplative life in *Scale II*[129] makes the following comment:

"Hilton in *The Scale* concerns himself with the whole range of contemplation. What he has to say about the entry into the Night is in accordance with the usual teaching of the mystics, but while the passages quoted above imply that the work of the discursive reason about God ceases at certain times, it is clear, I think, that he does not in *The Scale* teach the deliberate and conscious withdrawal from all reasoning about divine things which is the essence of the teaching of *The Cloud* and later of St. John of the Cross. The point is of interest in view of his possible authorship of *The Cloud*. The latter work insists so much upon it, that if Hilton was the author it is strange that he did not make explicit mention of it at least once in *The Scale*"[130].

We wish to call attention to the following passage from Walter Hilton which answers the above observation of Dom Sitwell.

"When thou feelest thine intent and thy will fully set for to desire God and think only on Him, thou mayest as it were first ask thyself in thine own thought, whether thou covet for to have anything of this life for love of itself, or for to have the use of any of thy bodily wits in any creature. And then if thine eye begin and answer thus, I would see right nought; and after that thine ear, I would hear right nought; and thy mouth, I would savour right nought, I would speak right nought of earthly things; and thy nose, I would smell right nought; and thy body, I would feel right nought, and after, if thine heart say, I would think right nought of earthly things, nor of bodily

of Prayer; once in *Discretion of Stirrings*; twice in *Knowing of Spirits*.
sekyrlyche—once in *The Cloud*.
sekerly—twice in *The Cloud*; once in *Privy Counsel*.
sekerist—once in *Privy Counsel*.
sekerliche—twice in *Epistle of Prayer*.
sekirli—once in *Epistle of Prayer*.
sikyrly—once in *Study of Wisdom*.
sekirly—three times in *Epistle of Prayer*.
In all, in various forms, the author used the word 70 times.

[128] *Homly*—once in *Study of Wisdom*; twice in *The Cloud*.
homely—once in *The Cloud*.
homlynes—twice in *Study of Wisdom*.
Then:
stabelnes—once in *Discretion of Stirrings*.

[129] G. Sitwell, "Contemplation in The Scale", *Downside Review*, Summer 1949, pp. 276-290.

[130] Ibid. p. 288.

deed, nor I would have affection fastened fleshly to no creature, but only in God and to Godward, if that I could"[131].

This passage is reminiscent of the emptiness of which *The Cloud* author speaks. We also see here the extreme concentration and singleness of object that *The Cloud* so insists upon. In noting the influence of Richard of St. Victor on Walter Hilton, Professor Helen Gardner makes the following comment:

"He uses also the famous Platonic image of Richard of St. Victor, when he speaks of the soul as a mirror, in which God can be seen, and urges his reader to keep that mirror clean and bright"[132].

She uses the reference from *Scale II*, Ch. 30, and *Benjamin Minor*, 72, (Migne, P.L. cxcvi. 51). Attention must here be called to the fact that in the very free paraphrase of *Benjamin Minor* of Richard of St. Victor, entitled *Study of Wisdom*, *The Cloud* author has chosen the passage on the image of the "mirror" to form part of what has become, as it were, a new treatise. It is a fact that the *Study of Wisdom* is a free translation and that the author had selected this "mirror" image from the many that Richard of St. Victor uses. We shall have occasion to see this manner of translation that the author employed. From the 62 columns of the text of Richard of St. Victor, Migne edition, the author has synthesized the message of *Benjamin Minor* to about 17 pages of text in the critical edition made by Professor Hodgson. A very highly selective mind was at work, and in this selection, the image of the mirror was retained. We ask the question, Why? The passage from *Study of Wisdom* follows:

"And wete thou well that he that desireth for to see God, him behoveth to cleanse his soul, the which is as a mirror in the which all things are clearly seen, when it is clean; and when the mirror is foul, then mayst thou see nothing therein; and right so it is of thy soul, when it is foul, neither thou knowest thyself nor God. As when the candle brenneth, thou mayst then see the self candle by the light thereof, and other things also . . .

---

[131] Walter Hilton, *Scale II*, Ch. 24, Underhill, p. 325. See also *Scale II*, Ch. 24, Underhill, pp. 321-324; *Letter to a Hermit*, translated by J. D. Russell-Smith, *The Way*, July 1966, p. 237; C. Pepler, *The English Religious Heritage*, p. 267.
[132] H. Gardner, "Walter Hilton and the Mystical Tradition in England", *Essays and Studies*, XXII (1937), p. 119.

And therefore cleanse thy mirror and proffer thy candle to the fire . . ."[133].

This "mirror image" is similarly used in *The Cloud* when the author likens God's Word to a mirror[134]. Here we notice that the author uses the "mirror" image in a sense different from that in *The Study of Wisdom*. We shall see that Walter Hilton employs very much the same technique of a free and running paraphrase of the writings of others. Miss Clare Kirchberger made annotations of the parts proper to Walter Hilton in her anthology *The Coasts of the Country*[135]. And in her edition of the *Goad of Love* she writes:

"For this reason the editor makes no apology for turning this edition of the *Stimulus* into a study of Walter Hilton, for when we have the good fortune of being able to see what an author does with a text in translating it, we acquire a singular insight into his mind and character, as well as of his literary powers, which will illuminate his original work when we return to examine it again. . . . But all that will be said in this inquiry could be reinforced by quotations from the Passion chapters and the final meditations, and the reader interested in the pursuit of the 'whole Hilton' will find in the bracketed passages of these parts ample matter for his own research"[136].

We wish to join Miss Kirchberger in her recommendation, and further add that much light can be shed on the problem of authorship if the parts proper to Hilton and to *The Cloud* author can be collated and studied. For these personal additions to the works of other authors give us an insight into the mind of the one who made them.

In her retraction, too, Professor Helen Gardner writes:

"What I once took to be Hilton's misunderstandings of the doctrine of *The Cloud*—his misuse of its terms—might be the result of a change of spiritual experience, a recognition of the danger of 'a naked thought of God', a return to the Johannine and Pauline conception of the fullness of the revelation of God in Christ"[137].

133 *Study of Wisdom*, Gardner, pp. 30-31; Hodgson, 43: 4-14.
134 *The Cloud*, Ch. 35, Underhill, p. 158; Hodgson, 72: 4.
135 C. Kirchberger, *The Coast of the Country*, London, Chicago, 1952.
136 Walter Hilton, *The Goad of Love*, (Ed.) Kirchberger, London, 1952, Introduction p. 14. See also H. Gardner, "Walter Hilton and The Mystical Tradition in England", *Essays and Studies*, XXII (1937), p. 117.
137 H. Gardner, "The Cloud of Unknowing", *Medium Aevum*, XVI (1947), p. 42.

C

Although *The Cloud* author does not entirely ignore the other traditional concepts of God in *The Cloud* and *Privy Counsel,* the whole burden of the teaching of *The Cloud* is on the "naked thought of God". Commentators on *The Cloud* have seen in this emphasis a justification for making the God of *The Cloud,* the God of the Sufis, Buddhists and Mohammedans[138]. This is true, of course, but not in the context of *The Cloud.* The heavy emphasis on a metaphysical and transcendental God has also been seen as a great cleavage between the Hilton mind and that of *The Cloud* author[139]. It is interesting to note an observation made by Miss Kirchberger.

"Miss Underhill, in her edition of the *Scale,* gives us some valuable indications of his life there and the conditions in the East Midlands of the time. To her we owe the important fact that the first book of the *Scale* was written in two versions, the one, A, earlier, the second, B, with many changes from the wording of abstract passages, by adding the words 'Jesus Christ' or 'Our Lord' to the term 'God', or changing the phrase, and by further addition of many Christocentric passages. This procedure has been found to have been carried out deliberately and in great detail throughout his translation of the *Stimulus Amoris,* a fact that confirms her conclusions and is of such importance for the understanding of Hilton's work as to warrant an examination of the possible reasons for the changes. It also justifies our presumption that this translation was made in the same period of his life. We have as yet no means of ascertaining whether this was before or after his entry at Thurgarton, but it was before the writing of Book II of the *Scale* which shows signs of the influence of the *Stimulus*"[140].

In the footnote she makes the following observation.

"Similar, though fewer, changes are found in the translation of *De remediis contra tentactiones,* MS Bodley 131, also elsewhere ascribed to Hilton; and numerous similar ones in the (as yet) anonymous translation of the pseudo-Jerome, *Epistle to Demetrias,* St. John's Coll. MS, 94, etc."[141].

138 J. Walsh, "The Cloud of Unknowing", in *Pre-Reformation English Spirituality,* p. 170; W. Johnston, *The Mysticism of The Cloud of Unknowing.* pp. 7, 67-68; C. Pepler, *The English Religious Heritage,* pp. 288-289.

139 D. Knowles, *The English Mystical Tradition,* p. 69. C. Pepler, *The English Religious Heritage,* p. 249. Cf. Hilton, *Scale II,* chs. 30, 32, 33; Underhill pp. 358-363; 370-371; 378.

140 Walter Hilton, *The Goad of Love,* (Ed.) Kirchberger, p. 21. Cf. E. Underhill, *The Scale of Perfection,* Introduction, pp. xliv-xlv.

141 Ibid. Note 3, p. 21.

Professor Phyllis Hodgson in her penetrating comparison of works of Hilton and *The Cloud* group has noted the different usage the two groups of works make of similar words and phrases[142]. We wish to add some observations of our own, and say that not only does *The Cloud* author use similar terms in a manner different from Walter Hilton but himself variously uses the same words and phrases. We shall note just one example. The virtue of "discretion" is a controlling idea and virtue for *The Cloud* author and following Richard of St. Victor he likens it to Joseph, son of Jacob. The term "discretion" has different meanings in *Study of Wisdom, The Cloud* and *Discretion of Stirrings*.

> "For why, without discretion may neither goodness be gotten nor kept, and therefore no wonder though that virtue be singularly loved, without which no virtue may be had nor governed . . . what wonder though this virtue be late gotten, when we may not win to the perfection of discretion without much custom and many travails of these other affections coming before? . . . And thus after many fallings and failings, and shames following, a man learneth by the proof that there is nothing better than to be ruled after counsel, the which is the readiest getting of discretion . . . and all after that a man knoweth himself, thereafter he profiteth in the knowing of God, of whom he is the image and the likeness"[143].

In *Study of Wisdom* "discretion" is profound self-knowledge by virtue of which one comes to the knowledge of God. In *The Cloud* we see a different use of the same term.

> "And furthermore, if thou ask me what discretion thou shalt have in this work, then I answer thee and say, right none! For in all thine other doings thou shalt have discretion, as in eating and in drinking, and in sleeping and in keeping of thy body from outrageous cold or heat, and in long praying or reading, or in communing in speech with thine even-christian. In all these shalt thou keep discretion, that they be neither too much nor too little"[144].

We quote another passage from *The Cloud*:

> "Do this work evermore without ceasing and without discretion, and thou shalt well ken begin and cease in all other works with

142 P. Hodgson, "Walter Hilton and The Cloud", *Modern Language Review*, October 1955, pp. 395-406.
143 *Study of Wisdom*, Gardner, pp. 27-29; Hodgson 39: 9-15, 42: 1-4.
144 *The Cloud*, Ch. 41, Underhill, p. 174; Hodgson, 79: 20-23; 80: 1-3.

a great discretion. For I may not trow that a soul continuing
in this work night and day without discretion, should err in
any of these outward doings; and else, me think that he should
always err"[145].

In these two passages from *The Cloud* we see "discretion"
used in the sense of a measure of doing things. Note however
that the acts mentioned are similar to those which brought
about the responses in *Discretion of Stirrings,* yet "discretion"
in this letter is used more in the sense of *Study of Wisdom,*
which is that of self-knowledge coming after long experience
of falling and rising.

"For I knew never yet no sinner that might come to the perfect
knowing of himself and of his inward disposition, but if he were
learned of it before in the school of God, by experience of many
temptations, and by many fallings and risings; for right as
among the waves and the floods and the storms of the sea, on
the one party, and the peaceable wind and the calms and the
soft weathers of the air on the other party, the sely ship at the
last attains to the land and the heaven . . . The crown of life
may be said on two manners. One for ghostly wisdom, for full
discretion and for perfection of virtue . . ."[146].

Again in the same letter, the author uses the term "discretion" in the sense of an instinctive knowledge of doing things
which results from the exercise of love of which *The Cloud*
speaks.

". . . so that thus, by experience of such a blind stirring of love
unto God, a contemplative soul cometh sooner to that grace of
discretion for to conne speak, and for to conne be still, for to
conne eat, and for to conne fast, for to conne be in company,
and for to conne be only, and all such other . . ."[147].

It will be seen that *The Cloud* author uses "discretion" in
three different ways.

Professor Phyllis Hodgson made a penetrating study of
similar expressions used by Hilton and *The Cloud* author.
The following observation regarding the usage that Walter
Hilton makes of terms and expressions is worthy of note:

"Unfortunately Hilton's use of terminology is not uniform. He
indulged in the mediaeval license of employing the identical term
to signify more than one concept. Moreover it will be remem-

---

[145] Ibid. Ch. 42, Underhill, p. 176; Hodgson, 81: 2-8.
[146] *Discretion of Stirrings,* Gardner, pp. 97-99; Hodgson 64: 4-26, 65: 1-5.
[147] Ibid. Gardner, p. 113; Hodgson, 76: 6-10.

bered that he was not inclined to use speculative systems. Hence the cardinal rule of interpreting his thought will be the understanding of the whole context and the comparing of parallel passages"[148].

This is another reason why we have preferred to allow *The Cloud* author to speak for himself, and that in the wider context of whole passages. Professor Hodgson has done a great service in collating all the passages from both groups of writings which she thought could be a help to the problem of authorship. Perhaps a study of Hilton's works as regards individual words and expressions, similar to what we have done with the expression "discretion", might be profitable and show that Hilton does not only differ from *The Cloud* author but that he variously uses the same words.

In concluding her learned and penetrating study of the philology of the two groups of writings, Professor Hodgson made the following picturesque observation.

"It is hoped to establish that, granted a common background of mystical theology and orthodox teaching, the likeness is not really deep, and, like the oncoming stranger who in the distance was thought to be a familiar friend, these treatises grow more unlike on a closer approach"[149].

The present writer thinks that very much has been made of the "common background of mystical theology", and to reduce the similarities of thought and expression between the two groups of writing to this explanation is to oversimplify the matter. We have noted that a highly selective mind was at work in making the translations, in the choice of figures, as well as the exegesis of passages from Sacred Scripture. We have to keep in mind, too, that *The Cloud* author stresses the fact that God is the source for his teaching, and that *felt experience* is the key to the proper understanding and appreciation of the passages from *The Cloud* and *Privy Counsel*.

These then are the reasons for the extensive quotation of parallel passages from *The Cloud* group and the writings of Walter Hilton. We would like to disagree on one point with Professor Hodgson and say that whilst we thought at a

---

[148] A. Hughes, *Walter Hilton's Direction to Contemplatives*, p. 37.
[149] P. Hodgson, "Walter Hilton and The Cloud", *Modern Language Review*, October 1955, p. 396.

distance that the oncoming figure might be a friend, we find that he becomes more and more familiar as he approaches.

F.   THROUGH THE CENTURIES

Before continuing with what is properly the subject of this dissertation it is worth looking at the impact of *The Cloud* through the centuries. First of all it is interesting to note the extent to which it captured the attention of readers at different periods. At times it received full attention, at others little or none, but the message of *The Cloud* seems to have retained its inner power to stimulate and to-day it is more widely read than ever before.

The principal reason for writing *The Cloud* remains in the 14th century. The full understanding of its message belongs to the author and the disciple alone. But down the centuries, from the time that *The Cloud* started to circulate (despite the strong prohibitions against its free circulation), men have caught glimpses of brilliant shafts of light from its teaching. This is not surprising for the author asserts that God is the Source of his teaching and this accounts for the spiritual unction that is so noticeable in passages of great beauty. The author recognizes this secondary sphere of influence, and it is this influence that commentators have considered through the years.

The 17 different texts of *The Cloud*[150] partially sums up its history from the end of the 14th century. It is the opinion of Professor David Knowles that ". . . *The Cloud* and its companions held the field till driven out by the full flood of the Reform, and were then carried into exile by more than one of the religious houses at the end of Mary's reign"[151].

In the 17th century, a milestone was reached in the history of *The Cloud*. Fr. Augustine Baker, O.S.B., made extensive use of *The Cloud* in his spiritual direction of the English Benedictine Dames of Cambrai. It seems that *The Cloud* has become some sort of a family book for the English Benedictines. The names that stand out in the history of *The Cloud* studies that mark real progress in the theological understand-

[150] P. Hodgson, *The Cloud of Unknowing* (E.E.T.S., 1958), Introduction, p. xix.
[151] D. Knowles, *The English Mystical Tradition*, p. 151.

ing of it, are those of Fr. Baker, Abbot Justin McCann, and Dom David Knowles.

Fr. Baker wrote a commentary on *The Cloud* which he called *Secretum Sive Mysticum*[152]. Although he meant it to be a commentary on the texts, he actually reveals his own particular spiritual experience based on them. The passages proved for Fr. Baker a springboard for his own particular way to God. The length of his commentary would not allow an extensive discussion of the entire *Cloud*, and his interpretation involves the more obvious meanings that can be gathered from the texts. He considers *The Cloud* as a mystical writing[153] and recognizes the personal experience of the author[154]. He identifies the *singular* degree of life as that "when God calleth a soul to an internal life, and to the exercise of it",[155] and this is done within the *religious life*. He attests to the difficulty involved in expressing mystical experiences[156]. Although he uses the terms *passive*[157], *ordinary*[158] and *extraordinary*[159] in a manner different from the accepted meanings nowadays, a careful reading of his commentary shows that he knew the distinctions that present-day terms admit. This is understandable for Fr. Baker did not have the advantage of the synthesis of Mystical Theology that has resulted from the scientific studies of the works of St. Teresa, St. John of the Cross and other mystics. We realize that he is speaking of his own particular experience, inspired by the passages of *The Cloud*, when he writes:

"And indeed all this exercise of the will, thus prosecuted throughout this book, is in effect and substance but the self-same course of spiritual life which I have so much intimated and inculculated to you by word of mouth and by writing under the terms of *immediate acts, proper aspirations,* and *elevations of the will*"[160].

This becomes clearer when he gives his own interpreta-

---

[152] Included in J. McCann, *The Cloud of Unknowing* (1947), pp. 150-214.
[153] Ibid. p. 150.
[154] Ibid. pp. 152, 207.
[155] Ibid. p. 183. See note 112, pages 101-102, infra.
[156] Ibid. p. 157.
[157] Ibid. pp. 170, 199.
[158] Ibid. p. 158.
[159] Ibid. p. 159.
[160] Ibid. pp. 162-163.

tion of the way involved in *The Cloud*. So he sums up the ascent to God in this manner:

"For, by the exercise of this knowledge in meditation, a man attaineth to the exercise of acts, and from them to aspirations, and by them to the foresaid abstraction, which only is the cause of true humility. And when you find spiritual writers exhorting their scholars to think of their own nothing, they mean that knowledge of their nothing and meditation upon it, which is a good exercise for beginners; and they do not mean the feeling, which is attained only by the perfect"[161].

Fr. Baker clearly recognizes the *call* needed to start this exercise, but he interprets the *tests* differently[162]. And some confusion could result from his use of the term *mystic active contemplation*[163], but a careful reading of the commentary reveals that he is on sure ground. His qualifications of the terms bear out his understanding.

One can read with profit this commentary of Fr. Baker as a spiritual writing. But one cannot rely on this commentary as a guide to the understanding of the teaching of *The Cloud* author.

Doubtless, many read and profited from the teaching of *The Cloud* from the time of Fr. Baker to the early years of our century. And the absence of written accounts must not be confused with the inactivity of the Spirit of God. "The wind blows wherever it pleases"[164], and judging from the popularity of *The Cloud* during the centuries prior to Fr. Baker, it would be safe to assume that many souls continued to be inspired by the lovely passages of *The Cloud* through the centuries following him. However, we are limiting our inquiry to the written accounts, and with the exception of the 1871 edition by Fr. Henry Collins there was a long silence from the time of Fr. Baker to the present century.

Writing in 1927 on the English spiritual writers of the 14th century, Professor David Knowles observed:

"They form a group of religious teachers of whom any country and any century might be proud, but of whom, for various reasons, their own country has been until recently almost

---

161 Ibid. p. 179.
162 Ibid. pp. 161-162.
163 Ibid. p. 164.
164 John 3: 8.

entirely oblivious. There are signs that this oblivion is passing"[165].

The first glimmerings of this new dawn of interest are seen in the work of Dean W. R. Inge[166]. Abbot Cuthbert Butler, O.S.B. in a select bibliography of *Mystical Books and Books on Mysticism,* noted the mystical character of *The Cloud* when he referred to "that remarkable mystical treatise, the *Divine Cloud,* the work, I believe, of an unknown English mystic of about the same epoch[167]. In 1910, Edmund G. Gardner included the translations of *The Epistle of Prayer, Discretion of Stirrings, Knowing of Spirits,* and *The Study of Wisdom,* in his Anthology entitled *The Cell of Self-Knowledge.* For the present writer this edition of the 4 treatises is the most satisfactory of the modern translations.

Great impetus was given to *The Cloud* studies with the modern translation by Evelyn Underhill based on the MSS Harleian 674 which "best represents the language of the original"[168]. This 1912 edition reached its sixth edition in 1956. The bibliography shows a number of editions of *The Cloud,* including one in French and one in German.

From these years of reawakening up to the present decade the main bulk of the studies on *The Cloud* group has been linguistic and philological. The interest of scholars was attracted to the problem of the authorship of *The Cloud,* and out of their discussions arose the *Hilton claim.* The theological study of *The Cloud* has not been neglected, but these studies are more in the line of introductions to editions, or brief guides to the whole group of English Mystics.

A brief study on *The Cloud* that deserves a special mention is that of Fr. Conrad Pepler, O.P.[169]. He puts the teaching in the context of Spiritual Theology, and more particularly Mystical Theology. His insight into the mystical character of *The Cloud* is of great value. This lucid study originally

[165] D. Knowles, *English Mystics,* (1927), Introduction, p. vii.
[166] W. R. Inge, *Studies of English Mystics,* 1906. A chapter is devoted to Walter Hilton, pp. 38-79, and a chapter to Julian of Norwich, pp. 80-123. But no mention is made of *The Cloud.*
[167] C. Butler, *Mystical Books and Books on Mysticism,* Reprinted from *Downside Review* for March 21, 1911.
[168] P. Hodgson, *The Cloud of Unknowing* (E.E.T.S., 1958), Introduction, p. xlix.
[169] *The English Religious Heritage,* 1958.

appeared as a part of a series of articles in *The Life of the Spirit*. In this series of studies on the English spiritual writers, starting with the *Ancren Riwle*, Fr. Pepler maps out a gradual ascent in the spiritual ladder. In this ascent he puts *The Cloud* in the "Perfection of Christian Life".

It seems to the present writer that the studies on linguistic and philological grounds are the abler ones during this period of the history of *The Cloud*. *The Cloud* has also inspired studies from different viewpoints[170]. Only recently have *ex professo* theological studies of *The Cloud* and Walter Hilton been published[171]. The work of Fr. William Johnston has been noted earlier in this chapter.

With this brief historical survey we proceed to the primary reason for this study.

---

170 See footnote 43 p. 15.
171 A. C. Hughes, *Walter Hilton's Direction to Contemplatives*, Rome, The Gregorian University Press, 1962. W. Johnston, *The Mysticism of The Cloud of Unknowing*, New York, Rome, Tournai, Paris, 1967.

Chapter II

A Textual Portrait of the Author

The study of the texts of *The Cloud* and its allied treatises, as well as the published works of Walter Hilton, has proved to be a very absorbing and interesting endeavour. Writers on *The Cloud* have tried to gather from the texts facets of the personality of the author, and they have drawn for us portraits of what they thought the texts revealed of their writer's personality.

"Fortunately, however, we are not left entirely in the dark as to the kind of man he was. If historical facts are denied us, we have some compensation in the many important details of the writer's character to be gleaned from his productions. These books are so charged with their author's spirit as to convey a definite impression of his personality"[1].

The object of this chapter is to make a portrait of *The Cloud* author based on the texts, similar to those already undertaken by other writers but on a wider and fuller scale. It is interesting to note the various portraits already drawn by other writers. One such characterization runs thus:

"He was a man of strong individuality. In disposition he was generous and genial, though at times the sunny landscape of his life could cloud over, and its shining serenity be broken by the rush of a passing storm. His mind was acute and vigorous: his penetrative intellect could sound the depths of metaphysical speculation, and his keen imagination was undaunted before the loftiest ranges of spiritual adventure. His sure touch in dissecting mental processes and tracing them to their roots marks him an expert psychologist. His humour—quaint, subtle, shrewd—was delightful; as occasion arose he could exercise a playful fancy or a mordant wit"[2].

A not too sympathetic picture of the author has also been elicited from the study of the texts.

"The author of *The Cloud*, and of the other treatises which he acknowledges as his, cannot help, as he writes, drawing for us a living self-portrait, and we see him as a quizzical and humor-

[1] T. W. Coleman, *English Mystics of the Fourteenth Century*, p. 85.
[2] Ibid.

49

ous observer of his fellow-men, vivacious to the point of
eccentricity, deeply engrossed with the psychological processes
involved in speculation and the attainment of mystical illumination: and this man is as different as well can be from Walter
Hilton, as we know him in his works"[3].

The following character sketch appears to the present writer
to be more supported by the texts. And we see in this portrait
how unlike he is to Richard Rolle.

"His style reflects a forceful, quizzical personality, tough-minded
and down-to-earth, with shrewd insight into psychological
difficulties, unsentimental, objective, and austere. How different he was from Rolle in temperament and outlook is obvious
from his stern emphasis upon the considerable danger of a
literal interpretation of Rolle's kind of teaching on the psycho-
physical rewards of contemplation"[4].

The above characterizations reveal that there is more than
ample proof of the high quality of mind and heart as well as
the warmth of personality of *The Cloud* author, that can be
gathered from his writings. With this we proceed to make
our own character sketch of the author, and this under two
main headings—as a director of souls and as a translator of
the works of other writers whom he follows in his directions.

A.   DIRECTOR OF SOULS

There are two main qualities required for the science of
spiritual direction which St. Gregory calls the "ars artium".
These are holiness of life and learning. We shall start by
looking at the man and his natural capabilities, that quality
of mind on which God builds the superstructure that crowns
all His works.

1.   LEARNING

The intellectual background of *The Cloud* author is highly
specialized as is clearly shown in his writings. The background
of the Pseudo-Dionysius, Richard of St. Victor, St. Bernard,
St. Gregory the Great, and St. Augustine which his writings
reveal is impressive. With a group of writers such as these
forming the intellectual background, there is no doubt as to
the quality of his intelligence and learning. Taken individually

---

3 E. Colledge, *The Mediaeval Mystics of England*, p. 65.
4 P. Hodgson, *Three 14th-Century English Mystics*, p. 22.

scholars on *The Cloud* and other writings have noted the clear signs of the influence of Richard of St. Victor[5]. *The Cloud* author acknowledges the Pseudo-Dionysius as his only authority[6]. He reveals a familiarity with the teachings of St. Augustine[7], St. Gregory the Great[8] and his free rendering of the two *Sermons* of St. Bernard reveals an intimate knowledge of them[9]. The teaching of *The Cloud* includes reminiscences of *De Vita* Moysis of St. Gregory of Nyssa[10]. His intention was not to clutter up his writings with acknowledgements of authorities, which was a form of disguised parade of erudition. He mentions St. Thomas by name only once in the *Epistle of Prayer*[11]. He reveals deep familiarity with Holy Scripture and his approach to problems is scriptural. His observations

5 P. Hodgson, *The Cloud of Unknowing* (E.E.T.S., 1958), Introduction, pp. lxii, lxix lxxiii-lxxvi; E. Underhill, *The Cloud of Unknowing*, pp. 6, 9; C. Kirchberger, *Richard of St. Victor*, pp. 65-74; D. Knowles, "The Excellence of the Cloud", *The Downside Review*, January, 1934, p. 74; D. Knowles, *The English Mystical Tradition*, p. 73; J. McCann, "The Cloud of Unknowing", *Ampleforth Journal*, Summer 1924, p. 193; H. Gardner, "Walter Hilton and the Authorship of The Cloud of Unknowing", *The Review of English Studies*, April 1933, p. 136; M. Noetinger, "The Authorship of the 'Cloud of Unknowing'," *Blackfriars*, March 1924, p. 1462; D. M'Intyre, "The Cloud of Unknowing", *Expositor*, 7th Series, IV, October 1907, pp. 375, 377, 382; E. Colledge, *The Mediaeval Mystics of England*, pp. 47, 49-50, 71, 74, 79; W. R. Inge, *Mysticism in Religion*, p. 125; C. Pepler, *The English Religious Heritage*, p. 222.

6 W. R. Inge, *Mysticism in Religion*, p. 125; C. Pepler, *The English Religious Heritage*, p. 222; *The Cloud*, Ch. 70, Underhill, p. 256; E. Underhill, *The Cloud of Unknowing*, Introduction, pp. 6-7; P. Hodgson, *The Cloud of Unknowing* (E.E.T.S., 1958), Introduction, pp. lviii-lxiii; D. M'Intyre, "The Cloud of Unknowing", *Expositor*, 7th Series, IV, October 1907, pp. 375, 377-383; M. Noetinger, "The Authorship of the 'Cloud of Unknowing'," *Blackfriars*, March 1924, p. 1462; J. McCann, "The Cloud of Unknowing", *Ampleforth Journal*, Summer 1924, p. 193.

7 *The Cloud*, Ch. 75, Underhill, p. 270; Hodgson, 133: 1-3; E. Underhill, *The Cloud of Unknowing*, Introduction, p. 10; P. Hodgson, *The Cloud of Unknowing* (E.E.T.S. 1958). pp. lxiii, lxix, lxx, lxxi, lxii, lxxiii; H. Gardner, "Walter Hilton and the Authorship of 'The Cloud of Unknowing'," *The Review of English Studies*, April 1933, p. 135; D. Knowles, "The Excellence of the Cloud", *The Downside Review*, January 1934, p. 74.

8 P. Hodgson, *The Cloud of Unknowing* (E.E.T.S. 1958), pp. lxix, lxx, lxxi; H. Gardner, "Walter Hilton and the Authorship of 'The Cloud of Unknowing'," *The Review of English Studies*, April 1933, p. 136.

9 St. Bernard, Sermones de Diversis, P. L. t. clxxxiii, cols, 600-3. Nos. xxiii, xxiv.

10 Migne, *Patrologiae Cursus Completus*, Series Graeca, Tom. 44, Cols. 1366-1382.

11 Gardner, *Cell of Self-Knowledge*, p. 81. In connection with this background of learning, it is interesting to note that Walter Hilton names expressly Richard of St. Victor and St. Bernard. *Letter to a Hermit*, translated by J. D. Russell-Smith, *The Way*, July 1966, p. 233.

regarding the quaint ways of those new in the religious life
are said to have been taken from Hugh of St. Victor's *Institutio
Novitiorum*[12]. We merely mention here in passing that in the
matter of the primacy of the will and its act of love, the
influence of Thomas Gallus is nearer in time and more apparent than that of the Pseudo-Dionysius himself, despite the
statement of *The Cloud* author. We believe that this fact will
prove a fruitful field of inquiry and that there could be more
of Thomas Gallus in *The Cloud* than is at present appreciated.

We see then that the background of knowledge of the author
is made up of the very specialized tradition of mystical
theology. It is not the purpose of this study to discuss extensively these Patristic influences. *The Cloud* author turns to these
authors in so far as he needs their vocabulary and turns of
expression to clothe his own experiences.

An important scholar on the 14th-century English spiritual
writers has noted "the undoubted influence of Thomist
theology"[13] as well as the fact that ". . . it is therefore very
noteworthy that the author of *The Cloud* holds throughout to
the Thomist position without any hesitation"[14] as regards the
doctrine of grace. We have seen the influence that certain
writers had on *The Cloud* author, and while the influence of
St. Thomas on *The Cloud* author is not a central and govern-
ing one, we believe that it would be a profitable study to
investigate the universality of acceptance of St. Thomas in 14th-
century England. We know that St. Thomas was not received
in England with open arms. His teaching was condemned in
Oxford by the Archbishop of Canterbury, the Dominican
Robert Kilwardby, in a special congregation of all the masters,
regents and non-regents of the University on March 18, 1277[15].
This condemnation remained in full force at Oxford even
after his resignation from the See of Canterbury to become
Cardinal-Archbishop of Porto[16].

The teaching of St. Thomas then had a checkered history
in the beginning, and it was not till 1325 that the Bishop of
Paris, Stephen de Bouret, proclaimed that the censure had no

---

[12] P. Hodgson, *The Cloud of Unknowing* (E.E.T.S. 1958), p. lxxvii.
[13] D. Knowles, *The English Mystical Tradition*, p. 76.
[14] Ibid. p. 95.
[15] D. Callus, *The Condemnation of St. Thomas at Oxford*, p. 11.
[16] Ibid. pp. 15-16.

canonical value[17]. It had been noted that the fifty-year period between 1326 and 1375 saw a "marked tendency away from Aristotelianism and hence Thomism toward Platonism and therefore Augustinianism"[18]. We think that such a state of affairs would surely have made any theologian, even of the temper of *The Cloud* author, wary of a full acceptance of doctrine which attracted such a censure in the University that had the primacy in the world of learning of the day.

With this consideration of the various influences that could have formed *The Cloud* author's mind, we move to the requirement of a good spiritual director that is more at the level of the supernatural and the life of grace.

2. HOLINESS OF LIFE

Considering the intellectual background of *The Cloud* author the specialized readings on mystical theology could not have had their impact on the mind alone. For in the context of the whole spiritual life one so engaged in this science of spiritual direction must nourish his own spiritual life from his readings.

The author reveals in his writings a very deep and intimate knowledge of the Godhead. And in his narrations we sense that caution and trepidation that accompanies the revelation of the deep secrets of God that is common to the authentic seers of the Divine Presence. The unwillingness of the author to speak of hidden things does not spring from any sense of false humility, ignorance of the experience or lack of knowledge as to the nature of the experience, but because of the fact that in such matters it is best to keep silent when the tongue is not equal in the telling.

"As to the first, I answer and I say that I dread full much in this matter and such others to put forth my rude conceit, such as it is, for two skills. And one is this: I dare not lean to my conceit affirming it for fast and true"[19].

And compared with this personal knowledge and encounters, "all their great learning should seem open folly. And therefore no wonder that I cannot tell the worthiness of this work with my boisterous, beastly tongue"[20].

17 Ibid. p. 34.
18 A. Hughes, *Walter Hilton's Direction to Contemplatives*, p. 20.
19 *Discretion of Stirrings*, Gardner, p. 97; Hodgson, 63: 16-19.
20 *Privy Counsel*, McCann, p. 123; Hodgson, 153: 15-17.

One cannot get near the fire without feeling its warmth, and this personal encounter with the Godhead could not fail to produce its searing and purging effect on the soul of the author. And this warmth does not end with the person involved, but radiates from him to those around him. We have occasion to see this when he practises the virtues which are the perfections of the soul. "For the tree can be told by its fruit"[21] is as valid a test for the mystic as for anyone else. We shall consider then some of these outward manifestations of an interior holiness shown by the author.

a.   CHARITY

The author was very deeply aware of the mercy of God, and his experience of that need operative in his life made him an apostle of great mercy and charity. In the same way that God had forgiven him his many sins and faults, so it behoved him to extend the same pardon to those who had wronged him. And one result of this merciful attitude is an overwhelming unwillingness to judge others, or to make any statement that tends to depreciate others[22]. However, he also realizes that faults and misdeeds have to be corrected. For this one must not assume the office, but leave the matter to those whose duty it is. So he makes the point by answering an anticipated question. This is a favourite device of the author.

> "But I pray thee, of whom shall men's deed be judged? Surely of them that have power, and cure of their souls: either given openly by the statute and the ordinance of Holy Church, or else privily in spirit at the special stirring of the Holy Ghost in perfect charity. Each man beware, that he presume not to take upon him to blame and condemn other men's defaults, but if he feel verily that he be stirred of the Holy Ghost within in his work; for else may he full lightly err in his dooms. And therefore beware: judge thyself as thee list betwixt thee and thy God or thy ghostly father, and let other men alone"[23].

21 Mt. 12:33-34.
22 *The Cloud*, Ch. 19, Underhill, p. 118; Hodgson, 49: 24-50:10.
23 *The Cloud*, Ch. 30, Underhill, p. 146; Hodgson, 65: 10-19. Hilton too is fond of using the device of anticipated questions and he has something very similar to say as regards the correction of others. "But now sayst thou, how may this be? since it is a deed of charity for to reprove men of their defaults; and for to deem them for their amending, it is a deed of mercy. As to this I answer as me thinketh, that to thee or to any other which hath state and the purpose of life contemplative it falleth not for to leave the keeping of yourself and behold and reprove other men of their defaults, but if it were full great need, so that a man should

This is not surprising in one who teaches the fulness of charity in both forms, that which he calls *imperfect* which has for its object his fellow-men, and that which is *perfect*, which looks to God only. It is the fulness of the first, *imperfect*, charity that has more interest for us in this chapter. The author calls this form of charity *imperfect* not because of any manner of poorer quality, but simply because the object, one's fellow men, when compared with God, the object of *perfect* charity, is clearly below God in the scale of values. We see that there is a fulness of this charity on which he insists.

"For why, in this work a perfect worker hath no special beholding unto any man by himself, whether that he be kin or stranger, friend or foe. For all men him thinks equally kin unto him, and no man stranger. All men him thinks be his friends, and none his foes. Insomuch, that him thinks all those that pain him and do him disease in this life, they be his full and his special friends: and him thinketh, that he is stirred to will them as much good, as he would do to the homeliest friend that he hath"[24].

Throughout his writings we see the fulness of charity shining through.

b. HUMILITY

While not overlooking the other virtues, there are two that the author emphasizes: charity and humility. We shall see that when he talks of the perfection of the teaching of *The Cloud* all the virtues will become synthesized into these two. Like charity, he classifies this virtue of humility into *imperfect* and *perfect*, based on the same object, namely, man himself,

perish but if he reproved him. But those men which are active and have sovereignty and cure over others, as prelates and curates and such other, they are bound by their office, and by way of charity, for to see and seek and deem right fully other men's defaults: not of desire and delight for to chastise them, but only for need, with dread of God and in His Name, for love of salvation of their souls". *Scale I*, Ch. 17, Underhill, p. 36.

[24] *The Cloud*, Ch. 24, Underhill, p. 134; Hodgson, 59: 7 -14. Hilton has a similar passage. ". . . but the more shame and villainy he doth to thee in word or deed, the more pity and compassion thou hast of him, as thou wouldst have of a man that were out of his wit or mind, and thee thinketh thou canst not find in thine heart for to hate him, for love is so good in the self, but pray for him and help him and desire his amending, not only with thy mouth as hypocrites can do, but with affection of love in thine heart, then hast thou perfect charity to thine even—Christian. This charity had Saint Stephen perfectly when he prayed for them that stoned him to the death" *Scale I*, Ch. 70, Underhill, p. 167. also *Scale II*, ch. 38, Underhill pp. 407-408.

and God. We shall consider the form of humility which looks
to man himself. The author uses the term "meekness" for
humility.

> "Meekness in itself is nought else, but a true knowing and
> feeling of a man's self as he is. . . . Two things there be, the
> which be cause of this meekness; the which be these. One is the
> filth, the wretchedness, and the frailty of man, into the which he
> is fallen by sin; and the which always behoveth to feel in some
> part the whiles he liveth in this life, be he never so holy"[25].

We see how well this teaching is lived by the author in his
dealings with others. He had such an intimate knowledge of
his own weakness that any other could easily be his superior.
And this is surely an overriding consideration for the need to
show mercy and forgiveness to others.

> "And also when I think on mine innumerable defaults, the
> which I have made myself before this time in words and deeds
> for default of knowing, me thinketh then if I would be had
> excused of God for mine ignorant defaults, that I should
> charitably and piteously have other men's ignorant words and
> deeds always excused. And surely else, do I not to others as I
> would they did to me"[26].

The author is not unwilling to open his heart and reveal the
sore state of his soul if, in doing so, he would encourage the
addressee to persevere in the difficult work of *The Cloud*,
and strengthen him in the mercy and love of God. We shall
see this more when we consider the providence God has
even for the most wicked sinner.

[25] *The Cloud*, Ch. 13, Underhill, pp. 100-101; Hodgson, 40: 8-14. Hilton
teaches the same thing regarding imperfect meekness. "The first
meekness a man feeleth of beholding of his own sins and of his own
wretchedness, through the which beholding he thinketh himself unworthy for to have any gift of grace or any need of God; but him
thinketh it enough that He would of great mercy grant him forgiveness
of his sins" *Scale II*, Ch. 37, Underhill, p. 397.
[26] *The Cloud*, Ch. 19, Underhill, pp. 119-120; Hodgson, 51: 2-8. Hilton
makes the same admission. "For soothly that is my life; I feel me so
wretched, so frail, and so fleshly, and so far in true feeling from that
that I speak and have spoken, that I can nought else but cry mercy, and
desire after as I may with an hope that our Lord will bring me thereto
of His grace in the bliss of heaven. Do thou so, and better after God
giveth thee grace. The feeling of this lowness shall put out from thine
heart unreasonable beholding of other men's misliving and deeming of
other men's deeds, and it shall drive thee only to behold thyself, as
there were no man living but God and thou; and thou shalt deem and
hold thyself more vile and more wretched than is any creature that
beareth life . . ." *Scale I*, Ch. 16, Underhill, p. 34.

"I grant well, that to them that have been in accustomed sins, as I am myself and have been, it is the most needful and speedful cause, to be meeked under the remembrance of our wretchedness and our before-done sins, ever till the time be that the great rust of sin be in great part rubbed away, our conscience and our counsel to witness"[27].

But for all this admission of weakness the author does not hesitate to assert his claim and present his credentials if such would put more heart into his disciple. It is not sham humility or the repetition of conventional phrases and expressions when the author makes the admission of weakness on his part. For with him humility is truth.

"Lo! here mayest thou see that I covet sovereignty of thee. And truly so I do, and I will have it. I trow love stirreth me thereto more than any ableness that I feel in myself in any height of knowledge, or yet of working, or degree of my living. God amend what is amiss, for he knoweth fully, and I but in part"[28].

He can be quite strong in his insistence that he is qualified to guide the disciple.

"And since it so is that God of his goodness stirreth and toucheth diverse souls diversely, as it is, some with mean and some without, who dare then say that God stirreth not thee in this writing, or any other like unto thee that it shall either read or hear, only by me as mean, though I be unworthy, saving his worshipful will that he liketh to do as he liketh?"[29].

It is because he is ever conscious of the source of his teaching that he attributes all to God, and would not deflect to himself the glory that should go to God. He knows his limitations and God is the principal figure in the ascent to Him. This is indeed a very good quality in a spiritual director, for

[27] *The Cloud,* Ch. 15, Underhill, p. 106. Hodgson, 43:13-17. Hilton reveals a like disposition and temperament in exposing his own weakness. *Letter to a Hermit,* Russell-Smith *The Way,* July, 1966, p. 241. Hilton also reveals the mercy that had been operative in his life. "Also for to think of the mercy of our Lord that he hath shewed to me and to thee, and to all sinful caitiffs that have been encumbered in sin, spered in the devil's prison. . . . But for love he spared us, he had pity on us, and sent his grace into our hearts and called us out of our sins; and by his grace hath turned our wills wholly to him and for to have him, and for his love forsake all manner of sin. The mind of his mercy and of his goodness, made with other circumstances more than I can or may rehearse now, bringeth into a soul great trust of our Lord and full hope of salvation, and kindleth the desire of love mightily to the joys of heaven." *Mixed Life,* Jones, pp. 63-64.
[28] *Privy Counsel,* McCann, p. 123; Hodgson, 153:5-10.
[29] Ibid. McCann, p. 125; Hodgson, 155: 15-20.

he will not be timid where he is convinced that a course of action is God's own way, neither would he be impetuous.

In concluding his commentary on *The Cloud* Fr. W. Johnston puts a judgment into the mind of *The Cloud* author which in the light of the previous quotations he would be very unwilling to make.

> "And so, from across the centuries, this English mystic speaks to a wicked and adulterous generation looking for signs and intoxicated with the mescalin of its own psychiatry, quietly warning us with apophatic conviction that God is above every sensible experience and that He must be loved in the darkness of the cloud of faith . . ."[30].

That he would speak of "a wicked and adulterous generation" seems not in keeping with the temper of one who "considers mine many defaults the which I have committed by unknowing", who continually begs for prayers for the difficult state in which he finds himself, who teaches that the most wicked sinner could sooner come to the perfection of the teaching of *The Cloud* than even the innocent soul. At the very least this observation gives a jarring note to the serene teaching of *The Cloud*, whose ending to the message is one of heroic hope and encouragement—"For not what thou art, nor what thou hast been, beholdeth God with His merciful eyes; but that thou wouldest be"[31].

3. BALANCED PERSONALITY

We have seen the gifts of grace, holiness of life, and learning, which helped to form the character of the author. Added to these two main virtues the author must surely have been a lovable person, even when he does not mince his words to point out the shortcomings of his disciple. For in this he protests that he is governed only by love. It is the purpose of the remaining part of this sketch to see the gifts of nature with which the author was endowed. For, indeed, grace builds on nature, and the more richly endowed is a person, the easier it is for grace to build on it. Not that we would put a limit to the power of grace, but that according to the ordinary laws of things, this is so. Some of the qualities

---

[30] W. Johnston, *The Mysticism of The Cloud of Unknowing*, p. 266.
[31] *The Cloud*, Ch. 75, Underhill, p. 269; Hodgson, 132: 19-20.

revealed by the author in his writings make us believe that
the author was endowed with a balanced personality.

a. OBJECTIVE

The author does not gloss over the difficulties of his teaching, even when he extols the excellence of the way he proposes.
In this he demonstrates a great fairness. While *The Cloud*
and *Privy Counsel* are essentially concerned with a particular
way to God, he does not close his eyes to the value of other
things which are not directly concerned with his teaching. And
even when he does make a gradation, he hastens to correct
the impression that he could think lowly of anyone. For while
he puts things in their proper scale, he admits that before God
who can really say that one is more precious than another?

> "I say not that such a naked sudden thought of any good and
> clean ghostly thing under God pressing against thy will or thy
> witting, or else wilfully drawn upon thee with advisement in
> increasing of thy devotion, although it be letting to this manner
> of work—that it is threfore evil. Nay! God forbid that thou
> take it so. But I say, although it be good and holy, yet in this
> work it letteth more than it profiteth"[32].

Following his insistence as regards the excellence of the
message of *The Cloud* over other things of which he does not
touch, the author sees clearly the relative value of them and
classifies them as *essential* and *accidental* as regards the
spiritual life. Yet while he makes the distinctions he insists
that the final judgment as regards their worth must be left
with God. Thus he does not depreciate the value of sensible
comforts and consolations, while he makes it clear that they
do not pertain to the essentials of the spiritual life.

> "And all this is after the disposition and the ordinance of God,
> all after the profit and the needfulness of diverse creatures. For
> some creatures be so weak and so tender in spirit, that unless they
> were somewhat comforted by feeling of such sweetness, they
> might on nowise abide nor bear the diversity of temptations and
> tribulations that they suffer and be travailed with in this life
> of their bodily and ghostly enemies. And some there be that
> they be so weak in body that they may do no great penance to
> cleanse them with. And these creatures will our Lord cleanse
> full graciously in spirit by such sweet feelings and weepings.
> And also on the tother part there be some creatures so strong

---

32 Ibid. Ch. 9, Underhill, p. 91; Hodgson, 35: 9-14.

in spirit, that they can pick them comfort enough within in their souls, in offering up of this reverent and meek stirring of love and accordance of will, that them needeth not much to be fed with such sweet comforts in bodily feelings. Which of these be holier or more dear with God, one than another, God wots and I not"[33].

We see likewise revealed in this passage a good knowledge which the author has of the capacities of different men. And we have an admirable example of how well he fits his approach to each of them depending on their individual strengths.

When he insists on the "naked Being of God" alone, he makes it clear that meditations do not have a part in his teaching. But he does not for all that say that they are worthless.

"Nevertheless yet be these fair meditations the truest way that a sinner may have in his beginning to the ghostly feeling of himself and of God. . . . And whoso cometh not in by this way, he cometh not truly . . ."[34].

The author similarly gives comfort and consolation to those who do not have the grace to follow the teaching of *The Cloud*.

"But if it be to those men, the which although they stand in activity by outward form of living, nevertheless yet by inward stirring after the privy spirit of God, whose dooms be hid, they be full graciously disposed, not continually as it is proper to very contemplatives, but now and then to be perceivers in the highest point of this contemplative act; if such men might see it, they should by the grace of God be greatly comforted thereby"[35].

The Cloud author never loses sight of the source of his teaching. He is equally insistent as regards the relative value of things, and though some acts may not have any bearing on his particular way to God, still they have their value and worth. From this general frame of mind results a like disposition to give freedom to the disciple to go wherever the Spirit leads him, and to follow some other course if the teaching is not akin to his attraction and disposition.

33 Ibid. Ch. 50, Underhill, pp. 200-201; Hodgson, 94: 3-18.
34 *Privy Counsel*, McCann, p. 128; Hodgson, 158: 17-25.
35 *The Cloud*, Prologue, Underhill, p. 41; Hodgson, 3:1-8. Walter Hilton likewise reveals this frame of mind. "Life contemplative is fair and meedful, and therefore thou shalt aye have it in thy mind and in thy desire; but thou shalt have in using life active, for it is so needful and so speedful" *Mixed Life*, Jones, p. 35.

With the recognition of the relative value of things, is the knowledge of the diversity of experiences in the spiritual life. The author warns his disciples against having a one-track mind, and thinking that everything is, or should be, the same.

"Lo! hereby mayest thou see that he that may not come for to see and feel the perfection of this work but by long travail, and yet is it but seldom, may lightly be deceived if he speak, think, and deem other men as he feeleth in himself, that they may not come to it but seldom, and that not without great travail. And on the same manner may he be deceived that may have it when he will, if he deem all other thereafter; saying that they may have it when they will"[36].

A spiritual director fired with these deep-seated convictions would not restrict the spiritual freedom of his disciple. The essential freedom of the disciple is assured as there would be no attempt to try to keep him when he feels that he is being drawn elsewhere. Nor will such a director insist on a particular course of action when the disciple is drawn to another course of action, equally good.

b. OTHER GIFTS OF NATURE

The author reveals in his writings other qualities which must have made him a very likeable person and a well-balanced spiritual director.

He shows his qualities as a teacher when he travels at the pace of development and progress of his disciple. He does not rush, neither does he anticipate further nuances of his teaching which the addressee is not ready to understand. He spares his disciple confusion arising from the difficult matter of The Cloud. This could be the underlying reason for all the seeming repetition as regards the ideas of The Cloud. The author does not want to be misunderstood, and he wants to be sure that the disciple understands him in turn. Hence his teaching on more specific matters of The Cloud is at the same pace as that of the interior progress of the disciple. This way the disciple is more ready and apt to profit from the more delicate nuances that a special grace like that of The Cloud teaching demands.

"But for methought that thou wast not yet able suddenly to be lifted up to the ghostly feeling of the being of God, for rudeness

36 Ibid. Ch. 72, Underhill, p. 260; Hodgson, 127: 14-20.

in thy ghostly feeling, therefore, to let thee climb thereto by degrees, I bade thee first gnaw on the naked feeling of thine own being, unto the time that thou mightest be made able to the high feeling of God by ghostly continuance in this privy work"[37].

Because of the knowledge the author has of his own interior life and of human nature, he reveals himself a good judge of men. He does not mince words to bring home a point to his disciple or to bring his attention to a defect. The author realizes that the insistence on the choice by God of those who could do the teaching of *The Cloud* might easily give rise to thoughts and feelings of pride. He wants to disabuse his disciple of this. In fact later on we shall see that this feeling of pride could be the reason for the withdrawal of grace by our Lord and His seeming absence from the soul.

"Beware, thou wretch, in this while with thine enemy; and hold thee never the holier nor the better, for the worthiness of this calling and for the singular form of living that thou art in. But the more wretched and cursed, unless thou do that in thee is goodly, by grace and by counsel, to live after thy calling"[38].

In *Discretion of Stirrings* he noted the impulsiveness of the disciple in practising austerities and the solitary life. He cautions his disciple to go slowly, and always to take care that he does not ruin his health. For while these practices are good, they are not God. Realizing well the inroads that the travail involved in the teaching of *The Cloud* can make on the spiritual and physical resources of the disciple, the author is insistent that the disciple take good care of his health. He reveals himself as a realist and is cognizant of the weakness of human nature.

"I say not that thou shalt continue ever therein alike fresh, for that may not be. For sometime sickness and other unordained dispositions in body and in soul, with many other needfulness to nature, will let thee full much, and ofttimes draw thee down from the height of this working. But I say that thou shouldest

---

37 *Privy Counsel*, McCann, pp. 125-126; Hodgson, 156: 3-8.
38 *The Cloud*, Ch. 2, Underhill, p. 61; Hodgson, 14: 20, 15: 1-3. We see that Walter Hilton is quite capable too of dishing out a similar form of tongue-lashing in pointing out to his disciple his faults. *Letter to a Hermit*, Russell-Smith, The Way, October, 1966, pp. 232-233. Like *The Cloud* author, Hilton always puts a saving clause to mitigate the pain brought about by a correction. *Letter to a Hermit*, Russell-Smith, *The Way*, July 1966, p. 232.

evermore have it either in earnest or in game; that is to say, either in work or in will. And therefore for God's love be wary with sickness as much as thou mayest goodly, so that thou be not the cause of thy feebleness, as far as thou mayest"[39].

But there are times when sickness cannot be avoided and when it does come through no fault of the disciple, then patience is essential.

"And if sickness come against thy power, have patience and abide meekly God's mercy: and all is then good enough. For I tell thee truly, that ofttimes patience in sickness and in other diverse tribulations pleaseth God much more than any liking devotion that thou mayest have in thy health"[40].

While the teaching of *The Cloud* is a very specialized one, the author uses ordinary examples and his teaching is salted with common sense and illustrated with homely figures. This shows his firm grasp of his teaching, for with all the heights reached and taught by *The Cloud,* there is that simplicity of narration and accompanying precision which reveals a thorough knowledge of what he is saying. Thus, in the matter of the shortness of prayer, he takes the analogy from the example of human distress, as in the case of emergency brought about by a sudden fire. At this time one so straightened cannot be expected to make a gracious speech, but simply shout out "fire" to arouse his neighbours.

"Ensample of this have we in a man or a woman afraid in the manner aforesaid. For we see well, that they cease never crying on this little word "out", or this little word "fire", ere the time be that they have in great part gotten help of their grief"[41].

39 *The Cloud,* Ch. 41, Underhill, pp. 174-175; Hodgson, 80: 6-14.
40 Ibid. Ch. 41, Underhill, p. 175; Hodgson, 80: 18-22. Walter Hilton shows the same attitude as regards sickness, as well as the same patience when sickness comes the way of the disciple. "For wit thou well that what man or woman shall be occupied ghostly in thoughts, reasonable pain of hunger wilfully taken, or sickness in the stomach or in the head or in other part of the body, for default of himself by too mickle fasting or in any other wise, shall mickle let the spirit and mickle hinder him from the knowing and the beholding of ghostly things, unless he have the more grace. For though it be so that bodily pain, either of penance or of sickness, or else bodily occupation, sometimes letteth not the fervour of love to God in devotion, but often increaseth it; soothly I expect that it letteth the fervour of love in contemplation, which may not be had nor felt soberly, but in great rest of body and of soul. For this do thou reasonably that longeth to thee, and keep thy bodily kind upon reason, and suffer God then send what that He will, be it health or sickness. Take it gladly, and grouch not against God wilfully". *Scale I,* Ch. 75, Underhill, p. 186.
41 *The Cloud,* Ch. 39, Underhill, p. 170; Hodgson, 78:5-8.

Likewise he uses a figure taken from an image of domestic peace and security.

"But I trow whoso had grace to do and feel as I say, he should feel good gamesome play with Him, as the father doth with the child, kissing and clipping, that well were him so"[42].

These are some aspects of the author's nature which show him as a balanced director of souls.

B. THE CLOUD AUTHOR AS A TRANSLATOR

In his spiritual direction the author makes use of the writings of other authors. However, he does so in such a way that he stamps on them the imprint of his own personality and makes of them some sort of an original treatise. In the three treatises which are actually paraphrases, namely, *Knowing of Spirits, The Study of Wisdom,* and *Denis Hid Divinity,* he displays a method of translation very peculiarly his own[43]. He has the main structure of the treatise he is using very much in mind, but then he works it out in such a way that his personal teaching and attitudes are silently incorporated into it. At this stage of our study we shall note the more obvious workings that the author did to the writings which he used. The finer points of doctrine will be used in the later sections to complement the teaching of *The Cloud*.

1. KNOWING OF SPIRITS

This is a paraphrase of two *Sermons* of St. Bernard, *De Diversis*[44]. By numbering the paragraphs in the critical edition,[45] we notice that paragraphs 1 to 5 are taken from *Sermon XXIII,* paragraphs 6 and 7 from *Sermon XXIV,* and paragraphs 8 to 16 are again taken from *Sermon XXIII.* Even from this physical examination we see that the author had a

---

42 Ibid. Ch. 46, Underhill, p. 188; Hodgson, 88:1-4. Walter Hilton likewise uses homely figures and examples. "But he is a simple master that cannot teach his disciple whilst he is learning but aye one lesson, and he is an unwise leech that by one medicine will heal all sores. . . . And also another reason is this: if there were one certain deed by the which a soul might come to the perfect love of God, then should a man ween that he might come thereto by his own work and through his own travail, as a merchant cometh to his meed by his own travail only, and by his own work" *Scale II,* Ch. 20, Underhill, pp. 298-299.

43 See also P. Hodgson, *Deonise Hid Diuinite* (E.E.T.S., 1958), Introduction, pp. xxxiii-xlvii.

44 Migne, P. L., t. clxxxiii, cols. 600-3.

45 P. Hodgson, *Deonise Hid Diuinite* (E.E.T.S., 1958), pp. 80-93.

practical purpose in mind. We feel tempted to believe that the addressee of this paraphrase is the same as that of *The Cloud*. The violence of the spirits revealed by this treatise can easily explain the travail that the disciple of *The Cloud* had to undergo. The pain is so intense that were it not for the grace of God, no one could have the strength to bear it. This paraphrase likewise reveals the same state of soul undergone in the experience narrated in the *Four Degrees of Passionate Love* of Richard of St. Victor.

The author follows the identification St. Bernard gives of the three spirits. But he gives further descriptions of their wiles and workings. Thus, he describes those of the "spirit of the world"[46]. He emphasizes the fact that the third spirit, the devil, is the "spirit of wrath and wickedness". As an antidote to the working of this wicked spirit, he stresses the need for peace and restfulness, which is also a dominant theme of the teaching of *The Cloud*. This third spirit is the most dangerous of all. While any of the three spirits can bring a soul to hell, yet there are varying degrees of danger from them. This part is a personal teaching of the author which is note-worthy for its length. We notice the preoccupation of the author as regards thoughts of peace and kindliness with one's neighbours. In the same way that the prince of hell is a "spirit of wrath and wickedness", so he says that God is charity Himself, and whoever "lacketh peace and restfulness of heart, lacketh the lively presence of the lovely sight of the high peace of heaven, good and gracious God, His own dear self"[47]. The author singles out one way by which this "spirit of wrath and wickedness" goes about sowing strife and discord. He does this by suggesting singularity in works of piety and holi-ness that manifests as the "holier than thou" attitude. This is quite effective in sowing strife and discord among people striving for great holiness[48]. The author reveals a personal experience in an autobiographical paragraph.

(St. Bernard) "But it is sorrow for to say, and more for to feel, that sometime our own spirit is so overcome per-adventure with each of these three spirits, of the flesh, of the

---

46 *Knowing of Spirits*, Gardner, p. 121, Hodgson, 82:4-9, 83:12-85:12
47 Ibid. Gardner. p. 123; Hodgson 84:19-85:2.
48 Ibid. Gardner. pp. 124-25.

world, and of the fiend, and so brought into danger, bounden
in bondage, in thraldom and in service to them all,

(*Cloud* author) that sorrow it is to wit. In great confusion
and loss of itself,

(St. Bernard) it doth now the office of each one of them
itself in itself.

(*Cloud* author) And this befalleth when, after long use, and
customable consenting unto them when they come, at the
last it is made so fleshly, so wordly, and so maliciously, so
wicked, and so froward,

(St. Bernard) that now plainly of itself, without suggestion
of any other spirit, it gendereth and bringeth forth in itself,
not only lusty thoughts of the flesh, and vain thoughts of the
world, but that worst of all these, as are bitter thoughts and
wicked, in backbiting, and deeming, and evil suspicion of
others"[49].

This is a typical example of the way the author treats the
texts of other writers so that there is an intimate blending
of ideas. One can see in these additions predominant ideas
and preoccupations of *The Cloud* author in matters regarding
the spiritual life. The condition of the soul described above is
reminiscent of the *Four Degrees of Passionate Love*, wherein
nothing in heaven or on earth could satisfy or please it. The
only thing it can do is to ask others to pray for him. But
grace is most powerful and in this straitened condition these
wicked spirits can be put to flight by the power of grace. This
too is a thought proper to *The Cloud* author[50].

The remaining and concluding paragraphs from paragraphs
10 to 16 with two short sentences proper to St. Bernard,[51]
are all proper to *The Cloud* author. This personal part is
significantly on *Confession* and the particular role it plays in
this violent fight against the three wicked spirits. *The Cloud*
gives importance only to *Confession* although there is no
intention of underestimating the other Sacraments. Like other
matters not germane to the teaching of *The Cloud*, the author
recognizes their value but says explicitly that for the teaching
of *The Cloud* they are not of much help. We think that it is in
this section that the author explains the value and efficacy of

49 Ibid. Gardner, p. 126. Hodgson, 86:22-87:12.
50 Ibid. Gardner, p. 127.
51 Ibid. Hodgson, 88:2-93:2.

the Sacrament of Penance in relation to the particular teaching
of *The Cloud*. Surely the pain involved in the travail of *The
Cloud* is described no less graphically. These treatises are
not meant for beginners, and yet we admire how these treatises
can be written for those in the higher reaches of the spiritual
life. But in the light of the daring claims of *The Cloud* that
God in His absolute freedom can choose even the most
wicked sinner, we can only admire the goodness and mercy
of God which is the only reason for the *Divine Choice* of the
soul to undertake the teaching of *The Cloud*. Then there are
the trials and harassments that one bent on loving only God
will surely meet with as he goes higher in the ascent. The
purifying action of fire on metal is a favourite expression
among spiritual writers. *The Cloud* author will speak of the
launching of the soul upon the spirit's sea[52].

2.   *STUDY OF WISDOM*

This is an even freer paraphrase judging merely from the
brevity to which the author has reduced the lengthy work of
Richard of St. Victor. The author does not divide his transcrip-
tion into chapters. He uses the title headings of Richard of
St. Victor for the most dominant ideas. Several paragraphs
of Richard are paraphrased into a paragraph, or even altogether omitted. Richard's work was unillustrated, whereas the
author of *The Cloud* made use of a visual aid to illustrate the
role of Jacob, his wives and children. Jacob stands for God,
Rachel for Reason and Lia for Affection. One striking difference is the fact that the author equated Jacob with God which
Richard does not. The emphasis is on the fact that the children
of Jacob's wives are the virtues. They would not be the children of Jacob—God, if they were not. *The Cloud* author
develops his own point of view by changing the emphasis of
Richard's teaching. The use of Scripture references is reduced
to the barest minimum. Only the most telling quotation is
used. The use of terms is not exactly the same as in Richard.
Synonyms and phrases are used to express the ideas contained
in the *Benjamin Minor* of Richard. Abridgements of chapters
to a single paragraph, rearrangements and afterthoughts are
the ways the unknown author used to achieve his particular
purpose.

[52] *Privy Counsel*, McCann, p. 136; Hodgson, 167:13-168:2.

The Study of Wisdom is an outline of the ascent to God. It starts with the things necessary for salvation and continues on to perfection. Union is the end to be achieved. This progressive road to God is illustrated by the story of the wives of Jacob and their children. The paraphrase gives the impression that the author had completely mastered the teachings of Richard, and was so steeped in the *Benjamin Major* and *Benjamin Minor* that he could write from memory, now and then consulting Richard to see if he had kept the order of his works. It is interesting to note that in Chapter 73 Benjamin is born and Rachel dies. From here on the matter of contemplation is developed in great detail by Richard and more fully in *Benjamin Major*.

The paraphrase reveals that the author used Richard only where there were common points which he wished to discuss. The conclusion to *The Study of Wisdom* shows that the author clearly intended to make a treatise, not simply a translation. It is tempting to believe that the author stopped precisely with the birth of Benjamin so that he could develop his own particular teaching contained in *The Cloud* and *Privy Counsel*. The author ends with the note on JHESU. Similarly it would be easy to find the sequel to *The Study of Wisdom* in *The Scale of Perfection*[53] where Hilton talks of the particular work of contemplation as the *Love of Jhesu*. One could take this part of *Scale II* and fit it into the *Study of Wisdom* and the ideas would run continuously without difficulty.

Richard of St. Victor uses the story of Jacob's children in relation to the powers of the soul. This insistence on the part that psychology plays in the ascent to God is never lost sight of by Richard. The six degrees of contemplation in *Benjamin Major* are analyzed acutely and in great detail always in relation to the powers of the soul. This insistence on psychology is absent in *The Study of Wisdom*. Both Richard and *The Cloud* author use the story of Moses and the Ark of the Covenant, but the emphasis is different. Richard picks out the Cherubim above the Mercy Seat to illustrate his teaching on contemplation. The author of *The Cloud* narrates the roles played by Moses, Aaron and Bezaleel to illustrate the gratuitousness of the gift of contemplation.

53 *Scale II*, Ch. 31, Underhill, p. 366-Ch. 46, p. 464.

3. *DENIS HID DIVINITY*

As regards this free translation of the *Mystica Theologia* of the Pseudo-Dionysius, we have this explicit declaration of the author:

"This writing that next followeth is the English of a book that Saint Denis wrote unto Timothy, the which book is called in Latin tongue *Mystica Theologia*. Of the which book, for that it is made mind in the seventieth chapter of a book written before —the which book is called the *Cloud of Unknowing*—how that Denis' sentence will clearly confirm all that is written in that same book: therefore, in translation of it, I have not only followed the naked letter of the text, but for to declare the hardness of it, I have much followed the sentence of the Abbot of Saint Victor, a noble and worthy expositor of this same book"[54].

The opinion has been given that the author could not "have grasped the outlook and meaning of the Syrian monk of the early sixth century . . . the author of *The Cloud* did not read Denis in the original Greek, but in two medieval Latin translations, those of Johannes Sarracenus (d.1160) and Thomas Gallus (d.1240), assisted by the latter's commentary"[55].

We shall see this in greater detail, especially as regards the primacy of the will and love in the teaching of *The Cloud*. We shall see whether for all his protestations of fidelity to the Pseudo-Dionysius, *The Cloud* is in fact Dionysian.

We may sum up this manner of translation employed by the author in the following words:

"Everything points rather to their being the work of an original mystical genius, of strongly marked character and great literary ability; who, whilst he took the framework of his philosophy from Dionysius the Areopagite, and of his psychology from Richard of St. Victor, yet is in no sense a mere imitator of these masters, but introduced a genuinely new element into mediaeval religious literature"[56].

54 *Denis Hid Divinity*, Prologue, McCann (1947), p. 130; Hodgson, 2:3-12
55 D. Knowles, *The English Mystical Tradition*, p. 73.
56 E. Underhill, *The Cloud*, p. 9.

CONCLUSIONS

While we make no claim that this textual portrait we have attempted to draw of *The Cloud* author is a complete one, yet from the sketch we have made we see some character traits more deeply etched than others. We think that there is enough of these more finely marked character traits to identify the main lines of the personality of the author. Hence the intellectual background of the author lies heavily on the less frequently trodden ground of mystical theology, and the influence of Richard of St. Victor, St. Bernard, the Pseudo-Dionysius and St. Augustine as well as Thomas Gallus is clear from his writings. In contrast to the rare atmosphere within which these writings move, we see the author using very homely examples and figures that reveal that he is not completely out of touch with the more ordinary and humdrum aspects of life. We see him richly endowed with gifts of nature which harmonize with his gifts of grace and make of him a balanced director of souls. We find him not an inflexible personality that would insist on any one course of action. His adaptable nature allowed him to bend to others, rather than force them to conform to his own ways of thinking. He is sensitive to the needs of others and thoughtful and aware of the weakness of human nature. Hence he exhibits a variety of approach to the problems of his disciples based on their actual needs and several capacities, rather than on his favourite theories. We notice a quiet suppleness and strength in his character that could so open his heart to the scrutiny of his disciple and make him behold his sorry state if this could encourage his disciple. Yet despite his admission of weakness he was adamant regarding his possession of the grace to do the teaching of *The Cloud*, and to be the teacher. He does not hesitate to present his credentials and we do not see in him a streak of false humility that would cover real pride under a protestation of humility. As regards other writers he exhibits very clearly his eclectic tendencies yet he is not a mere imitator, stamping on the works he uses the imprint of his own personality. It is hard to see any one author dominating his way of thinking and it would be safer to say that three or four have a heavy influence on him. And in all his translations there is so much of himself that shines through and he reveals himself as master and moulder of the

authorities he follows. While he has the particular ascent of
The Cloud always before him so pressingly insistent, and while
he can extol its excellence, nevertheless he does not depreciate
the value of other things and matters that have their proper
use in their particular spheres. We see him as being objective
and fair in this respect. He is an extremely grateful soul and
keeps on singing the praises of the Lord and what He has
done for him. And in the realm of grace and virtue he clearly
reveals himself as deeply humble and profoundly charitable.
Having had an intimate experience of the mercy of God operative in his life, he would in turn become an apostle of this
mercy, and this deep-rooted disposition would colour so much
of his dealings with others that would blossom in kindliness
and understanding. And in all that he writes and reveals of
himself, we see him engrossed only in God, a man whose sole
preoccupation is thinking and loving his God, ever aware that
he moves and lives in His Presence, absorbing and occupying
all the waking moments of his life and demanding a unified
attention that would brook no companionship with any other.

This is the portrait of *The Cloud* author as we see him
revealed in his texts. This too is part of our contribution to
the problem of the authorship of *The Cloud*. One thing does
strike us. We have said that Richard Rolle was not a mystic,
and we have followed the view that the Monk of Farne, John
Whiterig, was a mystic. Yet *The Cloud* author is so radically
different from Richard Rolle, as surely he is different in
temperament and dispositions from John Whiterig. Instead
he exhibits many similarities of temperament and disposition
to Walter Hilton, who is not a mystic himself. It is easy to
give as a reason a "common background" of reading to
account for the similarities. But in practice this is not so easy
to verify. In the spiritual life it is difficult to have two persons
attracted to the same virtues, the same readings, the same
influences. One has only to consider a cloister of Carmelite
nuns to realize that within this very small group, tuned to the
spirituality of St. Teresa and St. John of the Cross, each
nun's particular approach to the spirit of her Order has a
personal colour that distinguishes it from any other. Besides,
in the case of *The Cloud* author and Walter Hilton, there are
the coincidences of time, place, language and teaching, bear-

ing in mind that every coincidence narrows the field of choice. A starting point in appreciating the value of parallel passages from *The Cloud* group and the works of Walter Hilton is to examine them with regard to both quantity and quality. It will be profitable to see what proportion of the complete works of Hilton these parallel passages comprise. At the same time it will be good to examine those passages in Hilton which bear resemblance to the particular teaching of *The Cloud* author, namely, "the naked Being of God". The present writer thinks that the "love of Jesu" involved in Hilton's "reformation in faith and feeling" can easily be replaced by the concept of God only for Himself, without a great change of meaning. The fact that the addressees are not the same may account for the variance of meaning.

In this textual portrait we have exploited the inner depths which the texts reveal, which are unaffected by scribal errors or state of preservation of the manuscripts. What is surprising is that these interior dispositions have managed to remain, and still shine through despite repeated corruption of the originals. To ask that the two groups of writings be identical would be to demand that we have mere duplicates. To do this would be to deny the richness of the human personality that *The Cloud* author reveals. And so we simply wonder why!

Chapter III

"This Work"

A. DIFFICULTY OF EXPRESSION IN MYSTICAL EXPERIENCES

Is it not quite a common experience for many of us to grope for words and admit our inability to express what we feel? At such times as these we only hope that our hearer understands what we wish to convey. And when we go higher up the range of feelings, when we are face to face with a tragedy or some ineffable experience, we find that we can at best only stammer and search for words.

If this is so with our common experiences how much more difficult must it be when the vocabulary has to bear the full weight of things infinite, when experiences so rare and other-worldly must be translated into words. Our Lord, being true God and true man, had experience both of the Divine and the human. But what He knows as God He translated to the hearers of His time in terms they understood. So when He taught of the Kingdom of Heaven He likened it unto "a grain of mustard seed"[1], "a dragnet cast into the sea"[2], "ten brides-maids"[3], "a merchant looking for fine pearls"[4], "a treasure hidden in a field"[5]. Our Lord had to resort to figures in translating realities beyond the ken of ordinary experience, for obviously His hearers had no previous experience of them. Even St. Paul could burst out that *the things that no eye has seen and no ear has heard, things beyond the mind of man, all that God has prepared for those who love Him"*[6].

And when we go back farther into the Old Testament times, this predominant use of figures is even more arresting. In the New Testament we have our Lord who spoke on His own authority and knowledge, while the Prophets and writers of the Old Testament were acting as intermediaries and spokesmen, peering, as it were, into the future still hidden by the clouds

1 Mt. 13 : 31; Mk. 4 : 31; Lk. 13 : 19.
2 Mt. 13 : 47.
3 Mt. 25 : 1.
4 Mt. 13 : 45-46.
5 Mt. 13 : 44.
6 Isa. 64 : 4; 1 Cor. 2 : 9.

73

of centuries. Figures then were used to convey the reality underlying the expressions they used.

The mystics are those favoured souls who had the most intimate experiences of the Godhead. When they write they speak of a very deep and ineffable experience which they want to translate into words that they know. With the mystics too we find the predominant use of figures and images, and it is interesting to note that their choice of figures is not haphazard. One notices, on closer study of the figures that the mystics have used, that their vocabulary seems limited and mystics of different ages have resorted to the ones used by earlier mystics.

However, notwithstanding the mystics' problems of expression, and their use of figures, we must make every effort to discover the realities to which they are alluding.

"It cannot be doubted that the mystics mean to affirm that they have an experimental knowledge of God and of their supernatural life. All their descriptions and statements point in this direction. To see nothing more in them than modes of expression is to overthrow the whole science of mysticism at its base or to make it merely the science of ordinary Christian life"[7].

In the same way that we notice that the mystics narrate experiences shared by only very few, we realise, too, that this higher, different perception reveals a level of mind with which we are unfamiliar.

"What we must hold to, on the unanimous testimony of mystics and mystical writers, is that in contemplation the soul has something like spiritual senses, which put us in relation with the concrete realities of the spiritual world, as the bodily senses do with those of the sensible world"[8].

We do not labour this point, for we realize that this is not generally accepted. M. Saudreau, the principal representative of the group of Dominican writers ". . . does not admit that there is in the mystic states that experimental knowledge of God, that angelic mode of knowledge without sensible images, by infused intellectual 'species' of which the mystical theologians speak. The very explicit expressions of the mystics on this special mode of knowledge, which seems so strange

[7] J. V. Bainvel, Introduction to A. Poulain, *The Graces of Interior Prayer*, p. lviii.
[8] Ibid. p. lxii.

to themselves in their first experiences, are, in his eyes, only metaphors, manners of speaking"[9].

When dealing with matters of mystical theology the mind is drawn instinctively to the writings of St. John of the Cross. Not that St. John of the Cross is the only mystic, but he was the one who made a synthesis of principles of Mystical Theology on a more systematic basis. This study will note the similarity of teaching of St. John of the Cross to that of *The Cloud,* and hope to make a contribution to what has already been noted by an eminent scholar on the 14th-century English spiritual writers.

> "We may now pass to consider what is perhaps his greatest claim on our attention—the striking manner in which he anticipates the most characteristic teaching of St. John of the Cross"[10].

Between *The Cloud* author and St. John of the Cross are some 200 years. Theirs were conflicting periods of history. The 14th century was one of stress and decline, while the 16th century in which St. John of the Cross lived was the golden age of Spain. The author of *The Cloud* never revealed himself as having been involved in matters of state, whereas St. John of the Cross and St. Teresa of Avila were familiar with Philip II, to whose austere room in The Escorial flowed information and reports from all over the world and from which, in turn, orders and directives were issued to the administrators of the Empire. For all the diversity of circumstances of times and place, *The Cloud* author and St. John of the Cross reveal very striking similarity of teaching which could attest to the reality of their experiences. We have St. John of the Cross testifying to the difficulty of expression in mystical experiences and the manner of using figures to express the reality beneath.

> "For who can write down that which He reveals to loving souls wherein He dwells? And who can set forth in words that which He makes them to feel? And lastly, who can express that which He makes them to desire? Of a surety, none; nay, indeed, not the very souls through whom He passes. It is for this reason that, by means of figures, comparisons and similitudes, they allow something of that which they feel to overflow and utter

---

9 Ibid. p. lxviii.
10 D. Knowles, "The Excellence of the Cloud", *Downside Review,* January 1934, p. 80; also *The English Mystical Tradition,* pp. 86-93.

secret mysteries from the abundance of the Spirit, rather than explain these things rationally. These similitudes, if they be not read with the simplicity of the spirit of love and understanding embodied in them, appear to be nonsense rather than the expression of reason, as may be seen in the divine Songs of Solomon and in other books of Divine Scripture, where, since the Holy Spirit cannot express the abundance of His meaning in common and vulgar terms, He utters mysteries in strange figures and similitudes. Whence it follows that no words of holy doctors, albeit they have said much and may yet say more, can ever expound these things fully, neither could they be expounded in words of any kind. That which is expounded of them, therefore, is ordinarily the least part of that which they contain"[11].

And beneath these figures is a reality which the mystics want to describe and make known, so as to proclaim the wonders of the Lord.

"Let it not appear to the reader of this that in what we have said we are indulging ourselves in mere words, for in truth, if it were necessary to explain that which passes through the soul that arrives at this happy estate, all words, and time itself, would fail us, and still the greater part would remain to be expounded; for, if the soul is enabled to reach the peace of God, which surpasses all that is of sense, then all that is of sense will remain bereft and mute at having to expound it"[12].

With this note from St. John of the Cross regarding the difficulty of expression in mystical experiences, we shall proceed to annotate the leading ideas of *The Cloud* and other treatises with the teachings of St. John of the Cross, in places where they show striking similarity. With this introductory note, too, on the language of the mystics, we move closer to the particular teachings of *The Cloud*.

B. "THIS WORK"

Heretofore we have been referring to the teaching of *The Cloud* in general terms, as a "way", "teaching", "doctrine" or "exercise". To describe his particular teaching the author uses the words "Work"[13] or "Working"[14], and we shall see that

---

11 St. John of the Cross, *Spiritual Canticle,* Allison-Peers, pp. 23-24.
12 Ibid. p. 144.
13 A total of 172 times: in *The Cloud* 131 times; in *Privy Counsel* 35 times; in *Epistle of Prayer* 3 times; in *Denis Hid Divinity* 3 times. It is interesting to note that Walter Hilton uses the term "work" and its derivatives 11 times in Chapter 21 of *Scale II*. This chapter is one

The Cloud author invests them with a technical meaning of his own. It is interesting to note that in *Denis Hid Divinity* the author uses the same word to identify the teaching of the Pseudo-Dionysius[15]. The particular teaching of *The Epistle of Prayer* is also identified by the same words[16]. From the frequency with which he uses the word it is clear that he intends to identify his teaching with this term, which is remarkable for its generality.

But he invests it with a particularity and precision in relation to the teaching of *The Cloud*. By the use of demonstrative pronouns he links the term to "The Work of This Book"[17] or "This Writing"[18]. This emphasis is signified also by the use of the adjective "same"[19]. It is then not just any work to be done, but the "Work" that is the part of man in the ascent to God.

There are long passages of great beauty which describe extensively the different elements that go into "This Work". We also find short, pithy, and apt adjectives and modifiers that identify with strict economy "This Work".

Hence, in the expression "this lovely blind work"[20] the author gives the primacy to the will and its act of love. The will is considered as a "blind faculty" and in its working it follows the lead of the intellect.

"The gracious work of this book"[21] describes the need for a "special grace" to do "This Work". Like a haunting refrain "this ghostly work"[22] stresses the fact that this ascent must be made in the "sovereignest point of the spirit", and in the life that is "strictly contemplative". The presence of the *enabling grace* makes it "this light work"[23]. The secret and intimate nature of "This Work" is expressed by "this prive

---

of the central chapters of *Scale II*, and has to do with the journey of the Pilgrim to Jerusalem: see *Scale II*, Ch. 21, Underhill, pp. 303-310.

[14] A total of 21 times: in *The Cloud* 3 times; in *Privy Counsel* 9 times; in *Epistle of Prayer* 9 times.

[15] *Denis Hid Divinity*, Hodgson, 6: 10, 12, 26.

[16] *Epistle of Prayer*, Hodgson, pp. 48, 50, 52, 58.

[17] *The Cloud*, Hodgson, pp. 3, 4, 6, 7, 9, 11, 72-73, 100, 110.

[18] Ibid. Hodgson, p. 56.

[19] Ibid. Hodgson, p. 12, *Privy Counsel*, Hodgson, p. 148.

[20] *Privy Counsel*, Hodgson, 144: 29; also "meek blind stirring of love", *The Cloud*, Ch. 4, Underhill, p. 71; Hodgson, 22: 18.

[21] *The Cloud*, Hodgson, 6: 22-23.

[22] Ibid. Hodgson, 61: 2, 81: 10, 113: 12, 114: 15.

[23] *Privy Counsel*, Hodgson, 137: 17.

work"[24] and its excellence is shown by the expression "this precious working"[25]. "This high Divine work"[26] intimates its divine origin and, because of this, there must be great joy produced by this assurance. And so it is "this listi working"[27]. Finally it is God Who initiates, sustains and perfects it. God is the *Principal Doer* and the soul but the *consenter and sufferer*. In this is revealed that mark of *passivity* which truly characterizes the mystical life. Like a grand summing-up, the author describes his teaching as "the work of Only God"[28], "His Own Work"[29].

In the next section we shall see the nature of "This Work" through the use of descriptive phrases and paragraphs. In these pithy expressions as well as the longer passages, we notice a remarkable absence of strictly theological terms with their tendency to divide and subdivide. On the other hand we notice a clarity and a transparency shining through in the writings of *The Cloud* group. Everything flows and overflows spontaneously and the themes keep recurring in different nuances with effortless ease, like the ebb and flow of the tide. This manner of narration can be explained only by the author's mastery of the matter.

C.   NATURE OF "THIS WORK"

1.   *"BELIEF" AS THE FOUNDATION*

The author reveals a remarkable clarity and familiarity with the particular ascent to God that he teaches. Indeed he often attests to his personal experience, and says that the source of his teaching is God Himself. But this assertion must not simply be read and believed. We have to see in the writings of *The Cloud* author this mark of authenticity of personal experience, a *felt* and *experimental consciousness* of the Godhead, which Fr. Poulain says is the *first fundamental element* characterizing the mystical life.

A cursory reading of *The Cloud* and *Privy Counsel* gives this impression of a first-hand experience on the part of the author. The matter involved is difficult, yet there is an ease and

[24] Ibid. Hodgson, 156:8.
[25] Ibid. Hodgson, 148: 22.
[26] *Denis Hid Divinity*, Hodgson, 6: 10.
[27] *Privy Counsel*, Hodgson, 145: 3.
[28] *The Cloud*, Hodgson, 6: 21; 62: 2.
[29] *Privy Counsel*, Hodgson, 168: 11-12.

a fluidity in the narration. It is only on the basis of a detailed theological synthesis that we are slowly verifying the *fundamental* and *subsidiary* marks of the mystical life revealed in *The Cloud* and *Privy Counsel*. Since the 14th century many favourite theories and hypotheses have been discarded and superseded. The acceptable explanation is the reality of the experiences narrated by *The Cloud* author. In the highly specialized list of the marks of the mystical life verified in *The Cloud* and *Privy Counsel*, we find an economy and a concentration that is remarkable. One who is intent on proving a favourite theory would have been most careful in hedging all his statements so as to cover any possibility of a loophole. This would not have been in favour of economy. Neither would a simplicity and a fluidity of treatment result from this general frame of mind.

This general impression resulting from a reading of the texts is borne out by the observations of *the* expert on the texts of *The Cloud* group.

> "The author, describing an exercise of contemplative prayer, was obviously drawing from his own mystical experience. . . . Though his own mystical experiences are the unmistakable background of both these treatises yet, being schooled in the works of the Fathers and Doctors of the Church, he naturally shaped his thought according to the teaching of those writers who had most influenced him, because their experience was most akin to his own. Many of his turns of thought and phrases are traceable to known sources, but in their context they are so vividly personal that one must assume that such borrowed expressions best described his own mental and emotional experiences"[30].

Reflecting further on the style of *The Cloud* and *Privy Counsel*, Professor Hodgson has no doubt as to the personal experience of the author.

> "The young disciple for whom these treatises were written was not a scholar. The author having perfectly assimilated the teaching he wanted to communicate, and writing from very immediate personal experience, used simple everyday terms, deliberately avoiding all learned terminology . . . "[31].

The choice of a metaphor to describe some aspect of

---

[30] P. Hodgson, *The Cloud of Unknowing* (E.E.T.S., 1958), Introduction, p. li.
[31] Ibid, Introduction, p. lvii.

"This Work" is seen by Professor Hodgson again as revealing a personal experience.

"But there is a more individual kind of metaphor in *The Cloud* and *Priue Counseling* suggestive of an immediate experience. This particular kind conveys the sense of obstruction between man and God, and describes the exercise of contemplation as one of stripping and blinding"[32].

From this general observation we go to the texts themselves and see what the author says as regards the *experimental* quality of "This Work".

Firstly we have the author's declaration of intention as regards other people's works.

"On otherwise than thus, list me not cite him, nor none other doctor, for me at this time. For sometime, men thought it meekness to say nought of their own heads, unless they affirmed it by Scripture and doctors' words: and now it is turned into curiosity, and shewing of cunning. To thee it needeth not, and therefore I do it not. For whoso hath ears, let him hear, and whoso is stirred for to trow, let him trow: for else, shall they not"[33].

Here too his personal experience is suggested by the use of the expression "stirred for to trow . . .", and in his comparison of this mental state with that of "hearing". In this passage describing the personal experience of the author, we find verified the *second fundamental mark* of the mystical life, namely "this knowledge is the result of an impression, a spiritual *sensation* of a special kind"[34]. This *impression* and *sensation* will be seen more clearly in the *Personal Intervention* of God, which is the subject of Chapter VI of this study.

His intention to attest to this experience is borne out likewise by the expressions he uses. He uses the words "feeling" and "experience" to describe this interior reality. It would seem that the author was speaking lightly when he says that "This Work" is indescribable. But the key is in the "feeling".

". . . and yet it is no will, nor no desire, but a thing thou wottest never what, that stirreth thee to will and desire thou wottest never what. . . . It sufficeth enough unto thee, that thou feelest thee stirred likingly with a thing thou wottest never what, else

---

32 P. Hodgson, *Deonise Hid Diuinite* (E.E.T.S., 1958), Introduction, p. lvi.
33 *The Cloud*, Ch. 70, Underhill, p. 256; Hodgson, 125 : 15-22.
34 A. Poulain, *The Graces of Interior Prayer*, p. 88.

that in this stirring thou hast no special thought of any thing under God . . ."[35].

This passage confirms what he says about "This Work" when he admits that ". . . all that is spoken of it is not it, but of it"[36]. Yet we shall see in the succeeding sections that he gives a catalogue of the chief characteristics of the *nature* and *perfections* of his teaching, which show that he does know what it is all about. In this passage, as well as in other similar passages, we see verified the fourth characteristic of the mystical life, namely "the knowledge of God accompanying it is obscure and confused"[37].

This "feeling" of the "naked Being of God" is equated with the consciousness of other things that come to the mind, and their effect on the perfection of "This Work".

"For since a naked remembrance of any thing under God pressing against thy will and thy witting putteth thee further from God than thou shouldest be if it were not, and letteth thee, and maketh thee inasmuch more unable to feel in experience the fruit of His love, what trowest thou then that a remembrance wittingly and wilfully drawn upon thee will hinder thee in thy purpose?"[38].

It is not something merely theoretical. There are effects which can be verified. In this "feeling and experience", labour is required of the disciple. It is true that in the highest reaches of the Personal Invasion of the soul by God there is a different "feeling and experience" that is the result of extreme *passivity*. But still, it is the same *consciousness* that is involved.

"And therefore swink and sweat in all that thou canst and mayst, for to get thee a true knowing and a feeling of thyself as thou art; and then I trow that soon after that thou shalt have a true knowing and a feeling of God as he is. Not as He is in Himself, for that may no man do but Himself; nor yet as thou shalt do in bliss both body and soul together. But as it is possible, and as He vouchsafeth to be known and felt of a meek soul living in this deadly body"[39].

This "feeling" is described in comparison with other forms of personal experience of the same thing. The "feeling" in-

35 *The Cloud* Ch. 34, Underhill, p. 155; Hodgson, 70: 7-21.
36 *Privy Counsel*, McCann, p. 123; Hodgson, 153: 20.
37 A. Poulain, *The Graces of Interior Prayer*, p. 114.
38 *The Cloud*, Ch. 9, Underhill, pp. 90-91; Hodgson, 34: 23-24, 35: 1-4.
39 Ibid. Ch. 14, Underhill, pp. 103-104; Hodgson, 42: 1-7.

volved in "This Work" is distinguished from that which is granted to the Saints in the Beatific Vision: "Not as He is in Himself . . . nor yet as thou shalt do in bliss both body and soul together".

He stresses the fact of "this feeling" by distinguishing it from other mental states.

". . . then is it speedful to thee some time for to cease from these quaint meditations and these subtle imaginations of the qualities of thy being and of God's and of the works of thyself and of God (in the which thy wits have been fed, and with the which thou hast been led from worldliness and bodilyness to that ableness of grace that thou art in) for to learn how thou shalt be occupied ghostly in feeling of thyself or of God, whom thou hast learned so well before by thinking and imagining of thy doings"[40].

In this passage we see "feeling", "thinking" and "imagining" compared with each other.

The author has made a long list of the tests by which one could verify the presence of "the special grace" for "This Work". These have reference both to the inner testimonies of "the privy teaching of the Spirit of God" as well as to the overflowing effects of their presence into the exterior world so that others notice them. The strongest proof of the presence of "this special grace" is the effect of "the comings and the goings of the Lord" on the soul: "joy of the finding . . . sorrow of the losing"[41].

Again, he says:

"I suppose it shall be thus: the work shall witness when the proof worketh. And therefore, I pray thee, dispose thee for to receive this grace of thy Lord, and hear what he saith . . ."[42].

The different things that go to make these tests need not be verified all at once; it is sufficient that one or two are present[43].

Not only are these interior "feelings" compared with similar mental states and acts, but they are also compared with the experiences of others.

"Lo! hereby mayest thou see that he that may not come for to

---

40 *Privy Counsel*, McCann, pp. 138-139; Hodgson, 170: 15-23.
41 *The Cloud*, Ch. 75, Underhill, p. 269; Hodgson, 132: 15-16.
42 *Privy Counsel*, McCann, p. 125; Hodgson, 155: 20-22.
43 Ibid. McCann, p. 138; Hodgson, 170: 9-13.

see and feel the perfection of this work but by long travail, and yet is it but seldom, may lightly be deceived if he speak, think, and deem other men as he feeleth in himself, that they may not come to it but seldom, and that not without great travail. And on the same manner may he be deceived that may have it when he will, if he deem all other thereafter; saying that they may have it when they will"[44].

The personal experience of what he teaches is very evident in the passages on *pain* and *travail* involved in "This Work". Here they are described as actual and real, whether arising from the "forgetting of all creatures," or from the pain of actual or original sin.

As if this were one of the questions that the disciple put to the author, we see this fact unequivocably stated right in the beginning of *Privy Counsel*:

"Seek no further in him by subtlety of wit; let that belief be thy ground. This naked intent, freely fastened and grounded in very belief, shall be nought else to thy thought and to thy feeling but a naked thought and a blind feeling of thine own being . . .[45].

It is the opinion of Professor Hodgson that ". . . the theme of the whole passage is that the mind should be occupied only with God. That faith should be the basis of this work is an idea of secondary importance . . ."[46]. It is also her opinion that "a naked thought and a blind feeling of thine own being" means "mere consciousness"[47]. Indeed, this interpretation is supported by the context of *The Cloud* and *Privy Counsel*.

In an oblique way the author emphasizes the element of *perception, feeling* and *experience* in his surprise at those who

44 *The Cloud*, Ch. 72, Underhill, p. 260; Hodgson, 127: 14-20.
45 *Privy Counsel*, McCann, p. 106; Hodgson, 135: 23-24, 136: 1-3.
46 P. Hodgson, *The Cloud of Unknowing* (E.E.T.S. 1958), p. 204.
47 P. Hodgson, *The Cloud of Unknowing* (E.E.T.S. 1958), p. 205. In the light of this opinion the present writer begs to disagree with the interpretation of Fr. Johnston, seeing "belief" as something having to do with "faith" He writes: "The cloud of unknowing is thus seen to be that mystical knowledge that fills the mind when, void of images and concepts, it is grounded in *faith*, stirred by *love*, and suffused with *wisdom*. The Mary Magdalen motif makes the thing clear . . . Yet she had faith by which she 'regarded the sovereignest wisdom of his Godhead lapped in the dark words of his Manhood . . .' In this way, the contemplative sees the sovereignest wisdom of God lapped in the dark words of Christ in Scripture and the propositions of the Church, while love goes out to 'touch' the realities thus darkly apprehended". (W. Johnston, *The Mysticism of The Cloud of Unknowing*, p. 258; see also: pp. 3, 59-62, 64-65, 74-75, 125, 137, 140).

say ". . . that my writing to thee and to others is so hard and so high, so curious and so quaint, that scarcely it may be conceived of the subtlest clerk or witted man or woman in this life, as they say"[48]. In answer the author continues:

> "For I hold him too lewd and too simple that cannot think and feel that himself is—not what himself is, but that himself is. For this is plainly proper to the lewdest cow, or to the most unreasonable beast—if it might be said, as it may not, that one were lewder or more unreasonable than another—for to feel their own proper being. Much more then is it proper to man, the which is singularly endued with reason above all other beasts, for to think and for to feel his own proper being"[49].

It is then a question of *experience* and *perception* that is involved in "This Work". This the author says in his own down-to-earth way. And this *perception* and *feeling* is equated with the most fundamental of all one's awareness, one's consciousness of existence.

This fact of a personal experience is likewise drawn from the comparison with the experiences of Moses. Aaron and Bezaleel, who had most to do with the making of the Ark of the Covenant. In this connection he likens himself to Bezaleel. Apart from his direct claims this is the strongest allusion to his credentials. In this passage too he expressly attests to the presence of the "special grace" in his case and that of his disciple.

> "Lo! ghostly friend, in this work, though it be childishly and lewdly spoken, I bear, though I be a wretch unworthy to teach any creature, the office of Bezaleel: making and declaring in manner to thine hands the manner of this ghostly Ark. But far better and more worthily than I do, thou mayest work if thou wilt be Aaron: that is to say, continually working therein for thee and for me. Do then so I pray thee, for the love of God Almighty. And since we be both called of God to work in this work, I beseech thee for God's love fulfil in thy part what lacketh of mine"[50].

As proof of the reality of this interior world, wherein is heard "the privy teaching of the Spirit of God", the author gives the example of our Lord in His Ascension to Heaven. There is a reality and an experience in the "beholding and

48 *Privy Counsel*, McCann, p. 107; Hodgson, 137:8-11.
49 Ibid. McCann, pp. 107-108; Hodgson, 137: 26-30, 138: 1-3.
50 *The Cloud*, Ch. 73, Underhill, p. 263; Hodgson, 129: 4-12.

in the loving of his Manhood", but there is a reality and experience higher still.

"But for there was a higher perfection the which a man may have in this life—that is to say, a pure ghostly feeling in the love of his Godhead—therefore he said to his disciples, the which grudged for to forgo his bodily presence (as thou dost in part and in manner for to forgo thy curious meditations and thy quaint subtle wits): that it was speedful to them that he went bodily from them: *Expedit vobis ut ego vadam*"[51].

In concluding *Privy Counsel* the author reiterates his pre-occupation to stress the fact of *feeling* and *experience* in "This Work" by an interesting personal exegesis of a passage from St. Paul:

"And therefore, I pray thee, seek more after feeling than after knowing, for knowing oftentimes deceiveth with pride; but meek lovely feeling may not beguile: *Scientia inflat, caritas aedificat*. In knowing is travail, in feeling is rest"[52].

These passages, and comments made upon them, stress the fact of an *actual experimental knowledge* of the Godhead. This quality colours the treatment of *The Cloud* and *Privy Counsel*. As the theological analysis proceeds this fact emerges from the passages without any trace of a conscious effort.

In closing this section we make our own the answer of Fr. Poulain to a similar objection:

"I reply that no one can repeat so many difficult things without contradicting himself and wandering away from the point. . . . There are a thousand shades that cannot be invented"[53].

2.   GOD AS THE SOURCE

In his description of the Personal *Intervention* and *breakthrough* of God through the "cloud of unknowing", the author adds this comment:

"For of that work, that falleth to only God, dare I not take upon me to speak with my blabbering fleshly tongue: and shortly to say, although I durst I would do not. But of that work that falleth to man when he feeleth him stirred and helped by grace, list me well tell thee: for therein is the less peril of the two"[54].

[51] *Privy Counsel*, McCann, p. 139; Hodgson, 171: 1-7.
[52] Ibid. McCann, p. 140; Hodgson, 171: 26-172: 3. Cf. Hilton, *Scale* I Ch. 4, Underhill, pp. 7-8.
[53] A. Poulain, *The Graces of Interior Prayer*, p. 224.
[54] *The Cloud*, Ch. 26, Underhill, p. 140; Hodgson, 62: 19-23.

In fulfilment of this desire the author wrote *The Cloud* to his disciple, and in our opinion also *Privy Counsel*. Though the addressee of the *Epistle of Prayer* could not be positively identified as the same as *The Cloud* disciple, yet in view of the identification which the author makes in *Privy Counsel* regarding "the fruit" of the *Epistle of Prayer*, and "The Work" of *Privy Counsel* and *The Cloud*, the present writer thinks that it is legitimate enough to see this *Epistle of Prayer* also as part of "that work that falleth to man".

First in our discussions of the elements that make up "This Work" is a description of the *nature* and characteristic marks of this teaching. We have seen how the author uses the word "Work", a generic term, to describe his particular ascent to God. However, he invests it with a technical meaning all his own. Continuing this very general description he expressly states that it is indescribable. It is something which he does not know exactly how to describe, but with which he is familiar both as regards its presence and its workings:

> "Forasmuch as thou willest it and desirest it, so much hast thou of it, and no more nor no less: and yet is it no will, nor no desire, but a thing thou wottest never what, that stirreth thee to will and desire thou wottest never what"[55].

The author reveals his inability to define with precision what he has experienced. But, like other mystics, he knows that something actually took place, and this he shows with a remarkable clarity and familiarity.

> "For all that is spoken of it is not it, but of it"[56].

In this theological inquiry into the nature of "This Work" the first thing that comes to mind is the source of this teaching. Attempts have been made to trace the teaching to Patristic sources, as well as other mystical writings. And in the background of the two mainstreams of mystical tradition we see that *The Cloud* author gives the primacy to the will and its act of love, but in the higher reaches of his experience he reconciles the demands of the intellect and the will in the dynamic response of "the worker of This Work".

This study will show that the author belongs to the tradition

---

55 Ibid. Ch. 34, Underhill, p. 155; Hodgson, 70: 6-9.
56 *Privy Counsel*, McCann, p. 123; Hodgson, 153:20.

of *The Mystics of the Divine Essence* rather than to that of the *Trinitarian*. It is the blending of these different traditions, with some elements gradually shading into one another, that speaks very strongly for the originality of the message of *The Cloud*. It is for this reason too that we find it very difficult to accept the suggestion understandably made of the *common background* of mystical writing that make up the matter of *The Cloud*. For in the weaving of the elements of "This Work" a very highly selective mind was at work. We are saved the labour of much inquiry into possible Patristic sources, since the author tells us explicitly the source of his teaching. In this we are faithful to our intention to make the author speak for himself. The author then tells us that the source of his teaching is God Himself. This is a very daring statement, one that would easily invite the objection of being presumptuous. Presumption, however, is more in keeping with one not blessed with humility and the insistence on humility by the author and in its *perfect* form, is our answer to this objection. The claim may be presumptuous, but it is there, and for this reason we must take it seriously and subject it to severe scrutiny. If the claim stands the test we must be ready to accept it, if not, then we are obliged to abandon it. But certainly we cannot ignore it.

So the author makes an explicit testimony as to the source of his teaching, as well as to the gratuitousness of this gift.

"And if thou askest me by what means thou shalt come to this work, I beseech Almighty God of His great grace and His great courtesy to teach thee Himself. For truly I do thee well to wit that I cannot tell thee, and that is no wonder. For why, that is the work of only God, specially wrought in what soul that Him liketh without any desert of the same soul"[57].

He is aware of the dangers inherent in difficult teachings.

"Beware of error here, I pray thee: for ever, the nearer men touch the truth, more wary men behoveth to be of error. I mean but well: if thou canst not conceive it, lay it by thy side till God come and teach thee. Do then so, and hurt thee not"[58].

The Cloud author is not content to trace the source of his teaching in its entirety to God. He also traces the source for the individual elements that go to make up "This Work".

[57] *The Cloud*, Ch. 34. Underhill, p. 153; Hodgson, 68: 20-21, 69: 1-4.
[58] Ibid. Ch. 34, Underhill, p. 154; Hodgson, 69: 17-20.

One of the characteristics of "This Work" in its perfect
state is the "short prayer of the perfect worker". The source
for this is God.

"Have no marvel why I set these words forby all other. For if
I could find any shorter words, so fully comprehending in them
all good and all evil, as these two words do, or if I had been
learned of God to take any other words either, I would then
have taken them and left these; and so I counsel that thou
do. . . . And therefore take thou none other words to pray in,
although I set these here, but such as thou art stirred of God
for to take"[59].

This "short prayer" is also "this ghostly cry".

"This ghostly cry is better learned of God by the proof, than
of any man by word. For it is best when it is in pure spirit, without special thought or any pronouncing of word . . ."[60].

The "travail" and the "pain" involved in "This Work" can
be so intense that if God did not Himself alleviate the suffering the disciple could not endure it. But aside from this direct
alleviation by God, the author teaches his disciple some
devices with which he can temper the severity of this "travail".

"And if thee think that the travail be great, thou mayest seek
arts and wiles and privy subtleties of ghostly devices to put
them away; the which subtleties be better learned of God by
the proof than of any man in this life"[61].

The source of these devices is God. In distinguishing the
meditations of the "perfect worker" from those of "beginners
. . . and profiters", the author describes again this "short
prayer" and traces its source to God.

"But it is not so with them that continually work in the work of
this book. For their meditations be but as they were sudden
conceits and blind feelings of their own wretchedness, or of the
goodness of God; without any means of reading or hearing
coming before, and without any special beholding of any thing
under God. These sudden conceits and these blind feelings
be sooner learned of God than of man"[62].

The highest perfection of "This Work" is reached when
the "being of man" is drowned, as it were, in "the Being of

59 Ibid. Ch. 39, Underhill, p. 169; Hodgson, 77: 14-22.
60 Ibid. Ch. 40, Underhill, pp. 171-172; Hodgson 78: 19-22.
61 Ibid. Ch. 31; Underhill, pp. 147-148; Hodgson 66: 9-12.
62 Ibid. Ch. 36, Underhill, p. 160; Hodgson, 72:23, 73:1-6.

God", so that only the "Being of God" remain, without however any confusion of their respective natures and beings.
This "feeling of one's own being" which is also "deep ghostly
sorrow and good will and desire" can only be taught by God.

"This sorrow and this desire behoveth every soul have and feel
in itself, either in this manner or in another; as God vouchsafeth
for to learn to his ghostly disciples after His well willing and
their according ableness in body and in soul, in degree and
disposition, ere the time be that they may perfectly be oned
unto God in perfect charity—such as may be had here—if God
vouchsafeth"[63].

We note again the qualification that the author gives to his
teaching: "such as may be had here—if God vouchsafeth".
He puts the stamp of orthodoxy and accuracy to his teaching
in a personal, and almost casual way.

The author anticipates the doubts as to his credibility. It
will be noted that he speaks in his own favour, and therefore
what he says may be discounted. And so he explicitly distinguishes between the knowledge that he has and hearsay
evidence.

"For in misconceiving of these two words hangeth much error,
and much deceit in them that purpose them to be ghostly
workers, as me thinketh. Somewhat wot I by the proof, and
somewhat by hearsay; and of these deceits list me tell thee a
little as me thinketh"[64].

The author does not merely state a fact which must be
believed. He teaches his disciple the attitude he must take as
regards this inner testimony. There are the further checks to
verify their authenticity. For these the tests should prove a
safeguard.

"And if thou yet be in part astonished of them at the first time,
and that is because that they be uncouth, yet this shall it do
thee: it shall bind thine heart so fast, that thou shalt on nowise
give full great credence to them, ere the time be that thou be
either certified of them within wonderfully by the Spirit of
God, or else without by counsel of some discreet father"[65].

God is the source for "This Work". This is a daring claim,
made in such a direct manner as to leave no room for mis-

63 Ibid. Ch. 44. Underhill, pp. 182-183; Hodgson 85: 3-8.
64 Ibid. Ch. 51. Underhill, p. 203; Hodgson, 95: 10-14.
65 Ibid. Ch. 48, Underhill, pp. 195-196; Hodgson, 92: 7-13.

understanding. In contrast there is a playful quality which illuminates the letter with personal shafts of light. In this the credibility of the author is similarly revealed.

> "This is childishly and playingly spoken, thee think peradventure. But I trow whoso had grace to do and feel as I say, he should feel good gamesome play with Him, as the father doth with the child, kissing and clipping, that well were him so"[66].

But this is not for mere lightheartedness.

> "Look thou have no wonder why that I speak thus childishly, and as it were follily and lacking natural discretion; for I do it for certain reasons, and as me thinketh that I have been stirred many days, both to feel thus and think thus and say thus, as well to some other of my special friends in God, as I am now unto thee"[67].

It is good to remember that *The Cloud* is a letter and one marvels at the numerous shades of his personality that shine through. If I were to make my own objection to the *Hilton claim* to authorship of *The Cloud*, I would consider this lack of lightness in his character that is so evident in the author of *The Cloud*. But then, like the author, I say, that they are not contradictory. The seriousness of the *Scale,* and its dryness, can be accounted for by the particular reason Hilton had in writing it. Might not these apparent differences in character result from the way the author felt at the time of writing, for even he must have experienced the customary ups and downs. However, the present writer is not out to prove the *Hilton claim,* the purpose of this study being to examine available clues to the authorship problem.

On this note, as the author would say, "but forth of our matter". The author has given many detailed descriptions of "This Work", both with short, sharp sentences that sum up the qualities in a nutshell, and in long passages of great beauty.

3.   OTHER DESCRIPTIONS OF "THIS WORK"

While we have a good idea of the elements of "This Work" by these pithy descriptions, yet a deep and profound understanding of these different elements cannot be obtained from the brief syntheses. This deeper understanding is provided by

---

[66] Ibid. Ch. 46, Underhill, p. 188; Hodgson, 88: 1-4.
[67] Ibid. Ch. 47, Underhill, p. 189; Hodgson 88: 5-9.

the author in longer passages which describe the elements of
the ascent.

Having seen that the source of the teaching is God, we
likewise see that with this free gift comes a corresponding
ability and capacity of the soul to do "This Work".

> "The condition of this work is such, that the presence thereof
> enableth a soul for to have it and for to feel it. And that able-
> ness may no soul have without it. The ableness to this work is
> oned to the work's self without departing; so that whoso feeleth
> this work is able to thereto, and none else"[68].

Realizing the source of this grace, it clearly pertains to the
substance of the spiritual life and not to that which we call
accidental.

> "Such a good will is the substance of all perfection. All sweet-
> ness and comforts, bodily or ghostly, be to this but as it were
> accidents, be they never so holy; and they do but hang on this
> good will"[69].

Because God gives the corresponding ability it is the easiest
thing to do.

> "And yet it is the lightest work of all, when a soul is helped
> with grace in sensible list, and soonest done. But else it is hard,
> and wonderful to thee for to do"[70].

However, for all the gratuitousness of the gift of God, this
does not mean that the soul will not feel any labour or difficulty in pursuing this way. The grace of God is not a medal
of merit and the soul must pay the price for this choice of
God. Hence it is hard and strait in the beginning, as in all
matters secular or sacral, for this is the ordinary law of nature
and grace.

> "Travail fast but awhile, and thou shalt soon be eased of the
> greatness and of the hardness of this travail. For although it
> be hard and strait in the beginning, when thou hast no devotion;
> nevertheless yet after, when thou hast devotion, it shall be made
> full restful and full light unto thee that before was full hard.
> And thou shalt have either little travail or none, for then will
> God work sometimes all by Himself"[71].

And because God makes the work possible with His grace
and sustains it, it becomes likewise easy and pleasurable.

---

68 Ibid. Ch. 34, Underhill, p. 154; Hodgson, 69: 23, 70: 1-4.
69 Ibid. Ch. 49, Underhill, p. 197; Hodgson, 92: 21-22, 93: 1-2.
70 Ibid. Ch. 3, Underhill, p. 64; Hodgson, 16: 16-18.
71 Ibid. Ch. 26, Underhill, p. 139; Hodgson, 62: 5-11.

"In great commendation of this sweet subtle working, the which in itself is the high wisdom of the Godhead graciously descending into man's soul, knitting it and oneing it unto himself in ghostly subtlety and prudence of spirit, the wise man Solomon bursteth up and saith: *Beatus homo qui invenit sapientiam et qui affluit prudentia*. . . . He is a blissful man that may find this oneing wisdom and that may abound in his ghostly working with this lovely subtlety and prudence of spirit, in offering up of his own blind feeling of his own being, all curious knowledge of learning and of nature far put back"[72].

In these foregoing passages we see verified the eighth mark of the mystical life, namely "it demands less effort than meditation"[73]. The reason for the *ease* in "This Work" is the fact that it is God Himself who has given the "special grace" which has in turn produced the "ableness" in the soul for "This Work". With the *Absolute Freedom* and *Transcendence* of God in giving His gifts to whom and when He wants, we see nevertheless, that there are certain requisites on the part of the recipient which must be present.

". . . but if it be of such one, or to such one, that hath by thy supposing in a true will and by an whole intent purposed him to be a perfect follower of Christ not only in active living, but in the sovereignest point of contemplative living the which is possible by grace for to be come to in this present life of a perfect soul yet abiding in this deadly body; and thereto that doth that in him is, and by thy supposing hath done long time before, for to able him to contemplative living by the virtuous means of active living"[74].

We notice that the author is fond of using superlatives in describing "This Work". Hence it is the *easiest* thing to do, but still it can be the most *impossible* thing to do. These seeming contradictions and paradoxes are characteristic of the language of the mystics. The thing to remember is that we are dealing with a thing that is quite extraordinary, and there must be an overriding element which makes the difference, which makes the seeming contradictions blend and harmonize, and resolve them into one. Hence, the author explicitly says that this all-important element is God Himself, the special grace of God. With the grace of God "This Work" is the

---

[72] *Privy Counsel*, McCann, p. 115; Hodgson, 145: 3-19.
[73] A. Poulain, *The Graces of Interior Prayer*, p. 114.
[74] The Cloud, Prologue, Underhill, pp. 39-40; Hodgson 1: 14, 2: 1-7.

easiest thing to do; without the grace of God, it is *impossible* to do.

Now we see the author further describing "This Work" by another superlative. So he says that it is the *shortest* thing to do, equal to that of one atom. An "atom was used in the Greek Testament to signify 'the twinkling of an eye'. In medieval Latin its time-value was regularly fixed. It was the smallest medieval measure of time and equivalent to 15/94 of a second"[75],

> "This work asketh no long time or it be once truly done, as some men ween; for it is the shortest work of all that man may imagine. It is never longer nor shorter, than is an atom: the which atom, by the definition of true philosophers in the science of astronomy, is the least part of time. And it is so little that for the littleness of it, it is indivisible and nearly incomprehensible. This is that time of the which it is written: All that time that is given to thee, it shall be asked of thee, how thou hast dispended it. And reasonable thing it is that thou give account of it: for it is neither longer nor shorter, but even according to one only stirring that is within the principal working might of thy soul, the which is thy will. For even so many willings or desirings, and no more nor no fewer, may be and are in one hour"[76].

It sounds so short and simple, just one moment of time, equal to just one stirring of the heart. But when we consider that as the description of "This Work" progresses, we see that it requires every bit of stirring of the heart for the rest of one's life, then we realize that it is no simple matter. In the present fallen state of man, even with the grace of God, this requirement is unlikely to be fulfilled.

The author explains that "This Work" is the most natural thing for man to do in the state of Original Justice. It is very interesting to note that of all that man has to do in this life of knowing, loving and serving God, every thing that this purpose in life entails is contained in just one short stirring of love.

> "For this is the work, as thou shalt hear afterward in the which man should have continued if he never had sinned: and to the

75 P. Hodgson, *The Cloud of Unknowing* (E.E.T.S. 1958). p. 186.
76 *The Cloud*, Ch. 4, Underhill, pp. 65-66; Hodgson, 17: 14-20, 18: 1-7. In *Epistle of Prayer* the author describes "this working" as "little or less as a twinkeling of an eye", Hodgson, 49: 4-5.

which working man was made, and all things for man, to help
him and further him thereto, and by the which working a man
shall be repaired again"[77].

And because "This Work" involves extreme pain and
travail, which will make great inroads into the physical and
spiritual resources of the man, the author provides a physical
requirement.

"For I tell thee truly, that this work asketh a full great restfulness, and a full whole and clean disposition, as well as in
body as in soul"[78].

It is interesting to note that in his commentary on the
eighth character of the mystic union, namely that "it demands
less effort than meditation"[79], Fr. Poulain observes that "the
state of health is also a factor here"[80]. This is in connection
with the fatigue involved for man. We understand the preoccupation of the author as regards the health of the disciple:
"And therefore for God's love be wary with sickness as much
as thou mayest goodly, so that thou be not the cause of thy
feebleness, as far as thou mayest"[81].

But of all the elements which the author describes, there
is one which he stresses and develops again and again. This
is that "This Work" is "ghostly". The ultimate reason is the
fact that God is a Spirit, and if we are to be joined to Him
in oneness of love, it must be in spirit, "in the highest and
the sovereignest point of the spirit"[82].

"For He is even meet to our soul by measuring of His Godhead;
and our soul even meet unto Him by worthiness of our creation
to His image and to His likeness. And He by Himself without
more, and none but He, is sufficient to the full and much more
to fulfil the will and the desire of our soul"[83].

He stresses this further by the expression "the sovereignest
point of contemplative living"[84], "in the highest point of this
contemplative act"[85], "in purity of spirit"[86], "the purity and

[77] *The Cloud*, Ch. 4, Underhill, p. 68; Hodgson 19: 19-22, 20: 1.
[78] Ibid. Ch. 41, Underhill, p. 175; Hodgson 80: 14-16.
[79] A. Poulain, *The Graces of Interior Prayer*, p. 114.
[80] Ibid. p. 139.
[81] *The Cloud*, Ch. 41, Underhill, p. 175; Hodgson, 80: 12-14.
[82] *The Cloud*, Ch. 37, Underhill, p. 163; Hodgson, 74: 12-13.
[83] Ibid. Ch. 4, Underhill, p. 66; Hodgson, 18: 13-17.
[84] Ibid. Prologue, Underhill, p. 39; Hodgson, 2: 3.
[85] Ibid. Prologue, Underhill, p. 41; Hodgson, 3: 6.
[86] Ibid. Ch. 4, Underhill, p. 71, Hodgson 22: 21; Ch. 44, Underhill, p. 182,
Hodgson, 84: 12; Ch. 47, Underhill, p. 191, Hodgson, 89: 23; *Privy*

deepness of ghostly feeling"[87], "in deepness of spirit"[88], in purity and in deepness of spirit"[89], "the first point of thy spirit"[90], "the sovereign point of thy spirit"[91]. God is here described as "thy ground and thy purity of spirit"[92]. In stressing the "ghostly nature" of "This Work", the author attests to what Fr. Poulain describes as the *sixth character* of the mystic state, namely, "the union is produced neither by reasonings, nor by the consideration of creatures, nor by sensible images". The author describes this "ghostly nature" in two ways—that which it is not and that which it is.

"And here may men shortly conceive the manner of this working, and clearly know that it is far from any fantasy or any false imagination or quaint opinion: the which be brought in, not by such a devout and a meek blind stirring of love, but by a proud, curious and an imaginative wit. Such a proud, curious wit behoveth always be borne down and stiffly trodden down under foot, if this work shall truly be conceived in purity of spirit"[93].

And making explicit this ghostly nature, the author says:

"For the perfection of this work is so pure and so ghostly in itself, that an it be well and truly conceived, it shall be seen far removed from any stirring and from any place. And it should by some reason rather be called a sudden changing, than any stirring of place. For time, place, and body: these three should be fogotten in all ghostly working"[94].

Everything that has to do with "This Work" must be understood in its spiritual and not material context. The author explicitly mentions misunderstandings that can arise from this incorrect view.

"And therefore when they read or hear spoken of ghostly working—and specially of this word, 'how a man shall draw all his wit within himself' . . . they turn their bodily wits inwards to

Counsel, McCann, p. 110, Hodgson, 140: 24; *Privy Counsel*, McCann, p. 112, Hodgson, 142: 11; McCann, p. 124, Hodgson, 154: 16; McCann, p. 125, Hodgson, 155: 12-13; McCann, p. 138, Hodgson, 169: 23.
87 *The Cloud*, Ch. 47, Underhill, pp. 189-190; Hodgson, 88: 16.
88 Ibid. Ch. 47, Underhill, p. 190; Hodgson, 89: 3; Underhill, p. 191; Hodgson, 89: 16; Ch. 51, Underhill, p. 203; Hodgson, 95: 5.
89 Ibid. Ch. 47, Underhill, p. 190; Hodgson, 89: 10.
90 *Privy Counsel*, McCann, p. 113; Hodgson, 143: 9-10.
91 Ibid. McCann, p. 138; Hodgson, 169: 19.
92 Ibid. McMann, p. 114; Hodgson, 144: 18-19.
93 *The Cloud*, Ch. 4, Underhill, p. 71; Hodgson, 22: 15-21.
94 Ibid. Ch. 59, Underhill, p. 229; Hodgson, 110: 22, 111: 1-5.

their body against the course of nature; and strain them, as they would see inwards with their bodily eyes and hear inwards with their ears, and so forth of all their wits, smelling, tasting and feeling inwards. And thus they reverse them against the course of nature . . ."[95].

And in similar vein:

"For if it so be, that they either read, or hear read or spoken, how that men should lift up their hearts unto God, as fast they stare in the stars as if they would be above the moon, and hearken when they shall hear any angel sing out of heaven. These men will sometime with the curiosity of their imagination pierce the planets, and make an hole in the firmament to look in thereat. These men will make a God as them list, and clothe Him full richly in clothes, and set Him in a throne far more curiously than ever was He depicted in this earth"[96].

The author is derisive regarding the purely material interpretation of the words "inward" and "up" and his desire is to give a highly spiritualized meaning to the words in conformity with the nature of "This Work", to lead the disciple to the higher reaches of the *contemplative life*. Those who misunderstand these words reveal themselves to be lacking in the grace to do "This Work". They are open to the deceits and delusions brought about by the devil, which would end in their spiritual ruin. Mystics are realists and sensible people, and they do not expect the ordinary laws of nature to reverse themselves completely in favour of mystical experiences. Mystical grace presupposes the sound functioning of the powers of the soul, and while the lower powers are superseded and surpassed in their operations, yet their function and operation are still of importance. The functions may be suspended, but the powers remain whole and entire, to operate as normally as before the time when the mystical grace took possession.

4. *"AS A SPARKLE FROM THE COAL"*

Summing-up the author gives the dominant characteristics of "This Work", using the figure of the "sparkle from the coal". At the end of this study we shall see that the author uses

95 Ibid. Ch. 51, Underhill, p. 203, Ch. 52, p. 205; Hodgson, 95: 20-22, 96: 17-22.
96 Ibid. Ch. 57. Underhill, p. 220. Walter Hilton likewise notes the misunderstanding regarding "inwards" and "up". *Scale II*, Ch. 33, Underhill, pp. 375-377 See also C. Pepler, *The English Religious Heritage*, p. 296.

another image, "a beam of ghostly light, piercing this cloud of unknowing"[97]. This image of a *beam* refers to the part of God, the Source of this *Personal Breakthrough*. In the image of the "sparkle from the coal", the terminal of this *beam* is the aspect that is stressed. But we see the intimate connection between the two, for without the *beam* there is no *sparkle*. Everything that goes to make up "This Work" is synthesized as far as possible. *Nature* and *perfection* blend into one. This is only to be expected in a description of a mystical experience. And so we have the following description by the author of "This Work".

> "For if it be truly conceived, it is but a sudden stirring, and as it were unadvised, speedily springing unto God as a sparkle from the coal. And it is marvellous to number the stirrings that may be in one hour wrought in a soul that is disposed to this work. And yet in one stirring of all these, he may have suddenly and perfectly forgotten all created thing. But fast after each stirring, for corruption of the flesh, it falleth down again to some thought or to some done or undone deed. But what thereof? For fast after, it riseth again as suddenly as it did before"[98].

We see in this passage the *suddenness* and the *unexpectedness* of the *breakthrough* of God, which is a character of *passivity*. This is a characteristic quality of a mystical experience as described by mystical writers[99]. The passage is a

---

97 *The Cloud*, Ch. 26, Underhill, p. 140; Hodgson, 62: 14-15.
98 Ibid. Ch. 4 Underhill, p. 71; Hodgson, 22: 6-14. Hilton has a similar passage describing ... a sparkle springing out of a firebrand ... *Scale II*, Ch. 42, Underhill, p. 436. This is a significant coincidence.
99 L. Reypens, "Connaissance Mystique de Dieu", *Dictionnaire De Spiritualité*, III, Cols. 887, 893, 909. St. John of the Cross has some lovely passages similar to that of *The Cloud* author. "Even so, when a log of wood has been set upon the fire, it is transformed into fire and united with it; yet, as the fire grows hotter and the wood remains upon it for a longer time, it glows much more and becomes more completely enkindled, until it gives out sparks of fire and flame" (*Living Flame*, Allison-Peers, p. 14.) "And this flame the soul feels within it, not only as a fire that has consumed and transformed it in sweet love, but also as a fire which burns within it and sends out flame, as I have said, and that flame bathes the soul in glory and refreshes it with the temper of Divine life." (*Living Flame*, Allison-Peers, p. 18.)
"It is a marvellous thing: for, as love is never idle, but is continually in motion, it is ever throwing out sparks, like a flame, in every direction; and, as the office of love is to wound, that it may enkindle with love and cause delight, so, when it is as it were a living flame, within the soul, it is ever sending forth its arrow-wounds, like most tender sparks of delicate love, joyfully and happily exercising the arts and playings of love." (*Living Flame*, Allison-Peers, pp. 20-21.)
"But into the soul that is prepared love enters continuously, for the

lovely commentary on the *seventh* mark of the mystic act, namely "it varies incessantly in intensity"[100]. And when the author observes the "number of stirrings that may be in one hour wrought in a soul that is disposed to this work", he is also writing a commentary on the *eighth character* of the mystic act, namely "it demands less effort than meditation"[101]. This is not the only place where the author describes these qualities of the mystic state. We find these nuances coming up constantly in other passages. We have seen that one quality of "This Work" is that it is as short as an atom, the "twinkling of an eye". In *The Epistle of Prayer* the author describes this sudden and unexpected quality of the perfection of the "reverent affection".

> ". . . and ever the ofter that it is done suddenly, lustily, and likingly, without mean, the sweeter it smelleth, and the better it pleaseth the high King of heaven. . . . And yet is the perfection of this work sudden, without any mean"[102].

The shortness of the mystical experience is graphically described by the image of "sparkle from the coal". The sparks fly fast, are bright and scattered and quickly disappear. This is the underlying meaning of the image. And when we say that the sparks are scattered, this is not intended to suggest a lack of intensity or concentration, but rather a "stirring". In this passage, too, we see a recapitulation of the briefness of "This Work", as "short as an atom", equal to just one stirring of the heart. In view of this briefness we can see how many "stirrings" will be needed during the time that the soul is engaged in "This Work". Indeed, "This Work" would want every stirring of the heart for the rest of one's life. We have seen how the author compares the states of the "mights of the

spark seizes upon the dry fuel at its first contact; and thus the soul that is kindled in love prefers the short act of the breaking of the web to the duration of the act of cutting it or of waiting for it to wear away." (*Living Flame*, Allison-Peers, pp. 33-34.)
". . . the soul will be conscious of an assault upon it made by a seraph armed with a dart of most enkindled love, which will pierce that enkindled coal of fire, the soul, or, to speak more exactly, that flame, and will cauterize it in a sublime manner; and, when it has pierced and cauterized it thus, the flame will rush forth and will rise suddenly and vehemently, even as comes to pass in a white-hot furnace or forge . . ." (*Living Flame*, Allison-Peers, p. 39.)
100 A. Poulain, *The Graces of Interior Prayer*, p. 114.
101 Ibid.
102 *Epistle of Prayer*, Gardner, pp. 89-90; Hodgson, 57: 14-24, 58: 1-7.

soul" before and after the Fall. And so we see the alternating movements, upwards and downwards, of the soul engaged in "This Work". One moment there is this state like unto the "sparkle from the coal" when the perfection of experience is reached by the *breakthrough* of God. Then, at the next, there is the sudden realization of one's condition in this bodily life. This undulating movement can be something like the movements pictured by the image "upon the launching into the spirit's sea" which the author uses. There is also that alternating "coming and going of the Lord", the gladness upon the finding, the pining for the loss, and the subsequent gladness upon having found the Lord once again.

In *Privy Counsel* the author makes the following observation in connection with the tests for "This Work":

"and thou . . . be left as though thou wert barren, thou thinkest, as well from the feeling of this new fervour as from thine old wonted work, so that thou thinkest thee fallen down betwixt the two, having neither, but wanting them both. . . ."[103].

In this description, we see something of the expression "neither in heaven nor on earth". A description of this state can be found in *The Study of Wisdom*:

". . . because that, be he never so filled in soul of ghostly gladness and joy in God, yet, for corruption of the flesh in this deadly life, him behoveth bear the charge of the deadly body, as hunger, thirst. . . . And also a soul in this state is dwelling between the terms of deadly life and undeadly life. He that dwelleth between the terms hath nearhand forsaken deadliness, but not fully, and hath nearhand gotten undeadliness, but not fully;. . . Thus I trow that Saint Paul felt, when he said this word of great desire: 'Who shall deliver me from this deadly body?' And when he said thus: 'I covet to be loosed and to be with Christ.' And thus doth the soul that feeleth Issachar in his affection. . . . It enforceth it to forsake this wretched life, but it may not; it coveteth to enter the blessed life, but it may not; it doth that it may, and yet it dwelleth between the terms"[104].

And so from the heights of the experience of "this sparkle from the coal", always having in mind that all the previous descriptions and states are to be taken as included in one experience, the disciple then plummets down again to the physical level of his life.

---

103 *Privy Counsel*, McCann, p. 136; Hodgson, 167: 10-13.
104 *The Study of Wisdom*, Gardner, pp. 21-22; Hodgson, 31: 11-33: 1-5.

"But fast after each stirring, for corruption of the flesh, it falleth down again to some thought or to some done or undone deed. But what thereof? For fast after, it riseth again as suddenly as it did before"[105].

We cannot take this narration as something merely theoretical. With the background of the "deep ghostly sorrow", "the pain and travail", the "desire and chaste love", all these are real experiences which register on the soul like the atmospheric pressure on the barometer.

The full and final "forgetting" of creatures is possible only by the direct work of God. The soul can do all it can "to cover all creatures" with the "cloud of forgetting", but the full and final obliteration, even if it be but for a moment, is possible only by a special intervention of God. And we hear the author describing the complete forgetting of creatures in this mystical experience.

"And yet in one stirring of all these, he may have suddenly and perfectly forgotten all created thing"[106].

Can this passage be taken as a description of ecstasy? It is possible, but in the words of the author, "I wot not"[107].

The author uses the term ravishing once towards the end of *The Cloud* when he describes the perfection of "This Work". He gives the diversity of perfection of "This Work", which may or may not be ravishing, depending on God and the capacity of the soul.

"Some think this matter so hard and so fearful, that they say it may not be come to without much strong travail coming before, nor conceived but seldom, and that but in the time of ravishing. And to these men will I answer as feebly as I can, and say, that it is all at the ordinance and the disposition of God, after their ableness in soul that this grace of contemplation and of ghostly working is given to"[108].

We usually associate the highest mystical experiences with ravishment and ecstacy. But in *The Cloud* we find the author non-committal in this respect.

[105] *The Cloud*, Ch. 4, Underhill, p. 71; Hodgson, 22: 11-14. For Suso, "the imperfection of the experience is attributed to the fact of living in the body" (L. Reypens, "Connaissance Mystique De Dieu", *Dictionnaire De Spiritualité*, III, Col. 904.)
[106] *The Cloud*, Ch. 4, Underhill, p. 71; Hodgson, 22: 10-11.
[107] I do not know.
[108] *The Cloud*, Ch. 71, Underhill, p. 257; Hodgson, 125: 23, 126: 1-6.

This image of "a sparkle from the coal" clearly reveals the mystical character of "This Work". The various descriptions likewise reveal this intention, but with this image the author would seem to close all doors to any possible misunderstanding. This intention will again be revealed as the ascent progresses.

Having seen the dominant characteristics of "This Work", we move to a consideration of the state of life within which this must be done. We note the importance which the author attaches to the states of life when, in the first chapter, he names the "four degrees and forms of Christian men's living" and equates them with the life history of the addressee of *The Cloud*.

D.   "DEGREES AND FORMS OF CHRISTIAN MEN'S LIVING"

This is the expression which the author uses to cover the different states of life in Holy Church. This classification is based on the more general ways of living in their external aspects, following the traditional basis of whether one is living out "in the world" or in "religion", and within "religion" in a still more special form. These different states the author calls *Common, Special, Singular* and *Perfect*[109], and illustrates them from the life of the disciple. Thus, "Common" has reference to the life "when thou wert living in the common degree of Christian men's living in company of thy worldly friends . . .[110]"; "Special" has reference to the time when "He kindled thy desire full graciously, and fastened by it a leash of longing, and led thee by it into a more special state and form of living, to be a servant among the special servants of His . . ."[111]; and within this life in "religion" God called the disciple to a still higher state which the author designates "Singular". "Seest thou nought how listily and how graciously He hath privily pulled thee to the third degree and manner of living, the which is called Singular? In the which solitary form and manner of living, thou mayest learn to lift up the foot of thy love; and step towards that state and degree of living that is perfect, and the last state of all"[112]. From this passage we

109 See also C. Pepler, *The English Religious Heritage*, pp. 238-239, 241-242.
110 *The Cloud*, Ch. 1, Underhill, pp. 59-60; Hodgson, 13: 18-19.
111 Ibid. Ch. 1, Underhill, p. 60; Hodgson, 14: 3-5.
112 Ibid. Ch. 1, Underhill, p. 60; Hodgson, 14: 10-15. Professor Hodgson notes the varying interpretations of this passage. She observes that "Dom

see that the author equates the "Singular" form of living with "Solitary form and manner of living". And what was the reason for this further special call?

> "And what more? Yet it seemeth that He would not leave thee thus lightly, for love of His heart, the which He hath evermore had unto thee since thou wert aught . . ."[113].

The author insists that the only reason for the special call of the disciple to "This Work" is the Love of God. Nothing more is needed, and nothing less will do.

> "And insomuch thou shouldest be more meek and loving to thy ghostly spouse, that He that is the Almighty God, King of Kings and Lord of Lords, would meek Him so low unto thee, and amongst all the flock of His sheep so graciously would choose thee to be one of His specials, and sithen set thee in the place of pasture, where thou mayest be fed with the sweetness of His love, in earnest of thine heritage the Kingdom of Heaven"[114].

The author shows what a good teacher he is. Right at the beginning he sets before the disciple the grandeur of his life and calling. But as the message unfolds, the full price of this lofty calling is revealed.

The four "degrees and forms" the author further classifies, but now in relation to time and place. So he says that *Common, Special,* and *Singular* "may be begun and ended in this life"[115]. But the "perfect" degree is the link between heaven and earth, between time and eternity, and "may by grace be begun here, but it shall ever last without end in the bliss of heaven"[116]. He also stresses the fact that these four degrees come one after the other, and may not be jumped. So he says "first, Common, then Special, after Singular, and last Perfect"[117].

The author's delineation of the states of life has been seen as his reaction to the new attitudes concerning the traditional

---

Justin McCann . . . agrees with the interpretation of Fr. Baker . . . that 'solitary' here may refer only to a state of soul . . . Dom M. Noetinger found it difficult to believe that solitary referred only to a state of the soul". She concluded: "It would appear to be impossible to reach a conclusion". P. Hodgson, *The Cloud of Unknowing* (E.E.T.S.) 1958, p. 183

113 *The Cloud,* Ch. 1, Underhill, p. 60; Hodgson, 14: 8-10.
114 Ibid. Ch. 2, Underhill, pp. 61-62; Hodgson, 15: 3-9.
115 Ibid. Ch. 1, Underhill, p. 59; Hodgson 13: 11.
116 Ibid. Ch. 1, Underhill, p. 59; Hodgson, 13: 11-13.
117 Ibid. Ch. 1, Underhill, p. 59; Hodgson, 13: 14-15.

forms of monasticism and practices of the ascetical life[118]. The author's text, however, does not support this view. We have seen the equation of the "degrees and forms of living" with the life history of the disciple, and we shall see with even greater clarity the insistence of the author regarding the particular state of life within which "This Work" can be done. It is not the part of this study to say that "This Work" may not be done in any other state of life, but in the context of *The Cloud* the author expressly defines the area within which "This Work" can be accomplished. And, in connection with this, we see the identification of the "Singular form of living" as the "Solitary form and manner of living" and its significance to the teaching of *The Cloud*[119]. It is the opinion of the present writer that the disciple was a "solitary", that is, a *recluse*, who lived alone in a house which could be of several apartments with a garden attached. *The Cloud* was written at the time of the Golden Age of the English recluse, which roughly covered the period 1225-1400[120], and in the Rules of St. Benedict, St. Ailred and Grimlaic, "solitaries" were *recluses* as distinct from monks[121]. The term "solitary" then had a definite meaning at the time *The Cloud* was written. The following passage gives the tenor of the then prevailing opinion regarding the *recluse*.

"As a spiritual aristocrat, whose vocation was 'the height of perfection', the Recluse was set by Grimlaic before the coenobite or monk; and in the ninth-century list of benefactors of the Church of Durham the heading 'Names of Anchorets' comes before 'Names of Abbats', 'Names of Presbyters', 'Names of Monks'. This special respect arose no doubt from that aloofness, from the earthly vanities, supposed to be practised by the Recluse: 'Ancren have taken on Mary's part—which our Lord Himself commended . . .'"[122].

And for a proper appreciation of the message of *The Cloud* it is good to remember that the disciple could have been a solitary. This fact, too, might shed some light on other incidental questions relative to *The Cloud*.

The fact that *The Cloud* was written for someone striving

118 M. Noetinger, *Le Nuage de L'Inconnaissance*, p. 10.
119 F. D. S. Darwin, *The English Mediaeval Recluse*, pp. 2-6.
120 Ibid. p. 65.
121 Ibid. pp. 9, 30, 33, 42.
122 Ibid. p. 8.

for great holiness could give rise to some surprise regarding the relevance of Chapters 10 and 11, which are more a discussion of Moral Theology. The subject of mortal sins would seem out of place in *The Cloud,* which is mainly concerned with the "naked Being of God", but the author is not blind to the possibility that the flesh will sometimes attempt to claim the upper hand. And if refined thought of the attributes of God can hinder "This Work", how much more so the disciple's mundane thoughts of past events and acquaintances. The author warns the disciple that, for all his sheltered life, he is subject to temptations of body and mind.

> "And since a remembrance of any special saint or of any clean ghostly thing will hinder thee so much, what trowest thou then that the remembrance of any man living in this wretched life, or of any manner of bodily or worldly thing, will hinder thee and let thee in this work?"[123].

The emphasis is on the memory. And this is understandable in the context of the enclosed life of the disciple.

> "And this befalleth when thou or any of them that I speak of wilfully draw upon thee the remembrance of any man or woman living in this life, or of any bodily or worldly thing other . . ."[124].

It seems likely that one living in a high state of perfection in the exercise of the rarest virtues, doing away with even the slightest thought of the attributes of God, could be so psychologically conditioned that the slightest breath of sin could assume frightening proportions. Perhaps we could use an analogy from the world of medicine. One who has been well protected and sheltered from infection suffers a more severe attack of disease than one who has developed a natural immunity simply as a result of exposure to the infection. So it is with the situation of the disciple. Protected by the rules of the solitary life, shut in by the four walls of the enclosure, his engagements with the powers of darkness, and his ascent to God, must be in the spiritual realms. The author here demonstrates his adept handling of the problems of the spiritual life. In a consideration of the quality of the sins which could beset the disciple, he does not put emphasis on the two other elements which make a sin mortal, namely, *serious*

[123] *The Cloud,* Ch. 9, Underhill, p. 91; Hodgson, 35: 4-8.
[124] Ibid. Ch. 10, Underhill, p. 93; Hodgson, 36: 21-23.

matter and *full knowledge*. However, for the guidance of his disciple, the author places great emphasis on *consent*. It is difficult to have control over the thoughts and vagaries of the human mind, but the author insists on the age-old principle of spiritual writers for fighting temptations—"obsta principiis". It is easier to root out the temptation right at the start when it is still weak than when, by force of momentum and its attractiveness, it has become a force harder to combat. It does not take much to attract the heart.

> "For why, a naked sudden thought of any of them, pressing against thy will and thy witting, although it be no sin imputed unto thee—for it is the pain of the original sin pressing against thy power, of the which sin thou art cleansed in thy baptism—nevertheless yet if this sudden stirring or thought be not smitten soon down, as fast for frailty thy fleshly heart is strained thereby . . ."[125].

In the following passage it will be seen that the author distinguishes between similar thoughts entering the minds of men habitually living in sin, for whom the attraction can be mortal, and those living the life of perfection, when it is but venial.

> "The which fastening, although it may in fleshly living men and women that be in deadly sin before be deadly; nevertheless in thee and in all other that have in a true will forsaken the world, and are obliged unto any degree in devout living in Holy Church, what so it be, privy or open, and thereto that will be ruled not after their own will and their own wit, but after the will and the counsel of their sovereigns, what so they be, religious or seculars, such a liking or a grumbling fastened in the fleshly heart is but venial sin"[126].

But it will be seen that this distinction is qualified by a time factor. The disciple may not be quick in releasing the thought due to carelessness or natural slowness in his reaction, but when the action is long delayed a deliberate intent to entertain the evil thought is apparent. In this case the distinction does not apply.

> "But if it so be, that this liking or grumbling fastened in thy fleshly heart be suffered so long to abide unreproved, that then at the last it is fastened to the ghostly heart, that is to say the will, with a full consent: then, it is deadly sin"[127].

---

125 Ibid. Ch. 10, Underhill, p. 92; Hodgson, 35: 20-23, 36: 1-2.
126 Ibid. Ch. 10, Underhill, pp. 92-93; Hodgson, 36: 5-13.
127 Ibid. Ch. 10, Underhill, p. 93; Hodgson, 36: 16-20.

It is when the thought is deliberately entertained that the sin becomes mortal. But as long as it remains in the twilight zone, when the disciple cannot yet be sure as to its gravity, then he is given the benefit of the doubt. Why this indulgence?

"The cause of this is the grounding and the rooting of your intent in God, made in the beginning of your living in that state that ye stand in, by the witness and the counsel of some discreet father"[128].

The author emphasizes the need to fight these first impulses to sin.

"I would that thou travailedst busily to destroy the first stirring and thought of these things that thou mayest thus sin in"[129].

And there is nothing like knowledge to bring one to peace.

"I would that thou weighest each thought and each stirring after that it is . . ."[130].

One must see things objectively for what they are, neither minimizing nor exaggerating. This method of examination of conscience is different from that proposed in *Knowing of Spirits*. The author reveals his full grasp of the distinctions in moral theology regarding indeliberate venial sins, deliberate venial sins, and, of course, mortal. Depending on one's attitude one can find oneself deeper and deeper in sin. Indeliberate venial sins cannot be stopped, but there is no sin in them.

". . . that who weighest not, or setteth little by, the first thought —yea, although it be no sin unto him—that he, whosoever that he be, shall not eschew recklessness in venial sin"[131].

128 Ibid. Ch. 10, Underhill, p. 93; Hodgson, 36: 13-16.
129 Ibid. Ch. 11, Underhill, p. 96; Hodgson, 38: 3-4.
130 Ibid. Ch. 11, Underhill, p. 96; Hodgson, 38: 1-2.
131 Ibid. Ch. 11, Underhill, p. 96. Walter Hilton has similar passages on the Spiritual Capital Sins. Thus, he gives the same reason for the distinction between mortal and venial sins. "For that will that they set generally in their heart before to please God and for to forsake all manner sin, if they knew it, keepeth them there in such stirrings, and in all other that come of frailty, that they sin not deadly, and shall keep them as long as the ground of that will is kept whole". (*Scale I*, Ch. 60, Underhill, p. 145.) In another place Walter Hilton explains the reason for this distinction. "But another man or a woman which is in grace and in charity hath always a good general will to God in his soul, whether he sleep or wake, eat or drink, or what deed that he doth, so that it be not evil in the self; by the which will he chooseth and desireth God above all things and had liefer forbear all the likings of this world than his God, for love of Him. This will, though it be but general, is of so great virtue by the grace of our Lord Jhesu, that though he fall by frailty in lust and liking of meat, and drink, or such

One can never get rid of venial sins in this life. "The virtuous man falls seven times"[132], and St. John says that "if we say we have no sin in us, we are deceiving ourselves"[133]. *The Cloud* author has something similar to say. "Venial sin shall no man utterly eschew in this deadly life"[134]. But it is the attitude of the mind to these little things that the author insists on setting right.

> "But recklessness in venial sin should always be eschewed of all the true disciples of perfection; and else I have no wonder though they soon sin deadly"[135].

Like all other matters that seem at first sight extraneous to *The Cloud*, this section on Moral Theology is closely and intimately connected with "This Work". The author reveals this by following up the discussion on the analysis of sinful thoughts with a resounding conclusion in the opening lines of Chapter 12.

> "And, therefore, if thou wilt stand and not fall, cease never in thine intent: but beat evermore on this cloud of unknowing that is betwixt thee and thy God with a sharp dart of longing love, and loathe for to think on aught under God, and go not thence for anything that befalleth. For this is only by itself that work that destroyeth the ground and the root of sin"[136].

In the fight against sin, external exercises, according to the author, "would help thee right nought". Fasting, early rising, sleeping on hard boards, wearing of sharp chains, and other forms of discipline and mortification would not do in the fight against these stirrings of sin. Not that they have no value,

other sickness, either in excess of too mickle eating, or too often, or too greedily, or too lustily and delicately, or too soon in unseasonableness, it saveth and keepth him from deadly sin". (*Scale I*, Ch. 72, Underhill, pp. 179-180.) In this passage too, Hilton intimates the instinctive knowledge that results from the perfection of "This Work" which *The Cloud* author teaches. The acts enumerated likewise are reminiscent of *Discretion of Stirrings*, Hodgson, 38: 5-7. Hilton has an explicit reference to the *Spiritual Capital Sins*. "Thou hast forsaken riches and mickel having of this world, and art shut in a dungeon; but hast thou forsaken the love of all this? I expect not yet; it is less mastery for to forsake worldly good than for to forsake love of it. Peradventure thou hast not forsaken thy covetise, but thou hast changed it from great things into small, as from a pound into a penny and from a silver piece into a disc of one half-penny". (*Scale I*, Ch. 71, Underhill, p. 172.)

132 Proverbs 24: 16.
133 1 John 1: 8.
134 *The Cloud*, Ch. 11, Underhill, p. 96; Hodgson, 38: 7-8.
135 Ibid. Ch. 11, Underhill, p. 96; Hodgson 38: 8-10.
136 Ibid. Ch. 12, Underhill, p. 97; Hodgson 38: 11-16.

but in the context of *The Cloud* they do not help very much. For we see that "This Work" involves special *travail* and *pain,* and when we see this further in the context of the violence of the "three spirits", which echo the experiences narrated in *The Four Degrees of Passionate Love* of Richard of St. Victor, then we see the particularity of the matters connected with *The Cloud* in clearer relief. For "This Work" involves the fixing of the whole attention of the mind and love of the heart on the "naked Being of God". Since these stirrings arise from the mind, then the mind that is already full of the thoughts of God would have no room for these troublesome thoughts. The author reveals himself as master of the workings of the human mind, referring in his own way to what modern clinical psychologists term the centres and peripheries of attention, and the levels of concentration.

> "Fast thou never so much, wake thou never so long, rise thou never so early, lie thou never so hard, wear thou never so sharp . . . yet will stirring and rising of sin be in thee"[137].

E.   "TWO MANNERS OF LIFE"

The previous classification that the author makes with regard to the "degrees and forms of Christian Men's Living", which he equates with the life of the disciple, is peculiarly the author's own.

As the discussion of "This Work" gains in depth we see that the author makes a further classification seen in relation to the particular teaching of *The Cloud* and whereas before he made the classification on the basis of external circumstances of life in general, now he follows the more traditional classification of the states of life in the Church, that is the "active life" and the "contemplative life". However, he connects this classification with "This Work," giving it a highly spiritualized meaning. In this respect the author does not merely give the contrast between Mary and Martha in its general sense of the *active* and the *contemplative* lives. In his characteristic manner of anticipated questions and answers, he sees the relative values of various exercises and modes of prayer in connection with the traditional "two lives" in the Church.

137 Ibid. Ch. 12, Underhill, p. 97; Hodgson, 38: 16-20, 39: 1-3.

"And where that thou askest me, why that thou shalt put it down under the cloud of forgetting, since it is so, that it is good in its nature, and thereto when it is well it doth thee so much good and increaseth thy devotion so much. To this I answer and say —That thou shalt well understand that there be two manner of lives in Holy Church. The one is active life, and the other is contemplative life"[138].

The author continues his classification and identifies "active life" as "lower", and "contemplative life" as "higher". He is clearly thinking of their respective values as we customarily see them. But these two "manners of life" are not so far apart as to have no common ground. So the author explains that both the "active" and the "contemplative" lives have a higher and a lower part, and the two lives meet in the "higher part" of the "active life" and the "lower part" of the "contemplative life". "So that a man may not be fully active, but if he be in part contemplative; nor yet fully contemplative, as it may be here, but if he be in part active"[139].

The author makes a further classification according to the different objects and prayers of the "two lives" and their several "parts".

"The lower part of active life standeth in good and honest bodily works of mercy and of charity. The higher part of active life and the lower part of contemplative life lieth in goodly ghostly meditations, and busy beholding unto a man's own wretchedness with sorrow and contrition, unto the Passion of Christ and of His servants with pity and compassion, and unto the wonderful gifts, kindness, and works of God in all His creatures bodily and ghostly with thanking and praising. But the higher part of contemplation, as it may be had here, hangeth all wholly in this darkness and in this cloud of unknowing; with a loving stirring and a blind beholding unto the naked being of God Himself only"[140].

---

138 Ibid. Ch. 8, Underhill, p. 85; Hodgson, 30: 21, 31: 1-5. Walter Hilton makes a similar classification using likewise the terms "two manner of lives". "Thou shalt understand that there be in Holy Kirk two manner of lives, as Saint Gregory saith, in which Christian men shall be saved. One is called active, the other contemplative . . . Active life lieth in love and charity showed outward by good bodily works . . . Contemplative life lieth in perfect love and charity felt inwardly by ghostly virtues, and by soothfast knowing and sight of God and ghostly things . . ." Scale I, Ch. 2, Underhill, p. 3, Ch. 3, p. 5. He makes a detailed discussion of these "two manner of lives" and their different "parts" in Scale I, Chs. 2 to 9, Underhill, pp. 3-18.
139 The Cloud, Ch. 8, Underhill, p. 86; Hodgson, 31: 12-14.
140 Ibid. Ch. 8, Underhill, pp. 86-87; Hodgson, 31: 21-23, 32: 1-8.

We see then how the author indentifies the "higher part of contemplative life" with "This Work".

These different parts are more graphically illustrated by the author in the story of Martha and Mary. The author describes the different parts of the *two lives* with the terms "first and second part", which refer to the "lower and higher" parts of the previous classification. Thus the "first part" of *active life,* which is the part of Martha, has reference to "all the time that Martha made her busy about the dighting of His meat . . . full good and full holy"[141]. The "second part", which in the other classification is the *upper active* and *lower contemplative,* is engaged with the "preciousness of His blessed body . . . the sweet voice and the words of His manhood . . ."[142]. But the part of Mary, the *higher part* of the contemplative life, looks "to the sovereignest wisdom of His Godhead lapped in the dark words of His manhood . . ."[143].

The author makes a still further classification based on the relation of these different "parts" to the person himself.

"In the lower part of active life a man is without himself and beneath himself. In the higher part of active life and the lower part of contemplative life, a man is within himself and even with himself. But in the higher part of contemplative life, a man is above himself and under his God. Above himself he is: for why, he purposeth him to win thither by grace, whither he may not come by nature. That is to say, to be knit to God in spirit, and in onehead of love and accordance of will"[144].

The author insists on the separateness of these three parts, both in relation to the definite order they have to follow and to the form and manner of prayer and exercise involved in the ascent[145].

141 Ibid. Ch. 17, Underhill, p. 113; Hodgson, 47: 4-7.
142 Ibid. Ch. 17, Underhill, p. 113; Hodgson, 47: 8-9.
143 Ibid. Ch. 17, Underhill, p. 113; Hodgson, 47: 11-13. Richard of St. Victor uses the story of Martha and Mary, and equates the part of Mary with contemplation. "For while Martha as the Scripture saith. was occupied in serving, Mary sat at the Lord's feet and heard his word. For thus the highest wisdom of God hidden in the flesh, which she could perceive by the eye of the flesh, she understood by hearing and saw by understanding, and in this way, sitting and listening, she was occupied in contemplation of the highest truths. This is the part which shall never be taken away from the elect and the perfect. This is the work which will never come to an end in time or eternity. For the contemplation of truth begins in this life but is carried on perpetually in the next". *Benjamin Major,* Book I, Ch. 1, Ed. Kirchberger, p. 133.
144 *The Cloud,* Ch. 8, Underhill, p. 87; Hodgson, 32: 9-16.
145 Ibid. Ch. 8, Underhill, pp. 87-88; Hodgson, 32: 17-24, 33: 1-5.

By dividing the "two lives" into "three parts" the author is able to explain how it is that Mary's part is the best. For he clearly recognizes that there can be no "best" if there were only two to choose from. Thus he says:

"The first part is good, the second is better, but the third is best of all. This is the 'best part' of Mary. And therefore it is plainly to wit, that our Lord said not, Mary hath chosen the best *life;* for there be no more lives but two, and of two may no man choose the best. But of these two lives Mary hath chosen, He said, the best *part;* the which shall never be taken from her"[146].

The author uses the example of Martha and Mary to illustrate his teaching on the "contemplative and active lives", and gives it a highly spiritualized meaning in relation to the explanation of "This Work".

"Lo! friend, all these works, these words, and these gestures, that were shewed betwixt our Lord and these two sisters, be set in ensample of all actives and all contemplatives that have been since in Holy Church, and shall be to the day of doom. For by Mary is understood all contemplatives . . . And by Martha, actives on the same manner; and for the same reason in likeness"[147].

In *Discretion of Stirrings* the author comes once again to the role of Mary as the representative of the contemplative life[148]. The *best part* that Mary chose is invoked again, but with an altogether different interpretation. He gives an exegesis of the passage from Scripture, "one thing is necessary" in the light of the different spiritual exercises. The different degrees of *good, better, best,* are seen in the context of the different exercises of the spiritual life, as eating and fasting, living with others and living alone, waking and sleeping. Each of the two could be *good* or *better,* but the *best* part, which lies between the two, is God Himself. The author uses the phrase "The best is Almighty Jesu".

As a resumé of this extended discussion of the different stages of life, which the author describes as the "degrees and forms of Christian Men's Living" and "Manner of Lives" with

[146] Ibid. Ch. 21, Underhill, pp. 125-126; Hodgson, 54: 4-10. Cf. Hilton, *Scale I*, Ch. 45, Underhill, pp. 109-110.
[147] *The Cloud*, Ch. 17, Underhill, p. 115; Hodgson, 48: 10-16.
[148] *Discretion of Stirrings*, Hodgson, 73: 7-32, 74: 1-10.

their several "parts", a diagram will be helpful. In this way we can see more clearly the inter-relationships between the different states.

FOUR DEGREES OF LIFE

1. Common
2. Special
3. Singular

MANNERS OF LIVING

A. Active (Good)
B. Upper Active
   Lower Contemplative   (Better)
C. Contemplative (Best)
   i.   Contemplative Prentice
   ii. Profiter
4. Perfect   iii. Perfect

It can be said that *The Cloud* author does not talk of the *Mixed Life* which is a theme developed by Walter Hilton[149].

It is true that *Mixed Life* is not mentioned by *The Cloud* author, but we believe that this is because he had no reason for discussing this kind of life. All four letters, which we are inclined to believe were written to the same disciple, and the three paraphrases deal with the higher reaches of the spiritual life, whereas the known works of Hilton were intended for a much wider audience.

F.   THE CONTEMPLATIVE LIFE

From the diagram we have made of the different "degrees" and "manners of life" we see that the author has put his own

---

[149] We also give a diagram of the states of life as discussed by Walter Hilton. It is in this matter of the *states of life* that we find Hilton and *The Cloud* author differing greatly from each other.
TWO MANNERS OF LIFE
    1. Active
    2. Contemplative
    Three Parts
    A. By Reason
    B. By affection
       Two degrees
       i. Lower
       ii. Higher
    C. Perfect—Both in Cognition and Affection
J. E. Milosh discusses the different states of life according to Hilton in his book. *The Scale of Perfection and the English Mystical Tradition*, Chapter II, pp. 24-50. Also: A. C. Hughes, *Walter Hilton's Direction to Contemplatives*, pp. 59-66.

interpretation to the traditional divisions of *lives* in the Church. The distinction between "active" and "contemplative" lives is set in the context of the "singular degree" of living within which the disciple finds himself. And this division is made on the basis of prayer and other acts of piety. It is only the "higher part" of the "contemplative life" which the author considers as "contemplative", and this he equates with the "best part of Mary". One may be living the "singular degree" and still not be engaged in "This Work". Hence it is not true to say that the message of *The Cloud* is for everyone living the "singular degree".

The term "contemplative life" has assumed a special meaning in *The Cloud*. It is the "best part of Mary". It is "This Work" which is enveloped in the "cloud of unknowing". Later on we shall see specifically the dominant characteristics of this life.

Continuing the story of Martha and Mary the author gives us glimpses of the contemplative life in the concrete, practical day-to-day setting of 14th-century England. We see the "contemplative life" through the eyes of the author, who extols its excellence far beyond any other life. We also see that those who live the "contemplative life" are not free from failings. The author admits these shortcomings with his customary objectivity and charity, but has strong words for those who habitually criticize others for their faults.

". . . as fast, their own brethren and their sisters, and all their next friends, with many other that know not their stirrings nor that manner of living that they set them to, with a great complaining spirit shall rise upon them, and say sharply unto them that it is nought that they do. And as fast they will reckon up many false tales, and many true also, of falling of men and women that have given them to such life before: and never a good tale of them that stood[150].

The author records another objection to the life of the contemplative. This is the question of providing for the material needs of the recluse, and is something we can readily appreciate, for to this day the matter of providing for those who dedicate themselves to the service of God in the cloisters arouses much criticism.

---

150 *The Cloud*, Ch. 18, Underhill, pp. 116-117; Hodgson, 49: 4-11.

"And this I say in confusion of their error, that say that it is not lawful for men to set them to serve God in contemplative life, but if they be secure before of their bodily necessaries. For they say, that God sendeth the cow, but not by the horn. And truly they say wrong of God, as they well know"[151].

We see the great charity of the author when he answers this criticism. Mercy is a quality of the strong, not the strength that relies only on its physical powers but the strength that has been forged out of weakness. It is this strength that weathers all crises. We know that while suffering can embitter yet there can result from this a kindliness and an understanding of the suffering of others. *The Cloud* author knew what it was to be in need of mercy, and to have obtained it. And he understood that the complaints of the "actives" resulted from their ignorance of the "contemplative life".

"And so me thinketh that these worldly living men and women of active life should also full well be had excused of their complaining words touched before, although they say rudely that they say; having beholding to their ignorance. For why? Right as Martha wist full little what Mary her sister did when she complained of her to our Lord; right so on the same manner these folk nowadays wot full little, or else nought, what these young disciples of God mean, when they set from the business of this world, and draw them to be God's special servants in holiness and rightfulness of spirit. And if they wist truly, I daresay that they would neither do nor say as they say. And therefore methinketh always that they should be had excused: for why, they know no better living than is that they live in themselves"[152].

When Martha complained to Jesus about Mary, He answered for Mary. The author tells his disciple that Jesus would do the same for the contemplatives of his day.

"Our lovely Lord Jesus Christ, unto whom no privy thing is hid, although He was required of Martha as doomsman for to bid Mary rise and help her to serve Him; nevertheless yet, for He perceived that Mary was fervently occupied in spirit about the love of His Godhead, therefore courteously and as it was seemly for Him to do by the way of reason, He answered for her, that for excusing of herself list not leave the love of Him"[153].

151 Ibid. Ch. 23, Underhill, p. 131; Hodgson, 57: 6-11.
152 Ibid. Ch. 19, Underhill, p. 119; Hodgson, 50: 13-23, 51: 1-2.
153 Ibid. Ch. 20, Underhill, pp. 121-122; Hodgson, 51: 16-22.

The material needs of the contemplative would similarly be cared for.

"And as He will answer for us thus in spirit, so will He stir other men in spirit to give us our needful things that belong to this life, as meat and clothes with all these other; if He see that we will not leave the work of His love for business about them"[154].

The author is in no way idealistic in his comments on the "contemplatives" by the "actives". He admits the failings of others, but insists on charity.

"I grant well that many fall and have fallen of them that have in likeness forsaken the world. And where they should have become God's servants and His contemplatives, because that they would not rule them by true ghostly counsel they have become the devil's servants and his contemplatives; and turned either to hypocrites or to heretics. . . . Of the which I leave to speak at this time, for troubling of our matter. But nevertheless hereafter when God vouchsafeth and if need be, men may see some of the conditions and the cause of their falling. And therefore no more of them at this time; but forth of our matter"[155].

---

[154] Ibid. Ch. 23, Underhill, p. 131; Hodgson, 57: 3-6.
Professor Helen Gardner makes this observation: "The suggestion is of personal dependence on charity. If we accept that the disciple was a solitary, the natural explanation of the passage is that the author is a solitary too, and that both are living on the alms of their neighbours". ("The Cloud of Unknowing", *Medium Aevum*, XVI, 1947, p. 41.) This observation is indeed supported by the whole tenor of the defence of the contemplative life undertaken by *The Cloud* author. The present writer sees in this passage the reason why the author and the disciple could not have been Carthusians. The author explicitly mentions *meat*. The Carthusians are not allowed by Rule to eat meat, and this is a rigid provision which lasts to this day. While the Carthusians are very austere, they are never in want and surely none of the dire cases of poverty which required the intervention of the Bishops would be possible with them. They would not then depend individually on the "inspired charity" of other people, for the Order supplies their food and clothing. Similarly there would not be that "abundance of necessaries" of which the author speaks. The Carthusians would have a common supply and the context here gives the impression of putting stocks away to last for a while. It may never be proved that *The Cloud* author wrote *Discretion of Stirrings* to the same disciple as the addressee of *The Cloud*. However, it is noteworthy that the acts mentioned in *Discretion of Stirrings* (eating, fasting, being alone or with others, talking or keeping silent — all of which are to be governed by "freedom" given by the "Spirit of God"), are completely out of place in a Carthusian monastery. The approach by *The Cloud* author to the problem raised in this letter is a very significant clue to his spirituality, and it is inviting to think that this letter was written as a commentary on *The Cloud* teaching on "the naked Being of God", God only as IS, when the author gives the very lovely passage of what God IS NOT.
[155] Ibid. Ch. 18, Underhill, p. 117; Hodgson, 49: 12-22.

In the face of objections and criticisms, the author gives the clarion call that will give heart to the contemplative.

"For to them that be perfectly meeked, no thing shall defail; neither bodily thing, nor ghostly. For why? They have God, in whom is all plenty; and whoso hath Him—yea, as this book telleth—him needeth nought else in this life"[156].

Such encouragement would no doubt have put strength into any faint-hearted soul. This teaching of the author, based no doubt on his own experience, is a tribute to his heroic trust in the Providence of God and of the instinctive certainty of the grace for "This Work". However, the question of providing for the needs of the recluse had been the subject of the prescriptions of the *Constitutions* of Archbishop St. Edmund Rich of Abingdon. This was in 1236. "By this refreshingly ingenuous and sensible pronouncement coming from such an authority, the attitude of the English episcopate towards the pauper Recluse may well have been stiffened perceptibly during the last years of the waning Middle Age"[157]. There had been cases of dire poverty on the part of recluses which required the intervention of the Bishops[158]. But for the author the matter was a special one which required the *Personal Intervention* of God. Let us look at one or two different attitudes towards the recluse over the centuries.

"Your prudent and pious discretion knows exactly which are dearer to Christ: excellent prelates, solitary wandering hermits or pent-up Anchorets. The former feed: the two latter are fed. The former restore, with heavy interest, the talent entrusted by God; the latter, in a way, conceal the talent entrusted—intent on little more than their own salvation. To the Lord's granaries the former bring much fruit—true grains as it were of wheat, not of chaff: the latter, as solitaries, exist thus in truth and alone —without multiplication of fruit"[159].

But there has too been tender appreciation of the recluse.

"Recluses were swept away by the flood which carried off all that was in any way connected with monasticism. They had however fulfilled their purpose, and justified their existence. They were often men and women of strong and saintly character whose life commanded respect, and won gratitude from their

---

156 Ibid. Ch. 23, Underhill, p. 132; Hodgson, 58: 3-6.
157 F. D. S. Darwin, *The English Mediaeval Recluse*, pp. 54-55.
158 Ibid. pp. 55-56.
159 Ibid. pp. 83-84.

fellowmen—who recognized them as *workers*. At its best, the contemplative life was a career—and a noble one. There were of course some whose conduct brought discredit on their profession; but there were others who lived up to the high ideal"[160].

In the light of the foregoing passages it is interesting to note the interpretation that has been given to the objections and criticisms hurled at the contemplatives.

"On the other hand, it is also interesting to note that if the theologians criticize him, he also criticizes them; if they jibe at him, he jibes at them; he gives as much as he gets. But why the dispute? The answer, it seems to me, is first of all the historical fact that people who incline to vertical thinking and those who devote themselves exclusively to discursive or logical thinking have always had the greatest difficulty in understanding one another. In East and West, not a few mystics (even the most humble like the good author of *The Cloud*) have tended to look down on the less-favoured advocates of logic, despising them as poor, dull fellows who sit in self-satisfied ignorance within the dark and drab Platonic cave looking miserably at shadows when they should come out into the superb sunshine to contemplate the glorious reality. . . . And so against this there have always been reactionaries who, like the author of *The Cloud* wish to shake off the shackles of an excessive Aristotelianism to look for truth in silent and existential repose"[161].

Regardless of the respective merits of *vertical* and *horizontal* thinking, the problem to which the above passage calls attention is not the one that *The Cloud* author had in mind. The criticism levelled by the "actives" against "the contemplatives", refer to the morals of those who fail to live up to the high standard of the "singular life", as well as to the more practical problem of providing for the support of the recluse who is pent up in the anchorhold, and who by the Rules of St. Ailred must "live by the labour of her hands"[162]. The objection which the author of *The Cloud* noted could perhaps be translated by the modern expression of "God helps those who help themselves". This is still a common criticism of those who enter the service of God in Religion. There is still some feeling that one who enters the religious life becomes a drain on the financial resources of the community, for one so

---

160 Ibid. p. 86.
161 W. Johnston, *The Mysticism of The Cloud of Unknowing*, pp. 270, 272.
162 F. D. S. Darwin, *The English Mediaeval Recluse*, p. 56.

engaged in the life of prayer is not actively engaged in the production of material goods.

Having seen the different states of life according to the author, and the particular "degree and manner of living" within which "This Work" can be done, we move on to the question of the powers of the soul which are involved in the ascent to God.

G.   "MIGHTS OF THE SOUL"

As in the previous discussion on the different states of life, we see that the author has a special term for the powers of the soul, which he calls "the mights of the soul". These are the psychological and spiritual faculties of man by which a man may rise up to God and be united with Him in *spirit* and in *love*. The author names and classifies these "mights of the soul". They are *Memory, Reason, Will, Imagination* and *Sensuality*. Of the five three are "principal", namely *Memory, Reason* and *Will,* the other two are "secondary", namely *Imagination* and *Sensuality.* The "principal" powers are concerned with "all ghostly things", and the "secondary" powers with "all bodily things"[163]. "Memory is called a principal power, for it containeth in it ghostly not only all the other powers, but thereto all those things in the which they work"[164]. The author further classifies these five powers as to whether they are "working powers" or not. By a process of elimination the author excludes those "mights" which are not directly related to "This Work". Of the five it is *Memory* alone that is not a "working power", and because of the "ghostly nature" of "This Work" the author also removes the "secondary powers", *Imagination* and *Sensuality,* which "work beastly in all bodily things, whether they be present or absent, in the body and with the bodily wits. But by them, without help of Reason and of Will, may a soul never come to for to know the virtue and the conditions of bodily creatures, nor the cause of their beings and their makings"[165]. We shall therefore be dealing with the two "principal working powers", *Reason*

---

[163] *The Cloud,* Ch. 63, Underhill, p. 238; Hodgson, 115: 19-22.
       Cf. Hilton, *Scale II,* Chs. 30, 31, Underhill, pp. 364, 367.
[164] Ibid. Ch. 63, Underhill, p. 239; Hodgson, 116: 6-9.
[165] Ibid. Ch. 63, Underhill, p. 239; Hodgson, 115: 22-24, 116: 1-2.

and *Will,* but first the author describes the different "mights" in the light of the ascetical and moral life.

"Reason is a power through the which we depart the evil from the good, the evil from the worse, the good from the better, the worse from the worst, the better from the best. . . . Will is a power through the which we choose good, after that it be determined with Reason; and through the which we love good, we desire good, and rest us with full liking and consent endlessly in God. . . . Imagination is a power through the which we portray all images of absent and present things. . . . Sensuality is a power of our soul, recking and reigning in the bodily wits, through the which we have bodily knowing and feeling of all bodily creatures, whether they be pleasing or unpleasing"[166].

Looking back to the state of Original Justice, the author sees the functions of these powers as they were when they came from the Hands of God.

"Before ere man sinned, might Reason have done all this by nature . . . might not Will be deceived in his choosing, in his loving, nor in none of his works . . . was Imagination so obedient unto the Reason, to the which it is as it were servant, that it ministered never to it any unordained image of any bodily creature, or any fantasy of any ghostly creature . . . was the Sensuality so obedient unto the Will, unto the which it is as it were servant, that it ministered never unto it any unordained liking or grumbling in any bodily creature, or any ghostly feigning of liking or misliking made by any ghostly enemy in the bodily wits"[167].

And he immediately contrasts this ideal state with the present state of "Fallen Man" and the ravages that had been brought about to the "mights of the soul" by Original Sin.

"But now (Reason) is so blinded with the original sin, that it may not con work this work, unless it be illumined by grace . . . (Will) may not do so, unless it be anointed with grace. For ofttimes because of infection of the original sin, it savoureth a thing for good that is full evil, and that hath but the likeness of good . . . but now it is not so. For unless (Imagination) be refrained by the light of grace in the Reason, else it will never cease, sleeping or waking, for to portray diverse unordained images of bodily creatures; or else some fantasy, the which is nought else but a bodily conceit of a ghostly thing, or else a ghostly conceit of a bodily thing . . . for unless (Sensuality) be ruled by grace in the Will, for to suffer meekly and in measure

---

[166] Ibid. Chs. 64-66, Underhill, pp. 240-244; Hodgson, pp. 116-119.
[167] Ibid. Chs. 64-66, Underhill, pp. 240-245; Hodgson, pp. 116-119.

the pain of the original sin, the which it feeleth in absence of needful comforts and in presence of speedful discomforts, and thereto also for to restrain it from lust in presence of needful comforts, and from lusty plesaunce in the absence of speedful discomforts: else will it wretchedly and wantonly welter, as a swine in the mire, in the wealths of this world and the foul flesh so much that all our living shall be more beastly and fleshly, than either manly or ghostly"[168].

In equating the functions of the "mights of the soul" with their natural manner of working before the Fall, the author obliquely describes the *mystic way*. For, in the days before the Fall, our First Parents were described as "having walked with God", holding familiar converse with Him. The author gives the reason for this extended discussion on the "mights of the soul".

"Lo! ghostly friend! hereby mayest thou see somewhat in part, that whoso knoweth not the powers of their own soul, and the manner of their working, may full lightly be deceived in understanding of words that be written to ghostly intent"[169].

Carefully delineating their powers and limitations, the author proceeds from the lowest power of the soul to the highest. In this ascent each power gives way to the one above it, until that power is reached which is equal to "This Work".

"And therefore leave thine outward wits, and work not with them, neither within nor without: for all those that set them to be ghostly workers within, and ween that they should either hear, smell, or see, taste or feel, ghostly things, either within them or without, surely they be deceived, and work wrong against the course of nature. For by nature they be ordained, that with them men should have knowing of all outward bodily things, and on no wise by them come to the knowing of ghostly things. . . . On this same manner ghostly it fareth within our ghostly wits, when we travail about the knowing of God Himself. For have a man never so much ghostly understanding in knowing of all made ghostly things, yet may he never by the work of his understanding come to the knowing of an unmade ghostly thing: the which is nought but God. But by the failing it may: for why, that thing that it faileth in is nothing else but only God"[170].

The way is then cleared for the teaching of the author that

168 Ibid. Chs. 64-66, Underhill, pp. 240-245; Hodgson, pp. 116-119.
169 Ibid. Ch. 67, Underhill, p. 248; Hodgson, 120: 21-24.
170 Ibid. Ch. 70, Underhill, pp. 255-256; Hodgson, 124: 11-21, 125: 1-10.

in "This Work" it is the will that is involved. For when the *knowing power* fails, the *loving power* takes over. The author is most insistent on this primacy of will and love and makes explicit the limits that the "knowing power" can reach.

"For of all other creatures and their works, yea, and of the works of God's self, may a man through grace have fulhead of knowing, and well he can think of them: but of God Himself can no man think"[171].

With the limit of the "knowing power" reached, we end this general discussion on "the mights of the soul" and move to that "might" which, according to the author of *The Cloud* is the only one capable of doing "This Work".

H. THE PRIMACY OF THE WILL AND LOVE

The Cloud author expresses this primacy with this characteristic passage.

"And our soul by virtue of this reforming grace is made sufficient to the full to comprehend all Him by love, the which is incomprehensible to all created knowledgeable powers, as is angel, or man's soul; I mean, by their knowing, and not by their loving. . . . And therefore I would leave all that thing that I can think, and choose to my love that thing that I cannot think. For why; He may well be loved, but not thought. By love may He be gotten and holden; but by thought never. . . . For why, love may reach to God in this life, but not knowing"[172].

The author continues this teaching on the primacy of love in *Privy Counsel,* using the story of Rachel and her son Benjamin.

"By Benjamin contemplation, and by Rachel we understand reason. And as soon as a soul is touched with very contemplation—as it is in this noble noughting of itself and this high alling of God—surely and verily right then dieth all man's reason"[173].

While he echoes Richard of St. Victor in the interpretation of Rachel and Benjamin, he goes still further and equates it with "This Work". This illustration reveals both the thorough knowledge of *The Cloud* author, and the originality of his

---

171 Ibid. Ch. 6, Underhill, p. 77; Hodgson, 25: 18-19, 26: 1-2.
172 Ibid. Ch. 4, Underhill, p. 66, Ch. 6, p. 77, Ch. 8, p. 88; Hodgson, 18: 17-21, 26: 2-5, 33: 11.
173 *Privy Counsel,* McCann, p. 120; Hodgson, 150: 12-15.

teaching. The limitation of the intellect in knowing God is explained:

"And all the whiles that the soul dwelleth in this deadly body, evermore is the sharpness of our understanding in beholding of all ghostly things, but most specially of God, mingled with some manner of fantasy; for the which our work should be unclean. And unless more wonder were, it should lead us into much error"[174].

Based on the nature of the intellect and the will the explanation is enlarged.

"But be thou sure that clear sight shall never man have here in this life: but the feeling may men have through grace when God vouchsafeth. And therefore lift up thy love to that cloud: rather, if I shall say thee sooth, let God draw thy love up to that cloud and strive thou through help of His grace to forget all other thing"[175].

He uses a very homely figure to express this primacy when he likens the silencing of the intellect to a "sleep".

"And well is this work likened to a sleep. For as in a sleep the use of the bodily wits is ceased, that the body may take his full rest in feeding and strengthening of the bodily nature: right so in this ghostly sleep the wanton questions of the wild ghostly wits, imaginative reasons, be fast bound and utterly voided, so that the silly soul may softly sleep and rest in the lovely beholding of God as he is, in full feeding and strengthening of the ghostly nature"[176].

The author links this primacy of the will over the intellect with humility, calling on the authority of St. Bernard[177]. Scriptural acknowledgment of this primacy is given in passages from St. Paul and Solomon.

"For if it be wisely looked, the ground and the strength of this working shall be seen nought else but the glorious gift of love, in the which by the teaching of the Apostle all the law is ful-

---

174 *The Cloud*, Ch. 8, Underhill, p. 88; Hodgson, 33: 11-16.
175 Ibid. Ch. 9, Underhill, p. 90; Hodgson, 34: 17-22.
176 *Privy Counsel*, McCann, pp. 121-122; Hodgson, 152: 3-9. Fr. Poulain has a lovely commentary on the *sleep* of the faculties which he terms *quiescence*. "The faculties may be at rest and abstain from trying to add anything to that which they receive. The intellect is content to drink deep draughts of the experimental knowledge vouchsafed to it; it is wise enough to stop there. The memory and the imagination, having nothing to receive, seem to slumber; and as a rule this is the best thing that they can do" (*The Graces of Interior Prayer*, p. 125). In this, too, we can see how the mystic act "demands less effort than meditation". (*The Graces of Interior Prayer* p. 114.)
177 *Privy Counsel*, McCann, p. 122; Hodgson, 153: 2-5.

filled: *Plentitudo legis est dilectio*, 'the fulness of the law is love'. And this lovely law and this lively counsel, if thou keep it, as Solomon saith, 'shall be life to thy soul': within in softness of love to thy God, 'and grace to thy cheeks' without, in the truest teaching and the seemliest governance of thy bodily bearing in outward form of living to thine even Christian. And in these two, the one within and the other without, by the teaching of Christ, 'hangeth all the law and the prophets. . . .'"[178].

We find the same insistence on the primacy of will and love in *Discretion of Stirrings*. In so doing he takes his argument from the "Song of Songs" and thus moves his discussion from the field of reason, as shown in the previous passages, to the mystical life.

"Such a blind shot with the sharp dart of longing love may never fail of the prick, the which is God, as Himself saith in the book of love, where He speaketh to a languishing soul and a loving, saying thus: *Vulnerasti cor meum, soror mea, amica mea, et sponsa mea, vulnerasti cor meum, in uno oculorum tuorum*: 'Thou hast wounded mine heart, my sister, my leman, and my spouse, thou hast wounded mine heart in one of thine eyes.' Eyes of the soul they are two: Reason and Love"[179].

In his exegesis of this passage from the "Song of Songs" the author gives the reason for the primacy, now in relation to the Object of both powers of the soul, namely God. He intimately relates it to the aspect of God which is the only consideration of "This Work", that is, *God in Himself*.

"By reason we may trace how mighty, how wise, and how good He is in His creatures, but not in Himself; but ever when reason defaileth, then list, love, live and learn, to play, for by love we may feel Him, find Him, and hit Him, even in Himself. It is a wonderful eye, this love, for of a loving soul it is only said of our Lord: "Thou hast wounded mine heart in one of thine eyes"; that is to say, in love that is blind to many things, and seeth but that one thing that it seeketh, and therefore it findeth and feeleth, hitteth and woundeth the point and the prick that it shooteth at, well sooner than it should if the sight were sundery in beholding of many things, as it is when the reason ransacketh and seeketh among all such sere things as are these; silence and speaking, singular fasting and common eating, onliness or company, and all such other; to look whether is better"[180].

[178] Ibid. McCann, p. 116; Hodgson, 146: 11-22.
[179] *Discretion of Stirrings*, Gardner, p. 108; Hodgson, 72: 12-19.
[180] Ibid. pp. 108-109; Hodgson, 72: 19-26, 73: 1-6. St. John of the Cross notes this singleness of heart and fidelity on the part of the soul to-

The author brings this discussion down to the practical
level of the various exercises of the spiritual life. It is not a
mere dissertation he is writing, but a guide for a life to be
lived. And so he neatly links up his beautiful description of
"what God is not" to the life of the disciple seen in the light
of this primacy of love. He tells what form this primacy must
take in the level of the disciple's day-to-day life. "Choose Him
then"—this is the form and manner by which this love must
be expressed.

> "Such a lovely choosing of God, thus wisely lesinge and seeking
> Him out with the true will of a clean heart, between all such
> two leaving them both, when they come and proffer them to
> be the point and the prick of our ghostly beholding, is the
> worthiest tracing and seeking of God that may be gotten or
> learned in this life. I mean for a soul that will be contemplative;
> yea, though all that a soul that thus seeketh see nothing that
> may be conceived with the ghostly eye of reason; for if God be
> thy love and thy meaning, the choice and the point of thine
> heart, it sufficeth to thee in this life (though all thou see never
> more of Him with the eyes of thy reason all thy life time)"[181].

For *The Cloud* author it is the will and its act of love that
has the primacy in "This Work", in this ascent to God. The
author arrives at this conclusion by carefully delineating the
limits and capacities of the different "mights of the soul" and,
by a process of elimination, reaches finally the only "might"
which is equal to "This Work", namely the will. In giving
the primacy to the will and its act of love, we do not see
The Cloud author getting involved in the question as to
whether Love constitutes the essence of the mystical life. We
see him simply narrating a fact connected with "This Work".
In this connection, too, the will as a "might of the soul" is
presupposed, and it is the "impulsion to the virtue of Love"
produced in this mystic state that is stressed. Hence we verify

ward God in his exegesis of the same passage from the "Song of
Songs" . . . " . . . . because if the faith and the fidelity of the soul toward
God were not alone, but were mingled with respect or courtesy to some
other, she would not succeed in wounding God by love. Wherefore
it must be by but one eye alone that the Beloved is wounded. . . . And
the love wherewith the Spouse is taken captive by the Bride in this
singleness and fidelity that He sees in her is so intimate that, if He
was taken captive by the hair of her love, by the eye of her faith
His captivity is made closer with so fast a knot. . . ." *Spiritual
Canticle*, Allison-Peers, p. 117.
181 Discretion of Stirrings, Gardner, p. 108; Hodgson, 72:3-12.

the *tenth* characteristic of the mystic state, namely "it inclines the soul of itself and very efficaciously to the different virtues"[182]. We shall see this further in passages where he insists on *meekness* and *charity,* and wherein he says that ". . . all virtues they find and feel in God . . ."[183]. And at the end of his discussion he calls on the authority of the Pseudo-Dionysius to support his view.

"But by the failing it may: for why, that thing that it faileth in is nothing else but only God. and therefore it was that Saint Denis said, *the most goodly knowing of God is that, the which is known by unknowing.* And truly, whoso will look in Denis' books, he shall find that his words will clearly affirm all that I have said or shall say, from the beginning of this treatise to the end"[184].

1. *IS* THE CLOUD OF UNKNOWING *DIONYSIAN*?

Because of this express admission of Dionysian inspiration it might be said that *The Cloud* is specifically Dionysian, and "This Work" the "via negativa" of which the Pseudo-Dionysius writes in *Mystica Theologia.* Professor Knowles makes this comment on the above passage:

"This, however, is not precisely true . . . the author of *The Cloud* did not read Denis in the original Greek, but in two medieval Latin translations, those of Johannes Sarracenus (d. 1160) and Thomas Gallus (d. 1240), assisted by the latter's commentary. Gallus, abbot of St. Andrew's, Vercelli, and a canon of the Victorine order, had displayed even more than customary medieval skill in noiselessly adapting a work of ancient thought to medieval conditions, and had made love rather than understanding the characteristic occupation of the contemplative, thus rendering Denis viable among Thomists and Bonaventurans"[185].

Using the story of Moses the Pseudo-Dionysius tells us what happens on the mountain-top when Moses beholds "the place where God was".

". . . and then it breaks forth, even from the things that are beheld and from those that behold them, and plunges the true initiate unto the Darkness of Unknowing wherein he renounces all the apprehensions of his understanding and is enwrapped in

182 A. Poulain, *The Graces of Interior Prayer,* p. 114.
183 *The Cloud,* Ch. 40, Underhill, p. 172; Hodgson, 79: 7.
184 Ibid. Ch. 70, Underhill, p. 256; Hodgson, 125: 9-15.
185 D. Knowles, *The English Mystical Tradition,* pp. 73-74.

that which is wholly intangible and invisible, belonging wholly
to Him that is beyond all things and to none else (whether himself or another), and being through the passive stillness of all
his reasoning powers united by his highest faculty to Him that
is wholly Unknowable, of whom thus by a rejection of all
knowledge he possesses a knowledge that exceeds his understanding"[186].

In this passage we do not find the explicit admission of the
primacy of the will and love on which the author of *The
Cloud* insists. To the Pseudo-Dionysius the "Darkness of
Unknowing" takes place in the understanding but he does
not identify the "highest faculty" by which union is achieved
with "Him that is wholly Unknowable". In his characteristic
handling of this particular text we see how the author of *The
Cloud* neatly fits in his personal views and teachings, and
makes explicit the primacy of "affection" which the Pseudo-
Dionysius does not make. The parts personal to *The Cloud*
author are italicized in the following story of Moses.

"Ensample of this see by the story: How the godly Moses,
mildest of men first he is bidden to be cleansed, both in himself
and *also in his people, and after that to be separated from
occasion of defiling.* And then, after all cleansing of himself and
of his people, he heard trumps of many voices and saw many
lights with shining, sending out from them full broad and full
clean beams. Afterwards he was separated from the multitude
of this people, and with priests that were chosen, he attained to
the highness of the godly ascensions, *the which is the terms and
bounds of man's understanding, be it never so helped with
grace.* And yet in all this he was not with God, so as it accordeth
to the perfection of this divinity; but he had in contemplation
an object not himself, for he may not be seen by that eye. But
the place where he was, that was his object. *And that place
betokeneth the highest godly beholdings, passing above and
having in subjection all man's reasons, as the lady hath her
maidens. By the which godly beholdings, the presence of him
that is set above all thinking is sovereignly showed to man's
understandings, and setteth him above the natural terms of
himself. And then he is assoiled both from the understandable
working powers of his soul, and from the objects of them—that
is for to say, all those things in which they work.*

*In this time it was that Moses in singularity of affection was
separated from these beforesaid chosen priests, and entered
by* himself the darkness of unknowing, the which darkness is

186 Pseudo-Dionysius, *Mystical Theology*, Ed. Rolt, p. 194.

verily hid; in the which he shineth, all-knowable knowing. And surely he is made (in a manner that is invisible and ungropable) for to feel in experience the presence of him that is above all things, not having feeling nor thinking of no being thing nor yet of himself. But, in avoiding of all knowing that is still unknowing, he is knitted unto him in the best manner; and in that he knoweth no thing, he is made to be knowing above mind"[187].

We see from the personal additions which the author makes to the text of *Mystica Theologia* how well the observations of Professor Knowles are borne out. The explicit assertion "in singularity of affection" is a distinct progress from the Dionysian thought.

We have already discussed how to *The Cloud* author the state of the "cloud of unknowing" and the perfection of "This Work" is reached by the successive failures of the lower "mights" of the soul when a higher power takes over. And this process of elimination goes up till the only "might" left capable of "This Work" is the will.

Against this background we read the descriptions of the Pseudo-Dionysius of the "affirmative" and "negative" ways of reaching God outlined in *Mystica Theologia*.

"Unto this Darkness which is beyond Light we pray that we may attain unto vision through the loss of sight and knowledge ... which we shall do by denying or removing all things that are—like as men who, carving a statue out of marble, remove all the impediments that hinder the clear perceptive of the latent image and by this mere removal display the hidden beauty. Now we must wholly distinguish this negative method from that of positive statements. For when we were making positive statements we began with the most universal statements, and then through intermediate terms we came at last to particular titles, but now ascending upwards from particular to universal conceptions we strip off all qualities in order that we may attain a naked knowledge of that Unknowing which in all existent things is enwrapped by all objects of knowedge, and that we may begin to see that super-essential Darkness, which is hidden by all the light that is in existent things"[188].

The Pseudo-Dionysius distinguishes between the two ways, using as a basis the upwards and downward movements.

"But why is it, you will ask, that after beginning from the

187 *Denis Hid Divinity*, McCann, pp. 136-138; Hodgson, 4: 27-5: 24.
188 Pseudo-Dionysius, *Mystical Theology*, Ed. Rolt, pp. 194-196.

highest category when one method was affirmative we begin from the lowest category where it is negative? Because, when affirming the existence of that which transcends all affirmation, we were obliged to start from that which is most akin to It, and then to make the affirmation on which the rest depended; but when pursuing the negative method, to reach that which is beyond all negation, we must start by applying our negations to those qualities which differ most from the ultimate goal. Surely it is truer to affirm that God is life and goodness than that He is air or stone, and truer to deny that drunkenness or fury can be attributed to Him than to deny that we may apply to Him the categories of human thought"[189].

The "affirmative" and "negative" ways of the Pseudo-Dionysius involves successive operations of the mind, distinct psychological processes. This is not so with the state of "the cloud of forgetting", where, for all the *travail* and *work* involved in this act of *forgetting,* the final and complete forgetting and obliteration is possible only by the grace of God. These psychological processes are likewise different from the successive "failings" of the "mights of the soul" of *The Cloud.* The descriptions of the states of the soul in "the cloud of forgetting" and in "the cloud of unknowing" will further stress this difference between the Pseudo-Dionysius and *The Cloud* author. We hold that while the inspiration of *The Cloud* is Dionysian, nevertheless the author does not teach the "via negativa" of the Pseudo-Dionysius. We mention in passing that the perfection of prayer described as "the fruit" in the *Epistle of Prayer* is not the "affirmative way" of the Pseudo-Dionysius. In this the differences are more easily seen.

2.   *IS* THE CLOUD OF UNKNOWING *ANTI-INTELLECTUAL*?

Because of the insistence of *The Cloud* author on the primacy of will and love, the objection might be made that *The Cloud* is anti-intellectual. St. John of the Cross noted this possible misunderstanding of his own teaching[190]. We

---

189 Ibid. pp. 198-199.
190 "Here it is to be known, with respect to the saying of some that the will cannot love, save what the understanding first understands, that this has to be understood after a natural manner; for in the way of nature it is impossible to love if one understands not first that which one is to love; but in the supernatural way God can readily infuse love and increase it without infusing or increasing distinct knowledge, as is given to be understood in the passage quoted". *Spiritual Canticle,* Allison-Peers, pp. 98-99.

are aware that the question of the intellect and the will in the matter of the mystical life is not a simple one. Theologians as a whole have been divided on the question depending on whether they would give the primacy to the intellect or to the will. St. Thomas insists on the place of knowledge in this aspect of the spiritual life, and for him contemplation is in its essence a simple intuition of Truth, terminating in love. The Beatific Vision is for him the perfect intuition of the True. For the Franciscans, however, it is love that dominates[191]. In the face of this dichotomy of the intellect and the will, it is worth remembering the Jewish concept of man as a whole. For it is, after all, the whole man who loves and thinks and contemplates, and not just one segment of the whole. The admission of this primacy of the will, as well as its reconciliation with the other powers of the soul in the highest reaches of the spiritual life, can best be summed up by the maxim of St. Gregory the Great *amor ipse notitia est*[192].

From the foregoing passages we see that *The Cloud* author follows the school of St. Victor and William of St. Thiery. And in giving the primacy to the will, the author does not degrade the intellect. The extended discussions on the "mights of the soul" are proof of this. He insists that a right knowledge of the workings of these "mights" is necessary to avoid misunderstandings and delusions. And it is not an admission of weakness, but rather a recognition of the limitations of each power of the soul as regards a higher function, when he clearly shows their dividing lines.

This *primacy* which the author gives to the will and its act of love in "This Work" can be seen as an aspect of the *abbreviations* that the mystics use. Fr. Poulain makes a picturesque observation on the confusion and disputes arising from these *abbreviations*.

"Authors have wished to cut their explanations short, and their obscurity has resulted in interminable disputes. And then, to elucidate matters, all the treatises have been lengthened out; the question whether it is possible to love without knowledge having been the cause, especially, of the expenditure of a perfect flood of ink"[193].

191 C. Butler, *Western Mysticism*, pp. 23-24.
192 L. Reypens, "Connaissance Mystique de Dieu", *Dictionnaire De Spiritualité*, III, Col. 887.
193 A. Poulain, *The Graces of Interior Prayer*, pp. 129-130.

The Cloud author does not denegrate reason, and acknowledges the worth of knowledge, but for "This Work" they do not help.

"And where thou askest me thereof whether it be good or evil, I say it behoveth always be good in its nature. For why, it is a beam of the likeness of God. But the use thereof may be both good and evil"[194].

With his characteristic objectivity the author sees the relative value of things. He is not against learning and natural reason as such. But when they are wrongly used they lead men astray. Knowing how much he insists on humility, we can understand the strength with which he speaks against the pride of the intellect.

"But then is the use evil, when it is swollen with pride and with curiosity of much clergy and letterly cunning as in clerks; and maketh them press for to be holden not meek scholars and masters of divinity or of devotion, but proud scholars of the devil and masters of vanity and of falsehood. And in other men or women whatso they be, religious or seculars, the use and the working of this natural wit is then evil, when it is swollen with proud and curious skills of worldly things, and fleshly conceits in coveting of worldly worships and having of riches and vain plesaunce and flatterings of others"[195].

One result of this pride of the intellect is heresy and defection from the Church.

"Some there be, that although they be not deceived with this error as it is set here, yet for pride and curiosity of natural wit and letterly cunning leave the common doctrine and the counsel of Holy Church. And these with all their favourers lean over much to their own knowing: and for they were never grounded in meek blind feeling and virtuous living, therefore they merit to have a false feeling, feigned and wrought by the ghostly enemy. Insomuch, that at the last they burst up and blaspheme all the saints, sacraments, statutes, and ordinances of Holy Church"[196].

194 *The Cloud*, Ch. 8, Underhill, p. 84; Hodgson, 30: 5-8.
195 Ibid. Ch. 8, Underhill, pp. 84-85; Hodgson, 30: 11-20. Also *Privy Counsel*, McCann, 107-108.
196 *The Cloud*, Ch. 56, Underhill, p. 218; Hodgson, 104: 4-12. Walter Hilton speaks of the same pride of the intellect. "He should be able to hate the sin in all other men, for he hateth it in himself, but he could not love the man in charity for all his philosophy. Also if a man had knowing of clergy and of all divinity and is not soothfastly meek, he shall err and stumble and take that one for the other; but meekness is worthy to receive a gift of God, the which may not be learnt by kenning of man". *Scale 1*, Ch. 68, Underhill, p. 163. Also *Bonum Est*, Jones, pp. 188-189. These passages could easily have reference to Wycliffe and his followers who were university-trained intellectuals.

CONCLUSIONS

With this chapter we are starting to deal more intimately with the matter of this dissertation, namely, the teaching of the 14th-century English writer, on a particular ascent to God. We have proceeded in this study from the outside, dealing with those matters less concerned with the heart of the subject. We may call these questions secondary, but only in the sense of the relative value and importance which they have, as we see *The Cloud* author so often doing. For all these questions previously treated have a relevance all their own to the proper understanding of the whole message. In our approach of working from the outside towards the heart we are following the figure of the "stock" from *Denis Hid Divinity*.

We, too, can conjure up the picture of mountain-climbing, for, indeed, the circumference of the mountain tapers off as the ascent gets higher and the peaks become shrouded more and more with clouds as the heights are gradually reached.

"Here is a man having a sound stock of the greatest quantity without him, lying before him, and having within him intent and craft to make an image of the least quantity, of that place of the wood the which is (by measuring of right lining) in the centre and the middle of that same stock. First thou knowest well by natural wit that ere he may come for to see that image by clear bodily sight of his outward eye, or for to show it to be seen unto other, the which he hath in himself by clear craft of imagination, the stock yet being whole on every side, he must surely by craft and by instruments void away all the outward parts of that wood, being about and hindering the sight of that same image"[197].

This is our approach to the teaching of *The Cloud* proceeding step by step till we reach the heart of the matter, "the cloud of unknowing" itself.

In this chapter we discussed the nature and characteristic elements of the ascent and way to God which the author describes by the term "This Work". This expression has assumed a technical and personal meaning with the author and he uses it not in the sense of just any work to be done but in the sense of the specific "work" of *The Cloud*. The author reveals great familiarity with his teaching, which can be explained by the fact that it is a personal experience he

[197] *Denis Hid Divinity*, McCann, p. 138; Hodgson, 5: 33-6: 1-9.

narrates. He stresses the fact that "belief is the ground" of "This Work". By this he means an experience, a perception, "mere consciousness". This can be seen in the passages as one reads through the entire *Cloud* and *Privy Counsel*. This impression is greatly strengthened by the author's statement that this is so. In addition to this testimony of a *personal experience,* he says that it is God who is the Source of his teaching. This is a daring claim, but the fact that it is made commands our attention. It must be realized that the author means what he says, and whilst the statement may be too profound for our immediate understanding it must not be discounted because of this. In his explanations of the different characteristics he achieves great clarity by means of his two-way approach, namely describing first of all what a thing is not, and then specifically saying what it is. And he brings into focus the possible misunderstandings which can arise by his favourite device of anticipated questions and answers.

The grace to do "This Work" is freely given by God, and with this free gift comes the corresponding ability and capacity on the part of the soul to do "This Work". This being so, the particular teaching has reference to the "substance" of the spiritual life, and it is tempting to believe that *The Cloud* author must have been musing over the "calor, canor, and dulcor" of Richard Rolle as he wrote these passages.

In a manner characteristic of the mystics we see the author using seeming contradictions and paradoxes, as well as super-latives, in his descriptions of the nature of "This Work". Thus, it is the "easiest" thing to do, and yet it can be the "most impossible" thing to do, involving *pain* and *travail*. But there is a diminishing of this *pain* and *travail* as the perfection of "This Work" is gradually reached and a state of rest attained, which is a foretaste of the peace and rest of the heavenly Jerusalem. Because of the *pain* and *travail* involved in "This Work", "a full great restfulness" is required, and we see the relevance of his insistence that the disciple must be careful about his health.

As it is the "easiest" thing to do, so it is also the "shortest" thing to do, as "short as an atom", which is equivalent to the expression "a twinkling of the eye". It sounds a simple matter taken simply like that. But it must be remembered that this "twinkling of the eye", equivalent to just one stirring of the heart, must be maintained, moment by moment, for the rest of one's life. With this description we understand how the author can equate "This Work" with what was the most natural thing for men to do in the state of Original Justice. And it is interesting to note that of all the things that man may do "to know, love and serve God", the author has singled out "This Work" as the most natural.

The author insists on the "ghostly" nature of "This Work", which must be done "in the highest and the sovereignest point of the spirit". Anyone who misunderstands this nature and interprets his teaching in a material sense, does not have the grace to do "This Work". And with this insistence on the "sovereignest point of the spirit" we see very clearly the area within which "This Work" can be done, as well as the powers of the soul by which it may be effected.

In his discussion of the "states of life" the author uses his own terminology, which, like the expression "This Work" has assumed a technical meaning in *The Cloud*. Thus he describes the various "degrees and forms of Christian Men's living" in relation to the life history of the disciple. This extended discussion on the "states of life" was not intended by the author as an attempt at polemics, and we can see his explanations not as a reaction to the new attitudes concerning the traditional forms of monasticism and practices of the ascetical life, but as a precise description of the nature of "This Work". Of the four "degrees and forms of Christian Men's living" it is the "Singular degree" that has relevance for *The Cloud* author, as it is within this "degree" that the disciple finds himself. This "Singular degree" is the life of a recluse. And in the context of this life we find the relevance and importance of the Chapters on Moral Theology which is an anticipation of what St. John of the Cross would later say on *Spiritual Capital Sins*. This classification of "degrees and forms of Christian Men's living" has reference to the more external aspects of the life of the disciple. And in locating the "Singular degree" as that within which "This Work" can be done, the author further describes the "Two Manners of Life" which are now set in the context of the different forms of prayer and spiritual exercises. The "sovereignest point of the spirit" is equated with the higher part of the "contemplative life", which for the author is the one *strictly contemplative*.

The "ghostly" nature of "This Work" springs from the fact that God is a Spirit. The union with God in love must be by the spiritual faculties of man. The author calls the psychological faculties of man "the mights of the soul". And in his descriptions of these "mights of the soul", he uses his expressions according to whether they are "principal" or "secondary", "working" or "not working". And of the two "mights" which are "principal" for they work strictly on "ghostly things", the author gives the primacy to the will and its act of love. In doing so he does not downgrade the intellect and its act of knowing, but he stresses the limitations of the "knowing power".

Giving the primacy to the will and its act of love the author describes the ascent as a gradual yielding of the lower "mights of the soul" to those above until the highest power, that required to do "This Work", is reached. Both in this primacy of will and love and in the successive failures of the "mights of the soul", *The Cloud* and other treatises reveal very marked differences from the teaching of the Pseudo-Dionysius and his "via negativa". Whilst it seems that the inspiration for *The Cloud* is Dionysian, we submit that "This Work" is not specifically Dionysian, nor is it the "via negativa" as described by the Pseudo-Dionysius in his *Mystica Theologia*. The influence of Richard of St. Victor and Thomas Gallus as regards the primacy of will and love seems clear in *The Cloud*.

With *The Cloud* author's precise descriptions of the nature of "This Work" we have a clear picture of the particular way and ascent to God that he teaches. The picture is revealed with even greater clarity as we proceed.

CHAPTER IV

This Transcending God

The particular teaching of this 14th-century English spiritual writer deals with a distinctive way and ascent to God. The soul accomplishes this in the life which he calls strictly "contemplative". In this ascent the primacy is given to the will and its act of love. The Object and End of this ascent and way, which he calls "This Work", is no less than God Himself. We shall see what the author has to say about This God Who is the Term of "This Work", and with whom the soul aims to be united in Spirit and in Love.

The Cloud of Unknowing belongs to the tradition of *The Mystics of the Divine Essence*; we shall see how this is so as regards the *Object* of "This Work", God. In chapters V and VI we will discuss the *manner* of the ascent specifically in the light of this tradition of the *Mystical Life*. In this chapter we shall see how *This Divine Transcendence* is verified, both as regards *His Name*, "IS", and the manner of His Working. At the same time, too, the author does not overlook the *Transcendence* of God from His being the *Universal Cause of All Things*.

A. THE TRADITIONAL CONCEPTS OF GOD

The Cloud author does not go right away to the particular aspect under which he considers God as the Object of "This Work". Rather, he gives forth some traditional descriptions of God, as if he wanted to impress his disciple with the fact that for all his insistence on one particular aspect of God, this particular aspect is not the only one that he knows and teaches. In this we see the richness of the fund of his knowledge, as well as the universality and openness of his mind as regards approaches to matters of the spirit.

God is omniscient, "unto whom all hearts be open and unto whom all will speaketh, and unto whom no privy thing is hid"[1]. God is Triune and the author opens *The Cloud* with an invocation of the Trinity[2]. He describes the Trinity in the

---

[1] *The Cloud*, Prologue, Underhill, p. 37; Hodgson, 1: 1-2.
[2] Ibid. Prologue, Underhill, p. 39; Hodgson, 1:7.

F

manner of attributes proper to each Divine Person.

> "And if he ask thee, 'What is that God?', say thou, that it is
> God that made thee and bought thee, and that graciously hath
> called thee to thy degree"[3].

The God "that made thee" is God the Father, Creator; the
God "that bought thee" is God the Son, Redeemer, and the
God "that graciously hath called thee to thy degree" is God
the Holy Ghost, Sanctifier. God is a spirit[4] and "His dooms
be hid"[5]. He is the "Almighty God, King of Kings and Lord
of Lords, would meek Him so low unto thee, and amongst
all the flock of His sheep so graciously would choose thee to
be one of His specials, and sithen set thee in the place of
pasture where thou mayest be fed with the sweetness of His
Love, in earnest of thine heritage, the Kingdom of Heaven"[6].
He is the King of Angels[7], the Incarnate God Who is both door
and porter[8]. God is immutable: "Not that His sight may be
any time or in any thing more clear than in another, for it is
evermore unchangeable: but because it is more like unto Him,
when it is in purity of spirit, for He is a Spirit"[9]. Being Spirit,
He is likewise simple. "And truly, neither hath God nor
ghostly things none of these qualities nor quantities"[10]. The
singleness of mind and heart that "This Work" requires finds
its reason in an attribute of God himself.

> "He is a jealous lover and suffereth no fellowship, and Him
> list not work in thy will but if He be only with thee by Himself.
> He asketh none help, but only thyself. He wills, thou do but
> look on Him and let Him alone"[11].

And God is the Final Judge at the end of time: "And He
by His Godhead and His manhood together, is the truest
Doomsman, and the asker of account of dispending of time"[12].

For all the wealth of these Names of God, the author singles
out just one particular title and Name of God, just one aspect
of all the infinite splendours of the Godhead, which in *The*

---

3 Ibid. Ch. 7, Underhill, p. 79; Hodgson, 26: 16-18.
  Cf. Hilton, *Scale II,* Ch. 34, Underhill, p. 383.
4 *The Cloud,* Ch. 47, Underhill, p. 190; Hodgson, 88: 19.
5 Ibid. Prologue, Underhill, p. 41; Hodgson, 3: 4.
6 Ibid. Ch. 2, Underhill, pp. 61-62; Hodgson, 15: 4-9.
7 Ibid. Ch. 22 Underhill, p. 129; Hodgson, 55:20.
8 *Privy Counsel,* McCann, p. 128; Hodgson, 159: 6-8.
9 *The Cloud,* Ch. 47, Underhill, p. 191; Hodgson, 89: 21-24.
10 Ibid. Ch. 70, Underhill, pp. 254-255; Hodgson, 124: 10-11.
11 Ibid. Ch. 2, Underhill, p. 62; Hodgson, 15: 15-19.
12 Ibid. Ch. 4, Underhill, p. 70; Hodgson, 21: 12-14.

Cloud is "the naked being of God Himself only"[13], and in *Privy Counsel* he specifies further as "this little word is".

B. "THE NAKED BEING OF GOD"

This particular manner of expressing *This Name of God* may be personal to *The Cloud* author, but the Name Itself is not new. In the history of the Chosen People, we see Moses asking God for His name.

> "Then Moses said to God, 'I am to go, then, to the sons of Israel and say to them, "The God of your fathers has sent me to you". But if they ask me what his name is, what am I to tell them?' And God said to Moses, 'I Am who I Am.' This, he added, is what you must say to the sons of Israel: 'I am has sent me to you' "[14].

Because God Himself gave this Name, it has been considered as that which most properly belongs to God[15]. Biblical studies have shed much light on this passage of the encounter of Moses with God. Without striving to get involved in the philological and historical problems[16] connected with *This Name* of God, we give in rather summary fashion the more important theological meanings that have been put forward for *This Name* which God gave of Himself to Moses on Mount Sinai. While God is revealed as giving His Name in a definite historical situation, there is, however, indicated "the impossibility of defining God. This idea of indefinability, of the ineffable . . . is to remind us of the unbridgeable gulf which divides our idea of God from the reality which it strives to express. We can and should speak of God, but always with the realisation of the inadequacy of what we say"[17]. For Moses, the immediate necessity to be filled by the Name of God is the authenticity of his mission from God, the *credential*, as it were, to make the Israelites believe in his message. "This proof would consist in the fact that he is able to tell them the name of the one who sent him. For in ancient Eastern thought the name of the person who existed was a necessary part of his existence and one knew of a reality only if one was

[13] Ibid. Ch. 8, Underhill, p. 87; Hodgson, 32: 7-8.
[14] Exodus, 3: 13-14.
[15] St. Thomas Aquinas, *Summa Theologica*, Part 1, Q. 13, Art 11 (Burns Oates & Washbourne edition, 1920) p. 176.
[16] J. Plastaras, *The God of Exodus*, pp. 88-93.
[17] C.R.A. Cunliffe, "The Divine Name of Jahweh", *Scripture*, April, 1954, No. 4, p. 115.

able to pronounce its 'name'. In the same way Moses will only be able to make the Israelites believe in the reality of his encounter with God if he is able to tell them the name of the God who appeared to him"[18].

The *Sovereign Freedom* of God has been seen to be asserted in this passage: "At the very moment when Yahweh revealed his name to Israel, he also asserted his sovereign freedom. This fits perfectly into the context. There was always the temptation among the ancient Semites to regard a divine name as a magical means for gaining control over the god. . . . The Yahweh of the Mosaic revelation was radically different. There was nothing capricious about him and yet he was the God who was sovereignly free. The only limits to his freedom were imposed by his own justice and his fidelity to his own gracious promises. There were no limits to his power. . . . The manifestation of his power and the revelation of his inner nature would always be graciously free acts"[19]. In *His Sovereign Freedom* God then asserts *His Transcendence*. "He refuses to subject Himself to man but insists on His own transcendence. He will not curry favour or try to win acceptance by compromising His own Being. Nevertheless God makes known His intention of behaving as a propitious God, prepared to bless and to save His Chosen People"[20]. The *God of Exodus*, then, is "not pure being, pure existing, but an active being"[21] and "the reply is not an assertion of the Being of God in the metaphysical sense of aseity or His absolute existence. . . . Rather the emphasis here is upon the active presence of God in every here and now: He makes His Being known by the activity of His power in the present moment of man's history. . . . The saving quality of His presence is further described . . .[22]. The marvels of the "Divine I Am" (Present) are recounted in the subsequent turn of events after this encounter[23]. There is, however, that immediate effect of the *Divine Presence* first of all on Moses. "How explain the sud-

18 M. Noth, *Exodus*, p. 42.
19 J. Plastaras, *The God of Exodus*, pp. 99-100.
20 W. J. O'Rourke, "Moses and the Prophetic Vocation", *Scripture*, April, 1963, No. 30, p. 51.
21 M. Noth, *Exodus*, p. 45.
22 W. J. O'Rourke, "Moses and the Prophetic Vocation", *Scripture*, April, 1963, No. 30, pp. 50-51.
23 J. Plastaras, *The God of Exodus*, p. 100.

den transformation of this timid shepherd into a courageous leader of men? Whence came his zeal, his energy, his bravery and complete devotion? The secret of Moses' and the prophets' vitality lay not in himself but solely in the God who called him and chose him for His service. . . . Overcome by the realisation of this holiness and the transcendental personality of God, the prophet has a unique insight into the majesty and authority of God, as authority unlimited and independent"[24].

For *The Cloud* author likewise, "the naked Being of God", the "IS" of God, is not merely a Name, but *This Name* is conjoined with his own personal, particular experience. It is not some mere theoretical knowledge, but a *felt encounter* with the Godhead. So we hear him telling his disciple his particular description of God with its several nuances.

"Lift up thine heart unto God with a meek stirring of love; and mean Himself, and none of His goods. And thereto, look thee loath to think on aught but Himself. So that naught work in thy wit, nor in thy will, but only Himself"[25].

This is the dominant theme of *The Cloud* and other writings and they keep coming back like a refrain in lovely passages, in several different ways. Always intimately connected with this *Naked Thought of God* is the emptiness that must be produced in "the mights of the soul".

The author emphasizes this exclusiveness of God in "This Work" in the manner of an anticipated question and answer, which is a favourite device of his.

"And if any thought rise and will press continually above thee betwixt thee and that darkness, and ask thee saying, 'What seekest thou, and what wouldest thou have?' say thou, that it is God that thou wouldest have, 'Him I covet, Him I seek and nought but Him' "[26].

He gives a reason for this particular beholding of God that singles out just the thought of God only for Himself.

"Surely he that seeketh God perfectly, he will not rest him finally in the remembrance of any angel or saint that is in heaven"[27].

24 W. J. O'Rourke, "Moses and the Prophetic Vocation", *Scripture*, April, 1963, No. 30, pp. 52-53.
25 *The Cloud*, Ch. 3, Underhill, p. 63; Hodgson, 16: 3-6.
26 Ibid. Ch. 3, Underhill, p. 79; Hodgson, 26: 13-16.
27 Ibid. Ch. 9, Underhill, p. 91; Hodgson, 35: 15-17.

Seen in greater detail, we have this particular aspect of God intimately connected with the various descriptive elements of "This Work". It is the particular consideration of "the higher part of contemplation, as it may be had here, hangeth all wholly in this darkness and in this cloud of unknowing . . ."[28]. It is "the best part of Mary" wherein "all virtues shall truly be, and perfectly conceived, and feelingly comprehended . . ."[29]. The consideration of God Only for Himself makes the virtue of meekness "perfect"; "Another is the over-abundant love and the worthiness of God in Himself. . ."[30]. And this, too, makes the virtue of charity "perfect": "For charity is nought else to bemean to thine understanding, but love of God for Himself above all creatures, and of man for God even as thyself. And that in this work God is loved for Himself and above all creatures, it seemeth right well"[31]. Indeed all the virtues are contained in this Name of God.

> "For all virtues they find and feel . . . in God; for in Him is all thing, both by cause and by being . . . and mean God all, and all God, so that nought work in thy wit and in thy will, but only God"[32].

The thought of "this naked Being of God" is further developed in *Privy Counsel*. While in *Privy Counsel* there is the translation of the thought of "this naked Being of God" in the practical terms of spiritual exercises, we see the author likewise developing this central point in the more philosophical aspect of God as the *Universal Cause* of all things. The Immanence of God is here stressed.

> "And therefore think of God in this work as thou dost on thyself, and on thyself as thou dost on God; that he is as he is and thou art as thou art, so that thy thought be not scattered nor separated, but oned in him that is all; evermore saving this difference betwixt thee and him, that he is thy being and thou not his . . . He is being both to himself and to all. And in that only is he separated from all, that he is being both of himself and of all. And in that is he one in all and all in him, that all things have their being in him, as he is the being of all"[33].

---

28 Ibid. Ch. 8, Underhill, p. 86; Hodgson, 32: 5-6.
29 Ibid. Ch. 12, Underhill, p. 98; Hodgson, 39: 9-14.
30 Ibid. Ch. 13, Underhill, p. 101; Hodgson, 40: 14-15.
31 Ibid. Ch. 24, Underhill, p. 133; Hodgson, 58: 11-14.
32 Ibid. Ch. 40, Underhill, p. 172; Hodgson, 79: 7-12.
33 *Privy Counsel*, McCann, p. 106; Hodgson, 136: 11-23.

The author gives another reason for this excellence of *This Divine Name,* for no other name is equivalent to the *Eternity* of God.

"For know thou right well, that in this work thou shalt have no more beholding to the qualities of the being of God than to the qualities of the being of thyself. For there is no name, nor feeling, nor beholding more, nor so much, according unto everlastingness (the which is God), as is that the which may be had, seen and felt in the blind and the lovely beholding of this word is"[34].

We note the stress that the author gives to the *feeling* that is aroused with this name of God. Like a summing-up the author gives still another reason why this Name of God is most proper to Him, for the name "IS" contains all the other Names of God.

" . . . what other such thing that thou say of God: all it is hid and enstored in this little word *is.* For the same is to him only to be, that is all these for to be. And if thou add a hundred thousand such sweet words as these: good, fair, and all these other, yet went thou not from this little word *is.* And if thou say them all, thou addest not to it. And if thou say right none, thou takest not from it"[35].

The consideration of "the naked Being of God only" is compared to "gold and silver". The author also interprets the passage from Solomon as regards the *finding of wisdom* in the light of the pre-eminence of this Name of God "IS".

"The purchasing of this ghostly wisdom and of this subtle working is better than the getting of gold or of silver. By the which gold and silver is morally understood all other bodily and ghostly knowing, the which is gotten by curious seeking and working of our natural wits, beneath us, within us, or even with us, in beholding of any of the qualities that belong to the being of God or of any created thing"[36].

In extolling the excellence of this particular manner of beholding God, the author stresses its *ghostly* nature. In this passage, as in other passages stressing the *ghostly* quality of "This Work", we see the *sixth subsidiary character* that marks the mystical life, namely, that "the union is produced neither

---

[34] Ibid. McCann, p. 113; Hodgson, 143: 17-22.
[35] Ibid. McCann, pp. 113-114; Hodgson, 143: 25-30, 144: 1.
[36] Ibid. McCann, p. 115; Hodgson, 145: 19-25.

by reasoning, nor by the consideration of creatures, nor by sensible images"[37]. We see this quality even more stressed in the state described by the figure of "the cloud of forgetting". It is interesting to note that in this exegesis of the passage from Solomon, the author makes an addition of his own, namely, the line "primi et purissimi fructus ejus", in giving the reason for the excellence acquired at having found wisdom. And this he connects with the ghostly character of "This Work".

> "And why is it better, he addeth the cause and saith, *for primi et purissimi fructus ejus*. That is, for 'first and purest be the fruits of it'. And no wonder; for why, the fruit of this working is high ghostly wisdom, suddenly and freely raised of the spirit inwardly in itself and unformed, full far from fantasy, impossible to be strained or to fall under the working of natural wit. The which natural wit, be it never so subtle nor so holy, may be called (in comparison of this) but feigned folly formed in fantasy, as far from the very certainty when the ghostly sun shineth, as the darkness of the moonshine in a mist at midwinter's night from the brightness of the sunbeam in the clearest time of mid-summer day"[38].

There is in this passage, too, a description of the *suddenness* that characterises a mystical experience. *Nature, perfection* and *excellence* of "This Work" are blended intimately by the author in passages of great beauty. This is a distinctive mark of his personal experience of what he teaches.

In *The Cloud* the consideration of "the naked Being of God" as the *Object* of "This Work", may give the impression of being too abstract and theoretical. We think that this was precisely what the disciple pointed out to the author. And so, in *Privy Counsel*, aside from the wealth of the Names of God which the author gives, we see now the consideration of *God Only For Himself* translated into the more concrete and practical form of an offering, a spiritual exercise.

> "This naked intent, freely fastened and grounded in very belief, shall be nought else to thy thought and to thy feeling but a naked thought and a blind feeling of thine own being, as if thou saidst thus unto God within thy meaning: 'That that I am, Lord, I offer unto thee, without any looking to any quality of thy being, but only that thou art as thou art, without any more' "[39].

[37] A. Poulain, *The Graces of Interior Prayer*, p. 114.
[38] *Privy Counsel*, McCann, pp. 115-116; Hodgson, 145: 25-30, 146: 1-5.
[39] Ibid. McCann, p. 106; Hodgson, 136: 1-6.

It is interesting to note that this passage, which could have come from an observation of the disciple, is right at the beginning of *Privy Counsel*. The author plunges right away into the difficult problems of *The Cloud*. There is, too, a distinct progress in *Privy Counsel* from the idea in *The Cloud* as regards the "being of man". This "being of man" is in *Privy Counsel* made the object of an offering. The author stresses the *ghostly nature* of "This Work" from this consideration of "the being of man" and, in praise of its excellence, he gives an exegesis of a passage from Solomon[40] similar to that given above as regards the "Being of God". And just as the "IS" is the first of His Qualities and the Name that includes All Other Names, so the "being of man" is the first of all his qualities in which all his other qualities are contained.

> "The first of these gifts I call the first of thy fruits. The first gift in each creature is only the being of that same creature. For, though it be so that the qualities of thy being be so fast oned with the same being as they be without separation, yet because they hang all upon it, verily it may be called, as it is, the first of thy gifts. And thus it is only thy being that is the first of thy fruits"[41].

This "being of man" like "The Being of God" is made the object of an offering to God.

> "As if thou saidst thus in thyself in each one of thy beholdings, stirring thyself by the means of this beholding to the love and to the praising of thy Lord God—that not only gave thee to be, but so nobly to be, as the qualities of thy being will witness in thy beholding—saying thus: 'I am and see and feel that I am. And not only I am, but so I am, and so, and so, and so, and so,' reckoning up in thy beholding all the qualities of thy being in special. And then— that more than all this is—lap up all this in general and say thus: "That that I am and how that I am, as in nature and in grace, all I have it of thee, Lord, and thou it art"[42].

The *experimental* quality of "This Work" is never lost sight of by the author. This insistence verifies the *first fundamental character* of the mystical life, namely *God's Presence Felt*,[43] for in the perfections of "This Work" *The Presence of God*

40 *Proverbs* 3: 9-10.
41 *Privy Counsel*, McCann, p. 111; Hodgson, 141: 2-8.
42 Ibid. McCann, p. 111; Hodgson, 141: 12-21.
43 Poulain, *The Graces of Interior Prayer*, pp. 64 ss.

is clearly stressed and emphasized. Indeed, he makes this "belief" the "ground" and the foundation of "This Work"[44]. It is then the personal conviction, the "felt experience" of all that go to make "This Work" and more particularly this "naked intent stretching unto God" that is the touchstone of *The Cloud* and *Privy Counsel*. In this offering of one's fundamental being, there is very great apostolic efficacy and value. In this, too, are verified the *perfect* and *imperfect* forms of Charity, in so far as the Object and effect of this offering are concerned.

> "And all I offer it unto thee principally to the praising of thee, for the help of all mine even Christians and of me. And thus mayest thou see that the first and the point of thy beholding is most substantially set in the naked sight and the blind feeling of thine own being. And thus it is only thy being that is the first of thy fruits"[45].

In stressing the *ghostly* nature of "This Work", we see a gradual and progressive interiorisation and a profounder touching of depths revealed by the *objects* proposed as the main consideration of "This Work". We have seen these in the consideration of the *Divine Names* and the *qualities* of the "Being of God" and finally the "Being of God Himself". So, also, we see a parallel in the qualities of the "being of man", and finally "the being of man himself", firstly as a theoretical consideration, and then as the object of an "offering".

But while the "being of man" is the first gift on which all the other qualities and perfections of his being depend—just as the "Being of God" is the first likewise of His Attributes and the Name most proper to Him—the comparison ends there. To show this contrast the author uses an illustration from the world of medicine.

> "Take good, gracious God as he is, plat and plain as a plaster, and lay it to thy sick self as thou art. Or, if I shall say otherwise, bear up thy sick self as thou art and try for to touch by desire good gracious God as he is, the touching of whom is endless health, by witness of the woman in the Gospel, saying thus: Si tetigero vel fimbriam vestimenti ejus, salva ero. 'If I

----

44 *Privy Counsel*, McCann, p. 106; Hodgson, 135: 24, 136: 1-3.
  Cf. Hodgson, *The Cloud of Unknowing*, pp. 204-205.
45 *Privy Counsel*, McCann, p. 111; Hodgson, 141: 21-26.

touch but the hem of his clothing, I shall be safe' "[46].

We see this contrast likewise emphasized in God as the *Universal Cause of all Things*.

The author brings the consideration of "the naked Being of God" down to the very particular exercises of the spiritual life.

"But now thou askest me, what is that thing. I shall tell thee what I mean that it is: It is God: for whom thou shouldest be still, if thou shouldest be still; and for whom thou shouldest speak, if thou shouldest speak—and for whom thou shouldest fast, if thou shouldest fast; and for whom thou shouldest eat, if thou shouldest eat; and for whom thou shouldest be only, if thou shouldest be only; and for whom thou shouldest be in company, if thou shouldest be in company. And so forth of all the remenant, what so they be. For silence is not God, nor speaking is not God; fasting is not God, nor eating is not God; onliness is not God, nor company is not God; nor yet any of all the other such two contraries. He is hid between them, and may not be found by any work of thy soul, but all only by love of thine heart. He may not be known by reason. He may not be gotten by thought, nor concluded by understanding; but he may be loved and chosen with the true lovely will of thine heart"[47].

We see in this passage the dominant themes of *The Cloud* and *Privy Counsel,* namely the exclusiveness of God as the Only Object of these spiritual exercises, and the Primacy of the *will* and its act of *love*. In all these spiritual exercises, it is God Only that one must look for. The author continues:

"Choose thee Him, and thou art silently speaking, and speakingly silent, fastingly eating, and eatingly fasting, and so forth of all the remenant"[48].

In this passage, there is that reconciliation of the *intellect* and the *will,* as summed up in the lovely line of St. Gregory the Great, "Amor Ipse Notitia est"[49]. It is a *dynamic act* of the person himself expressed in all these different spiritual exercises. In giving the *primacy* to the *will* and its act of *love* we do not see the author getting involved in the question as to whether *love* constitutes the essence of the mystical life or not. We see him simply narrating a fact connected with

[46] Ibid. McCann, pp. 108-109: Hodgson, 138: 28-29, 139: 1-5.
[47] *Discretion of Stirrings,* Gardner, pp. 106-107; Hodgson, 71: 12-26.
[48] Ibid. Gardner, pp. 107-108; Hodgson, 71: 26, 72: 1-2.
[49] L. Reypens, "Connaissance Mystique de Dieu", *Dictionnaire de Spiritualité,* III, Col. 887.

"This Work". The author stresses the fact that in "This Work" it is *love* that prevails, wherein the "mights of the soul" are presupposed. It is, then, not *love* as the act of a "might of the soul" that is the character of the mystical life, which Fr. Poulain calls *subsidiary*, but rather *love* as an outpouring of "the impulsion to the virtues" that marks the mystical life[50]. It is the whole man that beholds the "naked Being of God Himself only", the "IS" of God. We see this vividly in the activity that is required of the soul in the state of "the cloud of unknowing".

"And thou shalt step above it stalwartly, but listily, with a devout and a pleasing stirring of love, and try for to pierce that darkness above thee. And smite upon that thick cloud of unknowing with a sharp dart of longing love; and go not thence for thing that befalleth"[51].

This "sharp dart of longing love" is one of the loveliest expressions characteristic of the part of man in "the cloud of unknowing". He further describes this act of love as ". . . such a blind stirring of love unto God for Himself, and such a privy pressing upon this cloud of unknowing . . ."[52]. Then in *Privy Counsel*, this beholding of "the naked Being of God Himself only" is put in the context of the "short and wordless" prayer which is a perfection of "This Work".

"And look that nothing remain in thy working mind but a naked intent stretching unto God, not clothed in any special thought of God, in himself, how he is in himself, or in any of his works, but only that he is as he is"[53].

"Choose thee Him" is the principal preoccupation of the soul in "the cloud of unknowing", as it is in *Discretion of Stirrings*[54].

This, then, is the God of *The Cloud of Unknowing*. Of all the wealth and many splendours of the Attributes and Names of God, the author singles out the first, most eminent and most proper Name of all, THAT HE IS, which in *The Cloud* is considered as "the naked Being of God only for Himself".

50 A. Poulain, *The Graces of Interior Prayer*, pp. 114, 151-165.
51 *The Cloud*, Ch. 6, Underhill, p. 78; Hodgson, 26: 8-12.
52 Ibid. Ch. 9, Underhill, p. 90; Hodgson, 34: 8-10.
53 *Privy Counsel*, McCann, p. 105; Hodgson, 135: 19-22.
54 Gardner, pp. 107-108; Hodgson, 71: 26, 72: 1-2.

But in so insisting on that One Name of God, the author does not overlook all the other Divine Names. He places them in the right relationship to this First Name of God. We see in this as in the other aspects of "This Work" the precision and the unity of teaching, as well as the openness and objectivity of mind which the author displays when he sees things in their relative places. And in all this, he does not depreciate them for the fact that they are seen as objectively lower in position in the spiritual life.

This is *The Transcendence of God* shown in the Name God gave of Himself to Moses, in the "naked Being", the "IS" of God as the Object of "This Work", and as *The Universal Cause of All Things*. With all these, the impression can perhaps be given that the God of *The Cloud* is heavily metaphysical[55]. And this would give rise to wonderment if we did not refer to the Humanity of Jesus for, indeed, The Word Incarnate broke the barrier of time and space to live with us in this World as the Carpenter's Son, who gave the assurance, "I have come so that they may have life and have it to the full"[56].

C. THE HUMANITY OF JESUS

While the author centres on *God for Himself* alone, nevertheless he makes Jesus also the object of this love.

"Right well hast thou said, for the love of JESUS. For in the love of JESUS; there shall be thine help. Love is such a power, that it maketh all thing common. Love therefore JESUS; and all that thing that He hath, it is thine. He by His Godhead is maker and giver of time. He by his manhood is the very Keeper of time"[57].

The story of Mary and Martha, although given a very highly spiritualised interpretation, nevertheless reveals our Incarnate Lord dealing with His special friends.   Prayers and meditations, which have for their object the Humanity of Jesus, belong to the "lower part of the contemplative life", and it is necessary to have gone through them before the "higher part of the contemplative life," which is *strictly contemplative,* can be reached.

55 See C. Pepler, *The English Religious Heritage,* pp. 289-290.
56 *John* 10 : 10.
57 *The Cloud,* Ch. 4, Underhill, pp. 69-70; Hodgson, 21 : 8-12.

"Nevertheless yet be these fair meditations the truest way that a sinner may have in his beginning to the ghostly feeling of himself and of God. And I would think that it were impossible to man's understanding—although God may do what He will—that a sinner should come to be restful in the ghostly feeling of himself and of God, unless he first saw and felt by imagination, and meditation the bodily doings of himself and of God, and thereto sorrowed for that that were to sorrow, and made joy for that that were to joy. And whoso cometh not in by this way, he cometh not truly; and therefore he must stand without and doth so, when he weeneth best that he is within"[58].

These meditations, then, on the Humanity of Christ are needed for all engaged in the life of prayer. For one called to "This Work", this early stage of prayer must have been passed. The author makes these meditations on the Humanity of Christ pre-requisites for the higher forms of prayer in "This Work". However, the author does not say that the grace for "This Work" will come for the reason that these states of prayer have been passed, neither does he assert that the Lord will not grant the grace for "This Work" for the reason that these meditations have not been gone through. There is always the absolute freedom of God, and the author puts in the saving clause, "although God may do what He will"[59]. However, it is for the usual way of doing things that the author speaks and he teaches that these meditations on the Humanity of Christ are stages to be passed before the higher reaches of prayer can be reached. Indeed, these meditations are the components of the life of prayer as a whole. It is when God calls one to a more special kind of prayer that one branches to a kind of prayer that God Himself teaches. Indeed, these meditations are the safeguards and the tests for the orthodoxy of the rarer kinds of prayer. He emphasizes this fact even more by his use of "a thief" and a "prowler".

"And whoso entereth not by this door, but climbeth otherwise to perfection, by the subtle seeking and the curious fantastic working in his wild, wanton wits, leaving this common plain

---

58 *Privy Counsel*, McCann, p. 128; Hodgson, 158: 17-27.
59 It seems that Fr. Johnston overlooked this passage when he wrote: "The tradition that underlies *The Cloud* and to which the author frequently refers is that no one can come to this mystical rest who has not spent a long time in ordinary meditation on the mysteries of Christ, devoting himself to penance and works of virtue". *The Mysticism of The Cloud of Unknowing*, p. 30.

entry touched before and the true counsel of ghostly fathers:
he, whatsoever he be, is not only a night thief, but a day
skulker"[60].

These meditations on the Humanity of Christ, then, are
like the lower rungs of a ladder that must be climbed before
one can go on higher to the more special forms of prayer, in
this case, the "short prayer of This Work".

The author further describes this intimate relationship and
interaction between the Human and the Divine in our Lord,
by the use of "porter" and "door".

"It is a marvellous household ghostliness! For our Lord is not
only porter Himself, but also the door: the porter by his Godhead, and the door by his Manhood"[61].

We have seen the richness with which the author abounds
in thoughts of God. For all the unity and insistence on "the
naked Being of God" as the main and only consideration of
"This Work", we see him nevertheless dealing in great fulness
with the other Names of God. The passages on the Humanity
of Jesus are enough to dispel any reservation that the God
of *The Cloud* is a God purely and solely metaphysical and
theoretical.

This fact of *Divine Transcendence,* as well as the nature of
"This Work", naturally gives rise to the conclusion that the
initiative for "This Work" must come from God Himself
only. For man by his own powers alone is not equal to "This
Work"; he cannot even have an idea of "This Work" without
God first taking the initiative. For it is God alone who
initiates, sustains, and perfects "This Work". This *Divine
Choice* shown in the manner of His working is another aspect

---

[60] *Privy Counsel,* McCann, p. 129; Hodgson, 160: 4-8.
[61] Ibid. McCann, p. 128; Hodgson, 159: 5-7. Walter Hilton teaches the
same inter-relationship between these meditations on the Humanity of
our Lord and what he calls "the working and the full use of contemplation". "Who so ween for to come to the working and the full use of
contemplation and not by this way that is for to say not (by steadfast
mind of the precious manhood and the passion of Jhesu Christ, nor)
by fullhead of virtues, he cometh not by the door, and therefore as
a thief he shall be cast out . . . For Christ is door and He is porter,
and without His life and His livery may there no man come in, as He
saith Himself: *Nemo venit ad Patrem nisi per me.* No man cometh
to the Father but by me. That is for to say, no man may come to the
contemplation of the Godhead, but he be first reformed by fullhead of
meekness and charity to the likeness of Jhesu in His manhood." (*Scale
I,* Ch. 92, Underhill, p. 221).

of the *Divine Transcendence*: "when he liketh and as he liketh".

D. THE DIVINE INITIATIVE

Just why God would call one in preference to another for "This Work" is not for us to enquire about. This is indeed a thing too high for us and we cannot hope to search the Mind of God. But one thing we know is that He does it only for Love, for with God nothing more is needed and nothing less would suffice. The author expresses this gratuitousness of the Divine Call in very succinct terms.

"And if thou asketh me by what means thou shalt come to this work, I beseech Almighty God of His great grace and His great courtesy to teach thee Himself. For truly I do thee well to wit that I cannot tell thee, and that is no wonder. For why, that is the work of only God, specially wrought in what soul that Him liketh without any desert of the same soul. For without it no saint nor no angel can think to desire it"[62].

Hence, the *Divine Initiative* springs from the fact that "This Work" is the "work of only God", in the working of which His *Sovereign Freedom* is paramount, "in whatever soul he liketh". This *Divine Choice* does not depend on anything that man may do. While earlier we noted the different opinions held by Fr. Poulain and M. Saudreau as regards the *fundamental* and *constitutive* element of the mystical life, we see, however, that in this aspect of the mystical state the two predominant schools of thought are in agreement, as exemplified by the definition of M. Saudreau ". . . and to which the soul, for all its efforts, can never raise itself"[63].

This exclusive role of God is described by the author by the figure of "stirring".

"And if it be thus, trust then steadfastly that it is only God that stirreth thy will and thy desire plainly by Himself, without means either on His part or on thine . . . So that thou mayest conceive here by these words somewhat (but much more clearly by the proof), that in this work men shall use no means: nor yet men may not come thereto with means. All good means

---

[62] *The Cloud*, Ch. 34, Underhill, p. 153; Hodgson, 68: 20, 69: 5. Also: Ch. 2, p. 62; Ch. 36, p. 160; Ch. 21, p. 126; Ch. 34, p. 156; Ch. 71, p. 257.

[63] J. V. Bainvel, in his Introduction to A. Poulain, *The Graces of Interior Prayer*, p. cv.

hang upon it, and it on no means; nor no means may lead thereto"[64].

The author stresses here the fact that this *Divine Initiative* can be better verified by experience. The human role is signified by the word "means".

He goes on to stress this exclusiveness of the part of God by ruling out the possibility of the actions of angels, good or bad.

"And be not feared, for the devil may not come so near. He may never come to stir a man's will, but occasionally and by means from afar, be he never so subtle a devil. For sufficiently and without means may no good angel stir thy will: nor, shortly to say, nothing but only God"[65].

St. John of the Cross attests to this helplessness of the devil in this regard, and gives the reason from the nature of *infused contemplation* as well as from the interior depths in which this *encounter* takes place[66]. St. Teresa of Avila on the other hand gives as her reason the fact that "His Majesty is so joined and united with the essence of the soul, that the evil one dare not approach, *nor can he understand this mystery*. This is certain, for the devil does not know our thoughts, much less can he penetrate a secret so profound, that God does not reveal it even to us"[67].

The author uses the term "full special grace" to describe this *Divine Role,* and he clearly distinguishes this "special grace" from "common grace"[68]. In making this distinction the

---

[64] *The Cloud,* Ch. 34, Underhill, p. 156; Hodgson, 70: 24-25, 71: 1-10. Walter Hilton has a lovely passage on the freedom of God expressed in His choices. "But then, for to have Him may no creature deserve only by his own travail; for though a man might travail as mickle bodily and ghostly as all creatures that ever were might, he might not deserve only by his works for to have God for his meed. Nevertheless on the tother side I say also, that I expect He giveth it not, but if a man work and travail all that he can and may, yea till he thinketh he may no more, or else be in full will thereto if he might". (*Scale II,* Ch. 20, Underhill, pp. 299-300.)

[65] *The Cloud,* Ch. 34, Underhill, p. 156; Hodgson, 71: 1-5.

[66] "The reason why the soul is free, *concealed from* the devil and his wiles in the obscurity of contemplation, is, that *infused contemplation,* to which it is now admitted, is passively infused into it, in secret, without the cognizance of the senses, and of the interior and exterior powers of the sensitive part . . . the more spiritual therefore the communication is, and the farther removed beyond the reach of sense, the less able is the devil to perceive it" (*Obscure Night,* as quoted by A. Poulain, *The Graces of Interior Prayer,* p. 235.)

[67] St. Teresa, *Interior Castles,* as quoted by A. Poulain, *The Graces of Interior Prayer,* p. 235.

[68] *The Cloud,* Ch. 2, Underhill, p. 138; Hodgson, 6: 18-21, 61: 14-15.

author uses the negative form. He describes how "special" this grace may be by the use of figures, but to remove it from the ambit of the "common grace", he simply does so by *simple negation*.

> "If I would now amend it, thou wottest well, by very reason of thy words written before, it may not be after the course of nature, nor of common grace, that I should now heed or else make satisfaction, for any more times than for those that be for to come"[69].

This grace to do "This Work" is also described by the author simply as "grace" without any qualification. From the context, however, the meaning is clear, setting in contrast the role of God and the part of man.

> "Above himself he is: for why, he purposeth him to win thither by grace, whither he may not come by nature"[70].

Later on the author will make further distinctions as regards this Role of God and describe the different interventions of God to make clear the fact that the distinction between "common grace" and the "special grace" to do "This Work" is one of *kind* and not merely of *intensity*.

The author uses also the term "reforming grace" to describe this special intervention of God.

> "And our soul by virtue of this reforming grace is made sufficient to the full to comprehend all Him by love, the which is incomprehensible to all created knowledgeable powers, as is angel or man's soul"[71].

The power of this "special grace" is set in contrast to what one's natural powers can do by themselves.

> "Study thou not for no words, for so shouldest thou never come to thy purpose nor to this work, for it is never got by study but all only by grace"[72].

To make his teaching even more vivid, the author always resorts to the use of figures of speech. So, he uses the figure of "pulling" to describe this fact of *Divine Initiative*.

69 Ibid. Ch. 4, Underhill, p. 69; Hodgson, 20: 20, 21: 1-3.
70 Ibid. Ch. 8, Underhill, p. 87; Also, Ch. 15, p. 106; Hodgson, 32: 13-15.
71 Ibid. Ch. 4, Underhill, p. 66; Hodgson, 18: 17-20.
72 Ibid. Ch. 39, Underhill, p. 169; Hodgson, 77: 18-20.

"Yet it seemeth that He would not leave thee thus lightly, for love of His heart, the which He hath evermore had unto thee since thou wert aught: but what did he? Seest thou nought how listily and how graciously He hath privily pulled thee to the third degree and manner of living, the which is called Singular"[73].

We cannot help but feel the concise hold the author has of his teaching when he tries to steer clear of any insinuation of force or violence on the part of God.

The author continues to stress this point in *Privy Counsel.* The reality of this special intervention of God is shown by examples from Church history.

"For since, in the first beginning of Holy Church, in time of persecution, divers souls and many were so marvellously touched in suddenness of grace that suddenly, without means of other works coming before, men of crafts did cast down their instrument from their hands, and children their tables in the school, and did run without ransacking of reason to the martyrdom with saints: why shall not men trow now, in time of peace, that God may, can, and will, and doth—yea! touch divers souls as suddenly with the grace of contemplation?"[74]

Together with the reality of the special intervention of God, there is in the passage a description of the suddenness of the *Divine Call,* as well as the absence of preparatory means on the part of those so called, aimed precisely at the reception of the call. In this allusion to martyrdom which the author makes, we see him perhaps slightly forcing an interpretation to show his point regarding the primacy of will and love over the intellect. But these are the shafts of light that reveal the author in more personal terms.

In the use of "porter and door", we see this *specific difference* between the "common grace" and "special grace". Our Lord is the "door" by his Manhood, and in Him we find a "common plain way and an open entry to all that will come . . . I have clothed me in the common nature of man and made me so open that I am the door by my Manhood, and whoso entereth by me, he shall be safe"[75]. The *Door to salvation* is for all. And for this state, the prayer life is made up of the beholding of the Humanity of Christ, and these

73 Ibid. Ch. 1, Underhill, p. 60; Hodgson, 14: 8-12.
74 *Privy Counsel,* McCann, pp. 120-121; Hodgson, 151: 1-9.
75 Ibid. McCann, p. 129; Hodgson, 159: 15-18.

correspond to the prayers and meditations of those in the "lower active" as well as for those in the "higher active" which is at the same time the "lower contemplative". For those in the "higher contemplative" which is purely "contemplative", the prayers and meditations are those which make up "the short prayer of This Work".

In this use of "Door", there is the distinction between "standing still at the door" and "entering in". "Finding and standing still at the door" signifies the "call to salvation". "Entering in" signifies the "call to perfection". We see the *specific difference* between the two which the author very clearly stresses. And while the "finding of the Door" is accomplished with the help of the "Porter", this assistance of the "Porter" in the "finding of the Door" is for all, although some find it sooner than others. But to "enter in" requires a special invitation and call by the "Porter", and this the author calls "the privy teaching of the Spirit of God".

> "What thereof if this be the door, shall a man when he hath found the door stand ever thereat or therein and come never innermore? I answer for thee and say: that it is good that he do so ever, until the great rust of his boisterous bodilyness be in great part rubbed away, his counsel and his conscience to witness. And specially, ever till he be called innermore by the privy teaching of the Spirit of God, the which teaching is the readiest and the surest witness that may be had in this life of the calling and drawing of a soul innermore to more special working of grace"[76].

The author gives a close analysis of this "privy teaching" which determines whether the one so affected by the "stirring" of the "Spirit of God" is called either to "salvation" or to "perfection". The key to this distinction is the quality of the "stirring" based on the content of the prayer, whether the matter is that which pertains to "This Work" or not.

> "Evidence of this touching a man may have thus: If he feels in his continual exercise as it were a soft growing desire to come near God in this life, as it may be by a special ghostly feeling,

[76] Ibid. McCann, p. 130; Hodgson, 160: 26-27; 161: 1-7. St. Teresa has a lovely passage describing this fact of the Divine Invitaton: "...If our Lord will have a soul to be Mary, *even on the first day*, there is nothing to be afraid of; *but we must not be self-invited guests* ..." *Life*, Ch. 22: 13, cited in Poulain, *The Graces of Interior Prayer*, p. 197.

as he heareth men speak of, or else findeth written in books. For he that feeleth him not stirred in hearing or reading of ghostly working, and especially in his each day's exercise by a growing desire to come near God, let him stand yet still at the door, as a man called to salvation but not yet to perfection"[77].

The intention of the author to make the distinction between the *common way* open to all as regards salvation, and the way and ascent to God mapped out in "This Work", cannot be more clear. He terms the *special grace* for "This Work" as a *call to perfection*. This distinction made by the author is worthy of some comment. In the same way as there is the *universal salvific* will of God, so there is likewise the *universal call to perfection*. The object and end of the mystical life is our *life in God,* and so "This Work" must be seen in its relation to *perfection*. This relationship between the *mystical life* and *perfection* has been noted by Fr. Bainvel. Indeed, this is a question that has been treated in good measure by writers on Mystical Theology. Having in mind the relation of the mystical life to perfection, the distinction has been made in an explanation of the Gospel words—*Estote perfecti, sicut et Pater vester coelestis perfectus est*—that "there is a call to all men to Christian perfection. . . . There is, on the other hand, a special call to perfection in the way of the counsels . . ."[78]. The Second Vatican Council in the *Dogmatic Constitution on the Church* reiterates and stresses this universal call to perfection enjoined by our Lord.

"Therefore in the Church, everyone belonging to the hierarchy, or being cared for by it, is called to holiness, according to the saying of the Apostle: 'For this is the will of God, your sanctification . . . The Lord Jesus, the divine Teacher and Model of all perfection, preached holiness of life to each and every one of His disciples, regardless of their situation: "You therefore are to be perfect, even as your Heavenly Father is perfect" . . . Thus it is evident to everyone that all the faithful of Christ of whatever rank or status are called to the fullness of the Christian life and to the perfection of charity"[79].

With this in mind, we see the significance of the distinction

---

77 *Privy Counsel, McCann,* p. 130; Hodgson, 161 : 8-15.

78 J. V. Bainvel, Introduction to A. Poulain, *The Graces of Interior Prayer,* p. cvii. see also p. cviii.

79 Dogmatic Constitution on *The Church,* in *The Documents of Vatican II,* Editor, W. M. Abbott, (1967), pp. 66-67.

which the author makes "between beginners and profiters" and "them that be perfect, yea as it may be here"[80] and "them that continually work in the work of this book"[81].

Nowhere does he say that "This Work" is the *only* way to perfection. The fact that he singles out "This Work" does not mean that he excludes all others. In the same way, too, he does not exclude all the other Sacraments in stressing the role of Confession.

On the other hand, *The Cloud* author never loses sight of the source of his teaching. From this general frame of mind, he gives the freedom to his disciple to go wherever the Spirit leads him and to follow some other course if the teaching is not akin to his attraction and disposition.

"And if thee think that this manner of working be not according to thy disposition in body and in soul, thou mayest leave it and take another, safely with good ghostly counsel without blame. And then I beseech thee that thou wilt have me excused, for truly I would have profited unto thee in this writing at my simple cunning; and that was mine intent"[82].

The bed-rock foundation for this attitude of the author is the deep-rooted conviction that he has on the *Absolute Freedom* and *Transcendence* of God. He gives the example of Moses, Bezaleel and Aaron as representing three different graces of contemplation[83]. And he makes this conviction ring in unmistakable terms.

"But not ever, nor yet no long time together, but when Him list and as Him list; and then wilt thou think it merry to let Him alone"[84].

---

80 *The Cloud*, Ch. 35, Underhill, p. 157; Hodgson, 71 : 18.
81 Ibid. Ch. 36, Underhill, p. 160; Hodgson, 72 : 23, 73 : 1.
82 Ibid. Ch. 74, Underhill, p. 264; Hodgson, 129 : 13-18. Hilton has a similar passage. "And if it be so, that through use savour of that lesseth, and thee thinketh another work savoureth thee more, and thou feelest more grace in another, take another and leave that". *Scale II*, Ch. 21, Underhill, p. 309. Also *Epistle of Prayer*, Hodgson, 59 : 6-13.
83 *The Cloud*, Ch. 73, Underhill, p. 262; Hodgson, 128-129.
84 Ibid. Ch. 26, Underhill, p. 139; Hodgson, 62 : 11-13. Walter Hilton has a similar passage. "For He is sovereign bliss and endless goodness, and passeth without comparison all men's deserts; and therefore may he not be gotten by no man's special work, as bodily meed may. For He is free and giveth Himself where He will and when He will, neither for this work nor for that, nor in this time nor after that time; for though a soul work all that he can and may, all his lifetime, perfect love of Jhesu shall he never have, till our Lord Jhesu will freely give it". *Scale II* Ch. 20, Underhill, p. 299.

In the light of the above passages, it is interesting to note the following observation.

"And, theologically speaking, it is possible to question the author's thesis that perfect love is found only in utter and complete forgetfulness of self and of all created things . . . My position, then differs only slightly from that of the English author. I believe that his contemplation is one way to perfection —and an ordinary way; but I do not believe it is the *only* way"[85].

The present writer wishes to point out that *The Cloud* author nowhere says that "This Work" is the *only* way. The difference intimated in the above passage is not slight at all. It is our intention to let the author speak for himself and, in the light of the previous passages from *The Cloud* author, we think that the above conclusion of Fr. Johnston is not supported by the texts. A passage from *The Epistle of Prayer* reveals the author giving this same freedom to the disciple.

"And therefore have I ordained thy climbing by these two thoughts; but if it so be that thy good angel teach thee within thy ghostly conceit, or any other man, any other two that are more according to thy disposition than thee thinketh these two be, thou mayst take them, and leave these safely without any blame. Nevertheless to my conceit (till I wete more) me thinketh that these should be full helply unto thee, and not much unaccording to thy disposition, after that I feel in thee. And therefore, if thou think that they do thee good, then thank God heartily, and for God's love pray for me. Do then so, for I am a wretch, and thou wotest not how it standeth with me"[86].

In this distinction, then, between the *call to salvation* and the *call to perfection,* the author gives further proof of the singleness of mind and unity of message. He also stresses his behest that he writes only for the disciple and those with the same special grace for "This Work". In identifying "This

85 W. Johnston, *The Mysticism of the Cloud of Unknowing,* p. 264. see C. Pepler, *The English Religious Heritage,* pp. 245-246.
86 Gardner, *Cell of Self-Knowledge,* pp. 91-92. Hodgson, 59: 4-14. Walter Hilton gives forth very much the same attitude. "Lo, I have told thee in this matter a little, as me thinketh, not affirming that this sufficeth, nor that this is the soothfastness in this matter. But if thou think it otherwise, or else any other man savour by grace the contrary hereto, I leave this saying, and give stead to him; it sufficeth to me for to live in truth principally, and not in feeling" *The Song of Angels,* Gardner, pp. 72-73. Also: *Letter to a Hermit,* Russell-Smith, *The Way,* July 1966, p. 241.

Work" as one that pertains to *perfection*, he does not conflict with the *universal call to perfection*. In the context of *The Cloud* and *Privy Counsel* in their entirety, the author identifies the way of perfection mapped out in "This Work" with the higher reaches of the *mystical life*.

In the immediate context of *Privy Counsel* we see this distinction stressing the *essential difference* between the "special grace" and all other forms of *Divine Aid* which the Lord gives for *salvation*.

Continuing this teaching on *special grace,* the author makes an exegesis of the passage "sine me nihil potestis facere" in the light of the work of contemplation, "This Work".

> "And thus I understand this word in the Gospel: *Sine me nihil potestis facere*—that is: 'Without me ye may do nothing'— on one manner in actives and on another manner in contemplatives . . . 'Without me'—either only suffering and not consenting, as in sinners; or else both suffering and consenting, as in actives; or (that more than all this is) principally stirring and working, as in contemplatives—'ye may do nothing' "[87].

The whole ascent to God in "This Work" is seen as one continuous way, and to even start on the way requires this "special grace". The figure of "doorkeeper and door", the distinction between the "call to salvation and the call to perfection", makes this teaching clear. And the *tests* to know the presence of this "special grace" will make the emphasis still clearer, for the tests presuppose the beginning of "This Work". Once this *special grace* to begin "This Work" is given, what happens to the one chosen? *The Cloud* author says that a corresponding ability to do "This Work" is given to the soul. For the grace of God is powerful indeed.

> "And yet He giveth not this grace, nor worketh not this work, in any soul that is unable thereto. And yet there is no soul without this grace, able to have this grace: none, whether it be a sinner's soul or an innocent soul"[88].

And in the perfection of "This Work", as regards the "naked being of man", we see again this interplay of "special grace" given by God, and "ableness" on the part of the soul.

> "But to this I answer thee and I say, that without a full special

---

[87] *Privy Counsel*, McCann, pp. 132-133; Hodgson, 163: 12-28, 164: 1-6.
[88] *The Cloud*, Ch. 34, Underhill, p. 154; Hodgson, 69: 12-15.

grace full freely given of God, and thereto a full according ableness to receive this grace on thy part, this naked witting and feeling of thy being may on nowise be destroyed"[89].

We see, then, the need for *this special grace to start, sustain,* and *perfect* this work.

The objection may arise to this insistence on the *special* intervention of God, as regards the fact of the freedom of the soul. Since it is God Who does everything, the soul might be said to have no choice in the matter, that it is forced or constrained to do "This Work" whether he likes it or not. The facts of the Divine Omnipotence and human freedom seem hard to reconcile. But this is an age-old problem and the author sees the difficulty. He goes to great length to discuss this interplay of Divine Power and human consent, but the solution he gives is more on the level of the practical, the actual dynamic response and experience of the soul. We do not see him engaged in the fine distinctions of speculative theologians, neither do we see him tracing the grace for "This Work" as proceeding from the "Gifts" of the Holy Ghost. For the author, it is God Alone, seen distinctly and differently from the human soul. Indeed, he gives the most fundamental explanation of this interplay and uses illustrations to emphasize his point. God does not do anything against the will of the person. Instead, he waits for the *consent* of the individual before "This Work" can be done.

"This desire behoveth altogether be wrought in thy will, by the hand of Almighty God and thy consent"[90].

Perhaps, if *The Cloud* author were asked just how precisely this can be done, we think that the author would answer in his characteristic fashion, "I wot not"[91]. For he is not one to search the Mind of God. He is a realist and accepts the presence of a fact once it is there. So, he resorts to the use of illustrations to stress his point.

"And if I shall shortlier say, let that thing do with thee and lead thee whereso it list. Let it be the worker, and you but the sufferer: do but look upon it, and let it alone. Meddle thee not therewith as thou wouldest help it, for dread lest thou spill

[89] Ibid. Ch. 44, Underhill, p. 180; Hodgson, 83: 9-12.
[90] Ibid. Ch. 2, Underhill, p. 62; Hodgson, 15: 14-15.
[91] "I do not know".

all. Be thou but the tree, and let it be the wright: be thou but the house, and let it be the husbandman dwelling therein. Be blind in this time, and sheer away covetise of knowing, for it will more let thee than help thee"[92].

We notice the contrasts that the *figures* give of God and the soul: worker — sufferer; carpenter — tree; husbandman — house. The author continues this teaching in *Privy Counsel*.

"For know thou right well, and all like unto thee that this writing shall either read or hear, that although I bid thee thus plainly and thus boldly set thee to this work, nevertheless yet I feel verily without error or doubt that Almighty God with his grace must always be the chief stirrer and worker, either with means or without, and thou only, or any other like unto thee, but the consenter and the sufferer. Saving that this consenting and this suffering shall be in the time of this work actually disposed and abled to this work in purity of spirit, and seemly borne up to thy Sovereign, as thou may be learned by the proof in the ghostly sight of thy spirit"[93].

God then, in "This Work", must be the "chief stirrer and worker", while the soul "but the consenter and the sufferer".

E. PASSIVITY, MAN'S RESPONSE

The teaching of *The Cloud* author on the *Divine Initiative* and God's part in *starting, sustaining,* and *perfecting* "This Work" brings us to the heart of the discussion on an overriding problem of the mystical life, that of *passivity*.

On this point, we have the following observations:

"Of the various points at issue around contemplation, the question of 'passivity' is probably the one that lies nearest to the root of the matter. Passivity has commonly come nowadays to be taken as the test of real contemplation. By passivity is meant that contemplation itself is wholly the act of God, the soul lying passive in the hands of God, receiving the gift and not resisting the divine action; yet accepting and responding by a vital act . . . There is common agreement that such passivity is the mark of the mystical experience in its strictest and fullest acceptation, so that it receives the name, among others of 'passive union' "[94].

To Fr. Poulain, *passivity* is "an absolute powerlessness to

---

92 *The Cloud,* Ch. 34, Underhill, p. 155; Hodgson, 70: 12-18.
93 Privy Counsel, McCann, pp. 124-125; Hodgson, 155: 5-14.
94 C. Butler, *Western Mysticism,* p. 28.

procure the mystic states for ourselves"[95]. In the list he gives of the *fundamental* and *subsidiary* marks of the *mystic state*, he gives *passivity* as the first of the *subsidiary* marks[96]. However, it is this character which he gives for the definition of the *mystic* or *extraordinary* prayer which distinguishes it from *ordinary*.

It is, then, this character that marks off the *infused, extraordinary, eminent,* which are terms synonymous with *mystical,* from the lower forms of prayer which is termed *acquired, active, ordinary.* It is in the light of this *fundamental distinction* that we beg to disagree with Fr. W. Johnston when he writes that "I believe that his contemplation is one way to perfection—and an ordinary way . . ."[97]. It is in this regard, too, that the present writer does not agree with the new meanings he gives to the term *ordinary.*

> "Again the mysticism of *The Cloud* may be called 'ordinary' because it follows a phenomenological pattern of supra-conceptuality that, in its broadest outlines, is common to many religions and to many cultures . . . Finally, the mysticism of *The Cloud* and its accompanying treatises may be called ordinary because of the assiduity with which the author eschews all extraordinary phenomena. His contemplative is a very ordinary person; and the author devotes pages of ridicule to the would-be mystic who acts as if he had a worm in his ear or looks like a silly sheep that has been banged on the head"[98].

Seen from another aspect: ". . . In the mystic state . . . something shows us more or less clearly that God is intervening"[99] and in all these there is "the feeling that she is entering a wholly new world"[100].

By *passivity,* then, "we merely wish to say that we receive something from another source, and render count of it to ourselves"[101]. It is with these particular nuances that we see the passages which *The Cloud* author gives to show *"God's action in us"*[102] of which the soul is *consciously aware*[103].

95 A. Poulain, *The Graces of Interior Prayer,* p. 115.
96 Ibid. p. 114.
97 W. Johnston, *The Mysticism of the Cloud of Unknowing,* p. 264.
98 Ibid. pp. 264-265; see also pp. 12, 13, 93, 177, 262.
99 A. Poulain, *The Graces of Interior Prayer,* p. 4.
100 Ibid. p. 72.
101 Ibid. p. 4.
102 J. V. Bainvel, Introduction to Poulain, *The Graces of Interior Prayer,* p. lxxxvii.
103 Ibid. p. lxxxviii.

In its historical context, we see that *The Cloud of Unknowing* was written at the time when the rumblings of dissent seemed a distant reality, although it might be said that the passages on the pride of the intellect that leads others astray in heresy could refer to Wycliffe. For the followers of Wycliffe were university-trained intellectuals. Comparable passages in the works of Hilton have been pointed out as having reference to "Master John Wyclif, Nicholas Hereford, John Aston and their followers"[104]. *The Cloud* author does not reveal in his writings the usage of the finer distinctions in terminology of latterday theology, and we agree with the observations that

" . . . It is recognized by all that the term 'acquired contemplation' first came into use at the beginning of the seventeenth century, 'contemplation' pure and simple, without qualification, being used by the earlier writers, as SS Augustine, Gregory and Bernard . . . that though the word 'acquired contemplation' was not employed, the distinction between the two kinds of contemplation was known to various early writers: in particular are cited Richard of St. Victor, Walter Hilton, Denis the Carthusian"[105].

To this enumeration of early writers, we can add the author of *The Cloud of Unknowing,* who locates "This Work" in the life that is "strictly contemplative", and who called his major work "A Book of Contemplation . . . in the which a soul is oned with God"[106]. It is by means of descriptions and comparisons with other mystical writings that he qualifies the state of "This Work" as that which we call by such different terms as *infused, extraordinary, passive, eminent, mystical.* In this part, we are particularly interested in the passages which show the character of *passivity* in *The Cloud* and other writings. For the sake of simplicity and clarity it is good to remember a key phrase in the matter of *passivity,* God's action in us, wholly, completely in the things that *distinctly* make the difference between *this action* of God and those which we might say God does in the ordinary way of His Loving Providence. Right from the start, then, this personal intervention is shown by His *Personal Choice* of the disciple,

---

104 E. Underhill, *The Scale of Perfection,* pp. xiii-xvi. Also Hilton, *Qui Habitat,* Jones, pp. 133-134; Hilton, *Bonum Est,* Jones, p. 226
105 C. Butler, *Western Mysticism,* p. 16.
106 *The Cloud,* Underhill, p. 35; Hodgson, p. 1.
    see P. Hodgson, *Three 14th-Century English Mystics,* p. 9.

the addressee of *The Cloud*: in all these passages, we must note the fact that God is the *Subject, The Doer* of the action described.

"Seest thou nought how listily and how graciously He hath privily pulled thee to the third degree and manner of living, the which is called Singular?"[107].

This personal intervention is contrasted with the part of the disciple after the call.

"In the which solitary form and manner of living, thou mayest learn to lift up the foot of thy love . . ."[108].

God's action comes first, those of the disciple come afterwards. Very early in *The Cloud,* the author stresses this *Divine Action* and the part of the soul[109]. Compared with the Work of God, the part of man, signified by his consent, covers those acts which, whilst of great value, are less important and decisive. The author then describes this consent, which is not a mere matter of saying "yes".

"He wills, thou do but look on Him and let Him alone. And keep thou the windows and the door, for flies and enemies assailing. And if thou be willing to do this, thee needeth but meekly press upon Him with prayer, and soon will He help thee"[110].

But this is not all. In the form of the anticipated question, he introduces the part which the desciple must do, in response to this Divine Choice.

"He is full ready, and doth but abideth thee. But what shall thou do, and how shalt thou press?"[111].

This is the main burden of *The Cloud* and *Privy Counsel.* From here on, the burden of the teaching of *The Cloud* author concerns the part of the disciple in "This Work" which is in contrast to the reticence with which he deals with those things which alone pertain to God.

"For of that work, that falleth to only God, dare I not take upon me to speak with my blabbering fleshly tongue: and shortly to say, although I durst I would do not. But of that work that

107 *The Cloud,* Ch. 1. Underhill, p. 60; Hodgson, 14: 10-12.
108 Ibid. Ch. 1, Underhill, p. 60; Hodgson, 14: 12-14.
109 Ibid. Ch. 2, Underhill, p. 62; Hodgson, 15: 14-15.
110 Ibid. Ch. 2, Underhill, p. 62; Hodgson, 15: 18-21.
111 Ibid. Ch. 2, Underhill, p. 62; Hodgson, 16: 1-2.

falleth to man when he feeleth him stirred and helped by grace, list me well tell thee: for therein is the less peril of the two"[112].

This consent is also shown by the docility to allow God to do *His Own Work*. There is always that contrast with the part of man.

"And therefore lift up thy love to that cloud: rather, if I shall say thee sooth, let God draw thy love up to that cloud and strive thou through help of His grace to forget all other things"[113].

The afterthought is revealing in that there is a groping for clarity and exactness in the mind of the author. This *Divine Choice* is shown in the description of "This Work" as the "best part" that Mary chose. Again, there is that afterthought that corrects his previous assertion in his desire for exactitude and clarity.

"But the third part that Mary chose, choose who by grace is called to choose: or, if I soothlier shall say, who so is chosen thereto of God. Let him listily incline thereto . . . "[114].

This *passivity* is shown in the various elements that make "This Work". So God is the author of "that devout stirring of love" which is the essence of "This Work".

"But I pray thee, wherein shall that travail be? Surely not in that devout stirring of love that is continually wrought in his will, not by himself, but by the hand of Almighty God: the which is evermore ready to work this work in each soul that is disposed thereto, and that doth that in him is, and hath done long time before, to enable him to this work"[115].

As God is the author, so He likewise sustains "that devout stirring of love". And this part is set in contrast to the travail which is the part of man, involved in the "cloud of forgetting". The contrast is made even more precise.

"In this is all the travail; for this is man's travail, with help of grace. And the other above—that is to say, the stirring of love —that is the work of only God"[116].

One of the consequences of this *powerlessness* which is

112 Ibid. Ch. 26, Underhill, p. 140; Hodgson, 62: 19-23.
113 Ibid. Ch. 9, Underhill, p. 90; Hodgson, 34: 19-22.
114 Ibid. Ch. 21, Underhill, p. 126; Hodgson, 54: 16-19.
    Also *Privy Counsel*, McCann, p. 131; Hodgson, 162: 5-7.
115 *The Cloud*, Ch. 26, Underhill, p. 138; Hodgson, 61: 16-21.
    Ch. 48, Underhill, p. 194; Hodgson, 91: 14-18.
116 Ibid. Ch. 26, Underhill, p. 139; Hodgson, 61: 24, 62: 1-2.

characteristic of passivity, is that the *mystic act* "cannot be foreseen, whatever preparation we may have tried to make. Beginners are often surprised at the *unexpected* manner of its arrival"[117]. We find this verified in *The Cloud of Unknowing* when the author describes the part of God in the lessening or the absence altogether of the travail involved in "This Work".

"And thou shalt have either little travail or none, for then will God work sometimes all by Himself"[118]. We have noted before that this *Sovereign Freedom* of God is another aspect of *His Transcendence*.

In our approach to the matter of *passivity* in *The Cloud* and other writings, tracing it from the first time of the *special grace, the call to perfection, the invitation to come inside the Door,* we notice that there is a progress in the matter of *passivity.* Not surely on the part of God, but on the part of the disciple. Hence, we notice the gradual diminution of the things which the soul must do in the matter of "This Work". In the beginning, we see that his part includes the keeping of "the windows and the door from flies and enemies assailing". We see this likewise in the matter to be covered down by the "cloud of forgetting". In the *travail* involved in "This Work", the *pain* and *travail* can be removed only perfectly by God Himself, just as the full and final forgetting of "all creatures" can be done by God alone. When this state is reached, the perfection of "This Work" is achieved. The passage just commented upon is one description of the state of perfection of "This Work". This is the highest state in which the powers of man are somehow involved although, in the course of the ascent, the part of man becomes less and less. This verifies the observation of Fr. Poulain that in the matter of *passivity* there is possibility of progress and "the passiveness is so much the greater as the mystic state is higher, because God's part in it is then more accentuated. But the activity is augmented at the same time"[119]. Finally, there comes a time when everything is, for a time at least, wholly and completely God's. In this, the soul has no part at all except to receive, and receive

---

[117] A. Poulain, *The Graces of Interior Prayer*, p. 115.
[118] *The Cloud*, Ch. 26, Underhill, p. 139; Hodgson, 62: 10-11.
[119] A. Poulain, *The Graces of Interior Prayer*, p. 5.

completely. This is *passivity* in its highest form, for it involves the *personal invasion* of the soul by God Himself. "Then will He sometimes peradventure send out a beam of ghostly light, piercing this cloud of unknowing that is betwixt thee and Him, and show thee some of His privity, the which man may not, nor cannot speak"[120]. This passage of great beauty and profundity will be discussed at great length in Chapter VI in the various passages describing the perfection of "This Work". There is verified in this passage the *unexpected* arrival of the mystic grace, as well as the *supreme powerlessness* of the soul to bring it about since it is completely God's own intervention. The author describes the breakthrough of God by the figure of a *beam of ghostly light*. In so describing this manner of Divine Intervention, the author does not mean to say that this "beam" is the Essence of God as HE IS in Himself. He affirms by this description that God was somehow perceived by some *spiritual sensation of a special kind*. We note that this is the second of the *fundamental* characters of the mystic state listed by Fr. Poulain and the *Presence of God is indeed felt* as the passage reveals. But more than this the author does not say. All he wants to convey by this revelation of the Godhead is that GOD IS HERE. It is only the PRESENCE of God he affirms. This is best seen in the word IS, which to *The Cloud* author is the best Name of God, and which is also the perfection of "This Work". And so, the verb IS assumes a Reality, a Presence, GOD IS HERE, and this is further abbreviated in "This Work" to IS. We have an analogy in the world about us when we say that "somebody is there" or "it is here", wherein the emphasis is on presence. But the difference lies in the fact that no *created* thing is supremely and completely identified with the presence, with the word *is,* whereas with God the Name and the Reality IS One. With this in view, we see the significance of the short prayer of the perfect worker of "This Work", one of which is simply "God". We could, perhaps, see the meaning of this "short prayer" by analogy with our own ways of doing things, as when we call out to a friend "John". We call a name and a person, who is *present*.

After this lovely passage describing the breakthrough of

---

[120] *The Cloud,* Ch. 26, Underhill, pp. 139-140. Hodgson, 62: 14-16.

God, what remains to be said seems to be an anti-climax. This drop in tone and development is in keeping with the manner of development which the author uses. So we have the author, after this height is reached, saying and reiterating his teaching in new forms and nuances. Thus he gives the reason for the Transcendence of God in His Actions.

"And this will He do, for He will be seen all merciful and almighty; and for He will be seen to work as Him list, where Him list, and when Him list"[121].

Passivity is tellingly asserted by the author as characteristic of "This Work" right at the beginning. He ties up this idea with the "special grace" as with the "ableness" of the soul for "This Work".

"The ableness to this work is oned to the work's self without departing; so that whoso feeleth this work is able thereto, and none else. Insomuch, that without this work a soul is as it were dead, and cannot covet it nor desire it"[122].

The author could not have chosen a clearer illustration. As regards the prayer of "This Work" the author says that ". . . these sudden conceits and these blind feelings be sooner learned of God than of man"[123].

This fact of *Passivity* is so intimately connected with the teaching of the author on the need for *special grace* that we have put the passages of *Privy Counsel* touching on *passivity* earlier in this discussion. However, we include here one passage on *passivity* which is as crisp and axiomatic as a principle of mathematics.

"But, in things contemplative, the highest wisdom that may be in man, as man, is far put under, so that God be the principal in working, and man but only consenter and sufferer"[124].

Just as the matter of *passivity* is intimately connected with the need for a *special grace,* so also we see this *passivity* intimately intertwined with the passages in which the author gives the tests for the presence of this grace. These passages will be more amply quoted in the later section on the *tests*. Here we draw from those passages the elements which most

---

121 Ibid. Ch. 34, Underhill, pp. 153-154; Hodgson, 69: 9-11.
122 Ibid. Ch. 34, Underhill, pp. 154-155; Hodgson, 70: 3-6.
123 Ibid. Ch. 36, Underhill, p. 160; Hodgson, 73: 4-6.
124 *Privy Counsel*, McCann, p. 132; Hodgson, 163; 9-11.

properly pertain to *passivity*. We have seen before how the author uses figures to demonstrate clearly the fact of *passivity*. To these figures, we add a picturesque one from *Privy Counsel*, a figure taken from the *sea*.

> ". . . but suffer meekly and bide patiently the will of our Lord. For now art thou in the ghostly sea (to my likeness) shipping over from bodilyness into ghostliness"[125].

Because the mystics have abundantly described the harassments that the *mystic soul* undergoes in the different "nights", it seems that the fact of *passivity* has become associated with this intense suffering. Perhaps we might say that this is the most graphic representation of this *passivity,* and most easily understood. The author in *Privy Counsel* likewise describes this state wherein the soul is pictured as one who has no say in a storm-tossed sea.

> "Many great storms and temptations, peradventure, shall rise in this time, and thou knowest never whither to run for sorrow . . . "[126].

These *Divine Harassments* have one purpose, the supreme docility of the *mystic soul* in the Hands of God. In this also is the perfection of passivity.

> "Yea! and if he after go, after will he come again; and each time, if thou wilt bear thee by meek suffering, will he come more worthlier and merrylier than other. And all this he doth because he will have thee made as pliant to his will ghostly as a roan glove to thine hand bodily"[127].

In addition to the *docility* that must be produced in the soul by these *comings and goings* of the Lord, there is the final aim for this manner of acting of God, namely, *union with Him*.

> "So that thus by patience in absence of these sensible feelings, the tokens of grace, and by that lively nourishing and that lovely feeding of thy spirit in their presence, he will make thee in both together so blithely bowing and so pleasantly pliant to perfection and the ghostly onehead to his own will—the which oneing is perfect charity—that thou shalt be as glad and as fain to

---

[125] Ibid. McCann, p. 136; Hodgson, 167: 13-16. See *Discretion of Stirrings*, Hodgson, 65: 4-23.
[126] *Privy Counsel*, McCann, p. 136; Hodgson, 167: 17-18.
[127] Ibid. McCann, p. 137; Hodgson, 168: 5-9.

forgo such feelings at his will, as for to have them and feel them in continuance all thy lifetime"[128].

Perhaps all these passages on *passivity* could be said to be highly theoretical. As if to remove the element of being *static* from God of Whom no motion can be predicated, the author describes this element of movement graphically, yet tenderly.

"And this meekness so obtaineth to have God Himself mightily descending, to venge thee of thine enemies, for to take thee up, and cherishingly dry thine ghostly eyen; as the father does the child that is in point to perish under the mouths of wild swine or wode biting bears"[129].

In *Privy Counsel*, the author identifies "this same work" with the *Epistle of Prayer*, as also with *The Cloud of Unknowing*. Hence, we shall see what the author has to say about *passivity* in this other letter of his. We leave out the *Discretion of Stirrings* and *Knowing of Spirits*, since the burden of their message is not mystical in character. They do complement *The Cloud of Unknowing* on certain points, but until it can be shown that they were written to the *same disciple* as the addressee of the *Privy Counsel*, it would be hard to see their mystical nature. On the other hand we notice a difference in the state described in *Epistle of Prayer* and that of *The Cloud of Unknowing* and *Privy Counsel*. For while the virtues synthesized in the perfection of "This Work" are *charity* and *humility*, we see that in the *Epistle of Prayer*, the author stresses *the fear of God* and *hope in His Mercy*. Without the identification made by the author in *Privy Counsel*, it would be difficult to see the unity of authorship in these letters. For in the mystical life, if we are correct in citing the works of the mystics, we shall see that there are no two lines we can cross. This essential difference would have proved a great difficulty to the problem of unity of authorship of these letters. But as the author would say, "but forth of our matter".

"For this same work, if it be verily conceived, is that reverent affection and the fruit separated from the tree that I speak of in the little *Epistle of Prayer*. This is the *cloud of unknowing* . . . "[130].

With this identification the present writer thinks it valid to

128 Ibid. McCann, pp. 137-138; Hodgson, 169: 9-16.
129 *The Cloud*, Ch. 32, Underhill, p. 150; Hodgson, 67: 10-14.
130 *Privy Counsel*, McCann, p. 124; Hodgson, 154: 13-15.

examine *The Epistle of Prayer* as regards the author's teaching on *passivity*.

The author affirms that the *reverent affection* in the *Epistle of Prayer* comes only from God without any intermediary of any sort.

> "For it is plainly known without any doubt unto all those that are expert in the science of divinity and of God's love, that as often as a man's affection is so stirred unto God without mean (that is, without messenger of any thought in special causing that stirring), as oft it deserveth everlasting life. And for that that a soul that is thus disposed that is to say, that offreth the fruit ripe, and departed from the tree) may innumerable times in one hour be raised in to God suddenly without mean, therefore more than I can say it deserveth, through the grace of God, the which is the chief worker, to be raised in to joy"[131].

In the same passage, too, we see the teaching of the author on the nature of "This Work", as well as its perfection. So also, in this section on *passivity,* we see the teaching of the author on the need for a *special grace,* on a *personal intervention* which makes up the *Divine Initiative.* There is such a compactness and a concentration in the teaching of the author, that all the various elements that go to make up "This Work" are intermingled with one another. It is not confusion that is the result. What is remarkable is that, in all this compactness and intermingling, there is a transparency that dominates the writings. This dissertation attempts to make a synthesis of the teaching of the author. In this synthesis we put one matter in one section, though it could be very well located in two or three other parts. There is a very great unity and singleness of purpose in *The Cloud of Unknowing* and *Privy Counsel.* And there is always that desire to synthesize and unify everything into one. So he says that the perfection of "This Work" is "Nought" just as it is also "The All". It is the "short prayer of the perfect worker", the "synthesis of the virtues", the "chaste love", "great peace and restfulness", "deep ghostly sorrow", "holy desire and good will", "as a sparkle from the coal", "a beam of ghostly light piercing this cloud of unknowing", just as all this is "The Cloud of Unknowing", *The Presence of God,* The *IS* of God.

In closing this section on *passivity* it is good to remember

---

131 *Epistle of Prayer,* Gardner, p. 87; Hodgson, 55: 19-25, 56: 1-3.

that in this mark of the mystical life, the predominant character is the *powerlessness* of the soul and the ALLNESS of
God in the mystic act. In this, too, *His Transcendence* is
revealed in the manner of working, "as Him list, where Him
list, and when Him list"[132]. It is in the light of the passages
commented upon above, on the *Divine Initiative* and the need
for a "special grace" insisted upon by *The Cloud* author, as
well as the nature of *passivity* which is verified in *The Cloud*
teaching, that the present writer finds it hard to agree with the
General Conclusion of Fr. W. Johnston.

> "The principal point I have made in this work is that the
> English writer's doctrine leads to a form of prayer that is no
> more than an intensification of the ordinary Christian life . . .
> The difference is only one of intensity"[133].

The above conclusion is not supported by the texts of *The
Cloud* and other writings. In making this dissenting opinion,
the present writer is fully aware of the controversy existing
between the two predominant schools of thought as regards
this aspect of mystical theology[134]. This is not an easy problem.
For the purposes of this dissertation it is suggested that on the
basis of the texts of *The Cloud of Unknowing* and other
writings by the same author the conclusion that "This Work"
of *The Cloud* is "ordinary" is simply not so. Fr. Bainvel gives
a lovely reconciliation of the *Sole Work* of God in the mystic
state, and the soul's *consent and correspondence* to God's
action in it.

> "The mystic graces are a powerful method of sanctification; this
> is beyond all question. We might quibble by saying that in the
> mystic act the soul is passive rather than active, and that it is
> not our *being moved* that sanctifies us, but *our own movement*
> towards God. True, it is not grace alone which does everything,
> but the grace to which we correspond, or, if we prefer, our
> correspondence to grace. No one, therefore, would try to make
> out that the mystic graces sanctify us without our aid: the
> mystics are there to remind us of this if anyone were tempted
> to forget it. But it remains that these graces attract the soul,
> uplift it, draw it to a world so beautiful, bring it into contact

---

132 *The Cloud*, Ch. 34, Underhill, p. 154, Hodgson, 69: 10-11.
133 W. Johnston, The Mysticism of *The Cloud of Unknowing*, pp. 257-259.
   See also pp. 28, 88, 93, 110, 113, 140-141, 180, 242.
134 J. V. Bainvel, Introduction to A. Poulain, *The Graces of Interior
   Prayer*, pp. civ-cxii; D. Knowles, *The English Mystical Tradition*,
   pp. 8-17.

with a force so gentle, provide it with such great lights on God and the nothingness of all that is not God, that, carried by the divine hand, leaning upon the Beloved, whom it feels as its sole possession and its all, the soul runs in the odour of these ointments, escapes from everything and even from itself, so as to belong entirely to Him, see nought but Him, and love none but Him"[135].

Having seen, then, the *Transcendence* of God, as well as the need for "special grace" and the passivity involved in "This Work", the question that naturally comes to mind is how one can know with some degree of certainty the fact of the *Divine Choice, This Divine Intervention,* this "call to perfection". The author has anticipated this and he says in the Prologue that there are tests by which this *Divine Choice* may be known.

> "This book is distinguished in seventy chapters and five. Of the which chapters the last chapter of all teacheth some certain tokens by the which a soul may verily prove whether he be called by God to be a worker in this work or none"[136].

F.   THE TESTS FOR THE PRESENCE OF "THE PRIVY TEACHING OF THE SPIRIT OF GOD"*.

For all the infinite gulf that yawns between God and His creatures, God of His own initiative does bridge this gap and takes the first step to approach whom He wishes, when He wishes and in whatever way He wishes. And when He does decide to take the initiative, He also makes known His desires in unmistakable terms. Moses had a glimpse of the Divine Presence in the burning bush[137]; the Chosen People followed him in the pillar of cloud by day and the pillar of fire by night[138]. They saw His might in the thunderbolts and lightnings that illuminated Mount Sinai. Elias knew His presence in the gust of wind[139]. St. John heard Him in the sound of many waters[140]. St. Paul was carried up to the third heaven and heard secrets which it is not for man to repeat[141]. St. Teresa

---

135 J. V. Bainvel, Introduction to A. Poulain, *The Graces of Interior Prayer*, pp. lxxxix-xc.
136 *The Cloud*, Prologue, McCann, p. 41; Hodgson, 3: 9-12.
* First published in the Summer 1969 issue of *Mount Carmel*.
137 *Exodus* 3: 2.
138 Ibid. 13: 21.
139 *1 Kings* 19:11.
140 *Apocalypse* 1: 15.
141 2 *Corinthians*, 12: 2.

and St. John of the Cross were carried out of themselves to have a glimpse of the Divine and they related their experiences in terms we can barely comprehend, even when they use the words we know.

And so, in his own way, we see *The Cloud* author giving the external signs by which one can know the presence of this "special grace" to do "This Work".

In the characteristic fashion of the author, we see him giving the negative aspect of the tests. So he narrates right in the beginning some classes of persons for whom *The Cloud of Unknowing* was never meant to be written[142]. The nature of "This Work" also gives an indication as to the presence or absence of the "special grace". In a negative way, then, those who misunderstand the *ghostly nature* of "This Work" and engage in unseemly practices especially in connection with the material interpretation of the words "in" and "up", can be sure that they are not meant for "This Work"[143].

In an affirmative way the author describes the tests for the presence of this "special grace". He does not describe something merely in the theoretical order. It is an experience, an objective reality in the interior of the soul that sets the person thinking what this "stirring" could be. It is a "liking stirring that they feel" that sets, as it were, the warning bells ringing. This "stirring" is not something hypothetical either, but connected with the reading or hearing of "This Work". A desire results from this hearing or reading.

> "Yea! and it seemeth impossible to mine understanding, that any soul that is disposed to this work should read it or speak it, or else hear it read or spoken, but if that same soul should feel for that time a very accordance to the effect of this work. And then, if thee think it doth thee good, thank God heartily, and for God's love pray for me"[144].

This attraction, when it comes, must be examined as regards its source. The reason for this is to see if this attraction is genuine and not just a passing fancy.

> "But if they will prove whence this stirring cometh, they may

142 *The Cloud,* Prologue, Underhill pp. 40-41; Hodgson, 2: 19-25, 3: 1-8.
143 Ibid. Ch. 53, Underhill, pp. 209-210; Hodgson, 99: 15-21, 100: 1-4, Ch. 62, Hodgson, 114: 3-10; Ch. 67, Hodgson, 120: 21-24, 121: 1-4.
144 Ibid. Ch. 74, Underhill, p. 265; Hodgson, 129: 22-25, 130: 1-2.

prove thus, if them liketh. First let them look if they have done
that in them is before, abling them thereto in cleansing of their
conscience at the doom of Holy Church, their counsel
according"[145].

Sacramental Confession comes right at the start of the
call to "This Work". This serves as a control to the attraction that the soul feels. This test is objective enough and easily
verifiable.

"And from the time that thou feelest that thou hast done that
in thee is, lawfully to amend thee at the doom of Holy Church,
then shalt thou set thee sharply to work in this work"[146].

In his characteristic fashion the author says the same thing
in another way.

"But if thou asketh me when they should work in this work, then
I answer thee and I say: that not ere they have cleansed their
conscience of all their special deeds of sins done before, after
the common ordinance of Holy Church"[147].

Knowing of Spirits discusses in detail the role of Sacramental Confession in the struggle against the three wicked
spirits. This section is proper to *The Cloud* author[148]. Sacramental Confession, then, is the first objective test. But it is not
sufficient. One does not get the assurance of the grace to do
"This Work" simply for having gone to Confession. There
are still other subsequent tests to be verified after having gone
to Confession. This is the reason why the author wants the
disciple to read *The Cloud* as a whole, and mentions explicitly
the need for such a complete reading as regards the time to
start "This Work".

"And I pray thee for God's love that thou let none see this book
unless it be such one that thee think is like to the book; after
that thou findest written in the book before, where it telleth what
men and when they should work in this work. And if thou shalt
let any such men see it, then I pray thee thou bid them take
them time to look it all over. For peradventure there is some
matter therein in the beginning, or in the midst, the which is
hanging and not fully declared there as it standeth. But if it
be not there, it is soon after, or else in the end. And thus if a

---

145 Ibid. Ch. 75, Underhill, p. 267; Hodgson, 131: 6-9.
146 Ibid. Ch. 31, Underhill, p. 147; Hodgson, 65: 20-21, 66: 1.
147 Ibid. Ch. 28, Underhill, p. 142; Hodgson, 63: 8-11.
148 *Knowing of Spirits,* Gardner, pp. 127-128; Hodgson, 88: 2, 92: 4.

man saw one part and not another, peradventure he should
lightly be led into error: and therefore I pray thee to work as
I say thee"[149].

The requirement of Confession having been met, the author
continues with the tests. These internal attractions and desires
must be closely scrutinized.

"If it be thus, it is well inasmuch: but if they will wit more near,
let them look if it be evermore pressing in their remembrance
more customably than is any other of ghostly exercise. And if
them think that there is no manner of thing that they do, bodily
or ghostly, that is sufficiently done with witness of their conscience, unless this privy little love pressed be in a manner ghostly
the chief of all their work: and if they thus feel, then it is
a token that they be called of God to do this work, and surely
else not"[150].

This internal attraction must have a continuing, absorbing
and intransigent quality. This quality is decisive; without it,
the attraction is but a passing fancy.

"All those that read or hear the matter of this book be read or
spoken, and in this reading or hearing think it a good and
liking thing, be never the rather called of God to work in this
work, only for this liking stirring that they feel in the time of
this reading. For peradventure this stirring cometh more of a
natural curiosity of wit, than of any calling of grace"[151].

We note how intimately intertwined the *tests* are to the
nature of "This Work", as well as to the *perfection* of it. It is
understandable for the author is describing in its entirety what
he knows for the guidance of his disciple. He does not do so
by doses, as it were waiting for the progress report of the
disciple. The circumstances of their lives would have made
this difficult[152].

However, it is not to be expected that this quality of the
attraction must always be present. It is possible that the grace
can be withdrawn at times, either for reasons of carelessness
on the part of the person himself, or because it is the wish of
our Lord to make the desire grow by such delays. With this
initial attraction and "stirring", there is the further experience
of waxing and waning, of disappearing and being found once

149 *The Cloud*, Ch. 74, Underhill, p. 265; Hodgson, 130: 3-13.
150 Ibid. Ch. 75, Underhill, pp. 267-268; Hodgson, 131: 9-17.
151 Ibid. Ch. 75, Underhill, p. 267; Hodgson, 130: 24, 131: 1-5.
152 Cf. supra, pp. 12, 103-104, 115.

again. For this there is a further check to verify the authenticity of this "stirring", namely, that when it comes again there is greater joy at having found it than when it was never lost at all.

> "I say not that it shall ever last and dwell in all their minds continually, that be called to work in this work. Nay, so it is not. . . . And this is one of the readiest and sovereignest tokens that a soul may have to wit by, whether he be called or not to work in this work, if he feel after such a delaying and a long lacking of this work, that when it cometh suddenly as it doth, unpurchased with any means, that he hath then a greater fervour of desire and greater love longing to work in this work, than ever he had any before. Insomuch, that ofttimes I trow, he hath more joy of the finding thereof than ever he had sorrow of the losing"[153].

The author gives the reason for this certainty as regards this test, taking as his authority St. Gregory the Great.

> "And Saint Gregory to witness, that all holy desires grow by delays: and if they wane by delays, then were they never holy desires. For he that feeleth ever less joy and less, in new findings and sudden presentations of his old purposed desires, although they may be called natural desires to the good, nevertheless, holy desires were they never. Of this holy desire speaketh Saint Austin and saith, that all the life of a good Christian man is nought else but holy desire"[154].

The author further develops this "holy desire" in his descriptions of the perfection of "This Work".

In *Privy Counsel* the author expounds on this continuing desire as a test for the presence of the grace to do "This Work". Now he puts them in the context of the concrete life of the disciple. We note again the use by the author of the anticipated question and answer, which is a favourite device of his.

> "Thou mayest ask me this question: By what one token, or more if thou likest, tell me, may I soonest know without error whether this growing desire that I feel in mine each day's working, and this liking stirring that I have in reading and hearing of this matter, be verily a calling of God to a more special working of grace, as is the matter of this writing; or whether it is a nourishing and a feeding of my spirit to bide

---

[153] *The Cloud*, Ch. 75, Underhill, pp. 268-269; Hodgson, 131: 18, 132: 16.
[154] Ibid. Ch. 75, Underhill, pp. 269-270; Hodgson, 132: 20, 133: 1-3.

still and work forth in my common grace, this that thou callest the door and the common entry of all Christian men?"[155].

To this anticipated question the author answers:

"To this I answer so feebly as I can. Thou seest well here that I set thee here in this writing two kinds of evidences, by the which thou shalt prove thy ghostly calling of God as to this work, one within and another without"[156].

And there is a further check on these two kinds of evidence. Both these evidences must concur, the presence of one without the other is not enough.

"Of the which two, neither may suffice in this case fully, as methinketh, without that other. But where they both be together one and according, then is thine evidence full enough without any failing"[157].

The author goes on to analyse these evidences.

"The first of these two evidences, the which is within, is this growing desire that thou feelest in thine each day's working. . . . Behold then busily to thine each day's exercise, what it is in itself. And then if it be the thought of thy wretchedness, the passion of Christ, or any such that belongeth to the common entry of Christian men touched before—then if it so be that this ghostly sight, that thus commoneth and followeth with thy blind desire, rise from these common beholdings, surely then it is a token to me that the growing of this desire is but a nourishing and a feeding of thy spirit to bide still and to work forth in thy common grace, and no calling nor stirring of God to any more special grace"[158].

The content of this "desire" is the criterion for the presence of this grace. This content is bound up with the object of the "prayer and meditations" of "This Work". In this case the content of the "desire" is that which makes up the "lower part of the contemplative life" as well as that of "imperfect meekness" which is not that of "This Work".

In the same manner the author gives certain indications regarding the *external evidence*, what they are not in connection with "This Work". We see, then, how consistently the author follows his predilection for discussing a matter in two

---

155 *Privy Counsel*, McCann, p. 133; Hodgson, 164: 15-23.
156 Ibid. McCann, p. 133; Hodgson, 164: 24-27.
157 Ibid. McCann, p. 133; Hodgson, 164: 27-28, 165: 1-2.
158 Ibid. McCann, pp. 133-134; Hodgson, 165: 3-20.

ways, that which it is not and, finally, that which it is.

"Now touching the second evidence, if it so be that this liking stirring, that thou feelest in hearing and reading of this matter, last nor continue no longer with thee, but only for the time of thy reading or hearing, and ceaseth then or else soon after, so that thou neither wakest nor sleepest therein nor therewith, and especially it followeth thee not in thy quotidian exercise, as it were going and pressing betwixt thee and it, stirrring and leading thy desire—then it is a true token in my conceit that this liking stirring, that thou feelest in hearing and reading of this matter, is but a natural gladness that every Christian soul hath in hearing or reading of the truth . . ."[159]

In a negative way, then, the author starts to intimate the characteristic quality of mystical experience, which is the *felt* dominance and intransigence of this continual presence of the Divine[160]. Furthermore, if the considerations regarding this external evidence have to do with less than the "naked Being of God", then there is proof again that one so occupied does not possess the grace for "This Work".

". . . (and especially of that the which touchest subtly and declareth verily the properties of perfection that most be according to the soul of man, and especially of God) and no ghostly touching of grace, nor calling of God to any other more special working of grace than is that the which is the door and the common entry to Christian men"[161].

We know that in the perfection of "This Work", the author identifies this "naked Being of God" with the "Presence of God". Needless to say that in this stage this *felt presence* need not be of the same *intensity* as that to be verified in its perfection. But then it must be already something of "this naked Being of God", different in kind from that of the lower forms of prayer. Perhaps we can use an analogy from the world of botany, and say that the difference must be in the same way as the seed of one plant differs from the seed of another.

Having described this external evidence by saying what it is not, the author gives a catalogue of objective signs by which this external evidence can be verified. The following passage deserves to be quoted at length:

[159] Ibid. McCann, p. 134; Hodgson, 165: 25-26, 166: 1-8.
[160] A. Poulain, *The Graces of Interior Prayer*, pp. 64-65.
[161] *Privy Counsel*, McCann, pp. 134-135; Hodgson, 166: 8-13.

"But if it so be that this liking stirring that thou feeleth in reading and hearing of this matter be so abounding in itself that it goeth with thee to bed, it riseth with thee at morrow, it followeth thee forth all the day in all that thou dost; it reaveth thee from thy quotidian wonted exercise and goeth between thee and it, it commoneth and followeth with thy desire, insomuch that thou thinkest it all one desire or thou knowest never what, it changeth thy gesture, and maketh thy countenance seemly; while it lasteth all things please thee and nothing may grieve thee; a thousand miles wouldst thou run to converse mouthly with one that thou knewest verily felt it; and yet, when thou comest there, canst thou nothing say, speak whoso speak will, for thou wouldst not speak but of it; few be thy words, but full of fruit and fire; a short word of thy mouth containeth a worldful of wisdom, yet seemeth it but folly to them that dwell in their own wits; thy silence is soft, thy speech full speedful, thy prayer is privy, thy pride full pure, thy manners be meek, thy mirth full mild, thy list is liking to play with a child; thou lovest to be alone and sit by thyself; men would hinder thee, thou thinkest, unless they wrought with thee; thou wouldst not read books nor hear books but only of it—then thine inward evidence and also thine outer were both according and knitting in one"[162].

It is interesting to note that the tests the author gives have relevance not only for one who is a *solitary*. The different descriptive acts can be verified also in one who does not live a *solitary life*, and when we know how well the author insists on a great care for recollection, for solitude, for simplification of everything that has to do with "This Work", for detachment, then we marvel how all these tests can be verified. But we think that the key to the understanding can be found in the qualification towards the middle of the above passage when he writes, "if you are willing to run a thousand miles to talk to someone else who, you know, hast truly felt all this". The test is in the *actual experiencing* of these various occurrences. However, we think that while the life of a *solitary* demands silence and solitude, there are times when all these acts can be seen to shine through, for we know that visitors used to come to the anchorhold to have conversations on the spiritual life with the recluse. We see, too, in this passage the *dominance* and the *intransigence* of the experience of the *habitual presence of* God which has engulfed the whole conscious life

162 Ibid. McCann, p. 135; Hodgson, 166: 14-26, 167: 1-7.

of the mystics. And there is, too, the application of the traditional monastic view of the mystical life prevailing in the 14th century which is quite simply the last rung on the ladder of charity, which is loving God to the highest degree possible in this life. This seems to be quite a long list, but we think that once the "special grace" is there, all these can somehow be verified. For these tests are inseparably linked with this "special enabling grace", so that once this "special grace" is granted, the fact of this Divine Intervention can be verified. And while we find difficulty in trying to explain the full meaning and impact of this passage, we think that the disciple whom the author said had the grace to do "This Work" would have understood it completely. For between them there must have been an area of understanding proper to them, which we as outsiders would not have any idea about. And so we leave the catalogue of these tests and let the author speak for himself as we have always desired. We think that one who had a comparable grace would be able to grasp the meaning and content of this passage[163].

In *Privy Counsel* the author further explains and amplifies the test which he gives in *The Cloud*. This concerns the temporary withdrawal of the grace, and subsequently finding it again. More specifically the author gives the reason for this temporary absence of The Lord, which is in the heart of mystical experiences.

"Yea! and if both these evidences with all their supporters written now here—from the time that thou once have had them all or any of them—cease for a time, and thou be left as thou wert barren, thou thinkest, as well from the feeling of this new fervour as from thine old wonted work, so that thou thinkest thee fallen down betwixt the two, having neither, but wanting them both: yet be not over heavy for this. . . ."[164].

In explaining this temporary absence of the Lord the author makes a clear distinction between the sensible feelings of consolation and the innermost experiences that take place in the soul which are not discernible to the senses.

"But all these sensible sweetnesses, these fervent feelings, and

---

[163] It is interesting to note the close similarity of description of the mystical life that the above passage gives, to that of a modern author. G. Thils, *Christian Holiness*. p. 544.
[164] *Privy Counsel*, McCann, p. 136; Hodgson, 167: 8-13.

these flaming desires—the which in themselves be not grace, but tokens of grace—these be oftentimes withdrawn in proving of our patience, and oftentimes for our other many ghostly profits, more than we ween. For grace in itself is so high, so pure, and so ghostly, that it may not be felt in our sensible part. The tokens thereof may, but not it. And thus sometimes our Lord will withdraw thy sensible fervours, both for increasing and proving of thy patience; and not only for this reason, but for many others, the which I set not here at this time"[165].

There is a further reason which lies with the Lord Himself. For He wants to know just how faithful the soul could be when He pretends to go away and abandon, seemingly, the soul.

"And since he sometimes goeth and sometimes cometh, therefore doubly in this double work will he privily prove thee and work thee to his own work. By the withdrawing of thy fervour, the which thou thinkest is his going, although it be not so, will he properly prove thy patience"[166].

The author makes a startling claim when he intimates the indefectibility of this grace once it has been given, as well as its efficacy to lead the soul to perfection.

"For know thou right well, that though God sometimes withdraw these sensible sweetnesses, these fervent feelings, and these flaming desires, nevertheless he withdraweth never the rather his grace in his chosen. For surely I may not believe that his special grace may ever be withdrawn from his chosen, that once have been touched therewith, unless deadly sin were in the cause"[167].

Finally the author makes a qualification regarding the verification of these tests. Like "This Work" which has varying degrees of intensity, so these tests need not appear all at the same time. But the presence of one or two of them gradually, progressively, is enough to assure the soul that it has the "special grace" for "This Work".

"And then from the time be that thou, or any other like unto thee as in spirit, have had very experience of all these tokens or any of them—for at the first time there be but full few that be so specially touched and marked with this grace that they may have soon or suddenly in very feeling the proof of them all; nevertheless it sufficeth to have some one or two, though a

165 Ibid. McCann, p. 137;Hodgson, 168: 19-24, 169: 1-4.
166 Ibid. McCann, p. 137; Hodgson, 168: 10-14.
167 Ibid. McCann, p. 137; Hodgson, 168: 14-19.

man have not all at the first time—and therefore if thou feel that thou hast true experience of one or of two, proved by true examination of Scripture, and of counsel, and of conscience: then it is speedful to thee some time for to cease from these quaint meditations and these subtle imaginations of the qualities of thy being and of God's, and of the works of thyself and of God (in the which thy wits have been fed, and with the which thou hast been led from worldliness and bodilyness to that ableness of grace that thou art in) for to learn how thou shalt be occupied ghostly in feeling of thyself or of God, whom thou hast learned so well before by thinking and imagining of thy doings"[168].

These then are the *tests* which the author gives to know the presence of this *Divine Initiative*, this *Direct Intervention of God*. In the bigger context of *Spiritual Theology* these tests, together with the treatises, *Discretion of Stirrings*, and *Knowing of Spirits*, make up the author's contribution to what spiritual writers call *Rules on the Discernment of Spirits*.

The next question that comes to mind is the person on whom this *Divine Choice* may fall, on whom these *tests* may be verified.

G.   WHO MAY BE CHOSEN FOR "THIS WORK"*.

For all the *Transcendence* and *Absolute Freedom* of God, we have seen that He can make known His desires and choices in favour of whom He wants, when He wants, and in whatever way He wants. In this section we shall see that the author teaches that this *Divine Choice* may fall on anyone. The only reason is His Love. But of course the author did not treat the matter as summarily and as simply as that. The *tests* apply the principle of Fr. Poulain that "we must have recourse to characters which are immediately verifiable",[169] and in answering the question as to who may do "This Work", the safe answer would be "the one on whom the tests may be verified". The author says that anyone could be called to "This Work".

"All those should work in this grace and in this work whatsoever that they be; whether they have been accustomed sinners or none"[170].

---

[168] Ibid. McCann, pp. 138-139; Hodgson, 170: 7-23.
* First published in the Autumn 1969 issue of *Mount Carmel*.
[169] A. Poulain, *The Graces of Interior Prayer*, p. 97.
[170] *The Cloud*, Ch. 27, Underhill, p. 141; Hodgson, 63: 6-7.

It does not depend on the personal worth and merit of the person so chosen. But there are certain conditions which must be met.

"If thou asketh me who shall work thus, I answer thee—all that have forsaken the world in a true will, and thereto that give them not to active life, but to that life that is called contemplative life"[171].

In stressing this condition the author merely restates his teaching that "This Work" can be done only in the life that is strictly "contemplative", as well as the "ghostly" character of "This Work". We do not limit the Ways of God in the sense that "This Work" may not be done in any other life. What we say is that as far as the teaching of *The Cloud of Unknowing* is concerned, "This Work" can be done only in the "contemplative life". The author mentions specifically himself and the disciple as having received the grace for "This Work".

"And since we be both called of God to work in this work, I beseech thee for God's love fulfill in thy part what lacketh in mine"[172].

The author emphasizes the fact that this grace is not given for anything that the soul has done. "For neither it is given for innocence, nor witholden for sin"[173]. Indeed, the author expressly says that a sinner could be called for "This Work" and could reach the perfection of "This Work" sooner than an innocent soul.

"Nevertheless, oftimes it befalleth that some that have been horrible and accustomed sinners come sooner to the perfection of this work than those that have been none. And this is the merciful miracle of our Lord, that so specially giveth His grace, to the wondering of all this world"[174].

This is indeed a daring claim. But that is what it is. Who can limit the *Divine Power* and *Mercy*? The author supports his statement with a look to the Last Day.

"Now truly I hope that on Doomsday it shall be fair, when that God shall be seen clearly and all His gifts. Then shall some that now be despised and set at little or nought as common sinners, and peradventure some that now be horrible sinners,

171 Ibid. Ch. 27, Underhill, p. 141; Hodgson, 63: 3-6.
172 Ibid. Ch. 73, Underhill, p. 263; Hodgson, 129: 10-12.
173 Ibid. Ch. 34, Underhill, p. 154; Hodgson, 69: 15-16.
174 Ibid. Ch. 29, Underhill, pp. 144-145; Hodgson, 64: 17-20.

sit full seemly with saints in His sight: when some of those
that seem now full holy and be worshipped of men as angels,
and some of those yet peradventure, that never yet sinned
deadly, shall sit full sorry amongst hell caves"[175].

This passage stresses the fact of the *Divine Mercy*. The
author does not depreciate those who live good and holy lives
as such. But he has other people in mind. This he makes clear.

"Hereby mayest thou see that no man should be judged of
other here in this life, for good nor evil that they do.
Nevertheless deeds may lawfully be judged but not the man,
whether they be good or evil"[176].

He stresses the fact obliquely when he names those who do
not possess the grace to do "This Work". Those who offend
against the virtue of Charity, which is one of the twin virtues
on which the author insists, are not meant for "This Work".

"Some men the fiend will deceive in this manner. Full wonderfully he will enflame their brains to maintain God's law and to
destroy sin in all other men. He will never tempt them with a
thing that is openly evil; he maketh them like busy prelates
watching over all the degrees of Christian men's living, as an
abbot over his monks. All men will they reprove of their
defaults, right as they had cure of their souls: and yet they think
that they do not else for God, unless they tell them their faults
that they see. And they say that they be stirred thereto by the
fire of charity, and of God's love in their hearts: and truly they
lie, for it is with the fire of hell welling in their brains and in
their imagination"[177].

On the other hand, the author does not exclude a converted
sinner. In fact he describes God's special action on their
behalf. In the passages where he makes a contrast between
"both sinners, and innocents that never sinned greatly",[178]
"those that have been sinners than they that have been
none",[179] "common sinners . . . horrible sinners . . . some of
those yet peradventure, that never yet sinned deadly",[180] he
does not mean simply that acute sense that mystics have of
their own sins as well as those of others[181]. He makes this clear

175 Ibid. Ch. 29, Underhill, p. 145; Hodgson, 64: 21-22, 65: 1-6.
176 Ibid. Ch. 29, Underhill, p. 145; Hodgson, 65: 7-9.
177 Ibid. Ch. 55, Underhill, p. 214; Hodgson, 102: 7-17.
178 Ibid. Ch. 29, Underhill, p. 144; Hodgson, 64: 14-15.
179 Ibid. Ch. 29, Underhill, p. 144; Hodgson, 64: 15-16.
180 Ibid. Ch. 29, Underhill, p. 145; Hodgson, 65: 1-5.
181 See C. Pepler, *The English Religious Heritage*, pp. 251-252.

in the story of Mary. He connects the story and example of Mary as regards the *Divine Choice*. One so chosen must not be afraid of "consenting to this grace" nor consider it presumptuous to undertake so high a work.

"Look that no man think it presumption, that he that is the wretchedest sinner of this life dare take upon him after the time be that he have lawfully amended him, and after that he have felt him stirred to that life that is called contemplative, by the assent of his counsel and his conscience for to profer a meek stirring of love to his God, privily pressing upon the cloud of unknowing betwixt him and his God. When our Lord said to Mary, in person of all sinners that be called to contemplative life, 'Thy sins be forgiven thee,' it was not for her great sorrow, nor for the remembering of her sins, nor yet for her meekness that she had in the beholding of her wretchedness only. But why then? Surely because she loved much"[182].

It is true that *The Cloud* author gives a very highly spiritualized interpretation to the story of Mary and Martha, equating "This Work" with the "best part that Mary chose". Still, we must not forget that the life history of Mary is part of the teaching of *The Cloud* author. He makes this even clearer in the incident between our Lord and Simon the Leper.

"And if a man list for to see in the gospel written the wonderful and the special love that our Lord had to her, in person of all accustomed sinners truly turned and called to the grace of contemplation, he shall find that our Lord might not suffer any man or woman—yea, not her own sister—speak a word against her, but if He answered for her Himself. Yea, and what more? He blamed Symon Leprous in his own house, for that he thought against her. This was great love: this was passing love"[183].

Surely Simon did not think of *Mary The Contemplative*. The Gospel describes her as "a woman . . . who had a bad name in the town"[184]. And what was the thought of Simon as he beheld Mary anointing our Lord, weeping? "If this man were a prophet, he would know who this woman is that is touching him, and what a bad name she has"[185]. Our Lord Who read Simon's thought, answered for, and defended, Mary.

[182] *The Cloud*, Ch. 16, Underhill, p. 109; Hodgson, 44: 16-22, 45: 1-4.
[183] Ibid. Ch. 22, Underhill, p. 129; Hodgson, 56: 3-10.
[184] *Luke*, 7: 37.
[185] Ibid. 7: 39.

The Gospel narrative ends with the forgiveness of Mary's sins, which again aroused a reaction from the others at the table with him.

"Then he said to her, 'Your sins are forgiven'. Those who were with him at table began to say to themselves, 'Who is this man, that he even forgives sins?' But he said to the woman, 'Your faith has saved you: go in peace' "[186].

The past sinfulness of Mary is distinguished from the sorrow she afterwards felt. *The Cloud* author makes this clear, just as there is the "deep ghostly sorrow" involved in the perfection of "This Work".

"Surely as Mary did. She although she might not feel the deep hearty sorrow of her sins—for why, all her lifetime she had them with her whereso she went, as it were in a burthen bounden together and laid up full privily in the hole of her heart, in manner never to be forgotten—nevertheless yet, it may be said and affirmed by Scripture, that she had a more hearty sorrow, a more doleful desire, and a more deep sighing and more she languished, yea! almost to the death, for lacking of love, although she had full much love (and have no wonder thereof, for it is the condition of a true lover that ever the more he loveth, the more he longeth for to love), than she had for any remembrance of her sins"[187].

The author makes the consideration of one's sinfulness and wretchedness the object of "imperfect meekness".

"One is the filth, the wretchedness, and the frailty of man, into the which he is fallen by sin; and the which always him behoveth to feel in some part the whiles he liveth in this life, be he never so holy"[188].

As regards the *pain* and *travail* involved in "This Work", the author distinguishes between "thy former special sins" and "the pain of the original sin".

"I mean, of the pain of thy special foredone sins, and not of the pain of the original sin. For that pain shall always last on thee to thy death day, be thou never so busy"[189].

The author then has chosen to develop in his teaching the choice of a sinner turned contemplative for "This Work". In

186 Ibid. 7: 48-50.
187 *The Cloud*, Ch. 16, Underhill, pp. 110-111; Hodgson, 45: 12-22.
188 Ibid. Ch. 13, Underhill, pp. 100-101; Hodgson, 40: 11-14.
189 Ibid. Ch. 33, Underhill, pp. 151-152; Hodgson, 68: 3-5.

the presence of such a tremendous grace involving a *Personal Choice* by God, what should be the attitude of the sinner now turned contemplative? The first attitude should be that of gratitude and to acknowledge that the choice did not depend on the personal worth of the soul.

"If thou be called, give praising unto God and pray that thou fall not"[190].

Despite his insistence on this *Personal Choice* by God and the need for a "special grace", the author likewise teaches that the grace for "This Work" is a legitimate object for prayer.

"And if thou be not yet called, pray meekly to God that he call thee when his will is"[191].

Surely, this *Divine Choice* cannot be an occasion for pride.

"Beware, thou wretch, in this while with thine enemy; and hold thee never the holier nor the better, for the worthiness of this calling and for the singular form of living that thou art in"[192].

Then, one so chosen should forget the past and look forward to the future.

"Look now forwards and let be backwards; and all what thee faileth, and not what thou hast, for that is the readiest getting and keeping of meekness"[193].

Another reason for forgetting past sins can be gathered from the psychological effect of dwelling on them. Thinking of them continually could easily bring about occasions for new sins. We know that in "This Work" any other thought than "the naked Being of God" can only distract the soul. How much more could the memory of past sins bring about uneasiness and restlessness?

"But what thereof? Came she therefore down from the height of desire into the deepness of her sinful life, and searched in the foul stinking fen and dunghill of her sins; searching them

---

190 *Privy Counsel*, McCann, p. 131; Hodgson, 161 : 24-25.
191 Ibid. McCann, p. 131; Hodgson, 161 : 25-26. It seems that Professor Knowles overlooked this passage when he made the following observation regarding *The Cloud* author and Walter Hilton: " . . . Neither of them directly faces and answers the question, which would seem to arise inevitably, whether all devout Christians may aspire, and hope to receive enablement, to attain to the mystical life". (D. Knowles, *The English Mystical Tradition*, p. 191).
192 *The Cloud*, Ch. 2, Underhill, p. 61; Hodgson, 14 : 20-21, 15 : 1.
193 Ibid. Ch. 2, Underhill, p. 62; Hodgson, 15 : 10-12.

up, by one and by one, with all the circumstances of them, and sorrowed and wept so upon them each one by itself? Nay, surely, she did not so. And why? Because God let her wit by his grace within her soul, that she should never so bring it about. For so might she sooner have raised in herself an ableness to have oft sinned, than to have purchased by that work any plain forgiveness of all her sins"[194].

The part that Sacramental Confession plays in "This Work" becomes clearer with this teaching of the author on sinners called to the contemplative life. It is in *Knowing of Spirits* that we have the teaching of the author as regards the efficacy of Sacramental Confession.

"For fast after confession a soul is, as it were, a clean paper leaf, for ableness that it hath to receive what that men will write thereupon. Both they do press for to write on the soul, when it is clean in itself made by confession: God and His angel on the one party, and the fiend and his angel on the other party, but it is in the free choice of the soul to receive which that it will . . . for why, there is no such thing written in thy soul, for all it is wasted away before in thy shrift, and thy soul left naked and bare; nothing left thereupon, but a frail and a free consent, more inclining to the evil, for custom therein, than it is to the good, but more able to the good than to the evil, for cleanness of the soul and virtue of the sacrament of shrift . . ."[195].

The author then describes this transformation of a sinner turned contemplative.

"Nevertheless yet, for all this thraldom to sin and devilishness in office, it may by grace of contrition, of shrift, and of amending, recover the freedom again, and be made saveable—yea, and a full special God's saint in this life, that before was full damnable and full cursed in the living"[196].

Finally the author looks far beyond the barrier of time and sees the reason for the choice of a sinner for "This Work". Now the whole picture is seen in the context of the Last Judgment. For in this life the sinner turned contemplative had only one desire and that was to show that God is ALL. So now in the end God will glorify the soul in turn in the presence of all men.

---

194 Ibid. Ch. 16, Underhill, p. 111; Hodgson, 46: 5-14.
195 *Knowing of Spirits*, Gardner, pp. 130-131; Hodgson, 90: 22, 91: 1-15. Walter Hilton describes the role of Sacramental Confession in relation to the "reforming in faith". *Scale II*, Chapters 7, 8, 9, 10, Underhill, pp. 245-259.
196 *Knowing of Spirits*, Gardner, p. 129; Hodgson, 90: 7-11.

"And this I trow he will do full graciously in chosen souls. For he will worthily be known in the end, to the wondering of all the world. For such a soul, thus lovely noughting itself and thus alling his God, shall full graciously be kept from all casting down by his ghostly or bodily enemies, without business or travail of itself, only by the goodness of God. As the godly reason asketh, that he truly keep all these that for business about his love forsake and care not to keep themselves. And no wonder that they be marvellously kept, for they be so full meeked in boldness and strength of love"[197].

CONCLUSIONS

In this chapter we have seen that the author was, as it were, bursting with thoughts of God. God is the end of "This Work", this ascent to God which the author teaches. But for all his insistence on "the naked Being of God only for Himself" as the one and only consideration of "This Work", nevertheless he does not overlook the other traditional concepts of God. In fact he incorporates them all in *The Cloud* and *Privy Counsel* and other treatises, and makes reference to the works of the Pseudo-Dionysius where the Names of God are discussed and elaborated. "The naked Being of God" which the author discusses in *The Cloud* is further elaborated in *Privy Counsel* with the Proper Name of God as IS. For this Name is the Name that God gave of Himself to Moses. In *Privy Counsel,* the author explains the excellence of this Name of God. The "IS" of God stresses the *Immanence* of God as the *Universal Cause of All Things,* and is equivalent to the *Eternity* of God. This Name of God contains all the other Names and Attributes of God and is interpreted in the exegesis of the passage of Solomon, as the *primi et purissimi fructus eius.* And in *Privy Counsel* too, "the naked Being of God" is translated into terms of concrete reality as an offering, a spiritual exercise, and in *Discretion of Stirrings* all the different exercises of the spiritual life are seen in relation to God.

For all the insistence on the *Immanence* of God as the *Universal Cause of all Things,* the author likewise stresses the

---

[197] *Privy Counsel,* McCann, p. 121; Hodgson, 151 : 9-18.

Transcendence of God. A cursory reading of *The Cloud* can easily give the impression that the God of *The Cloud of Unknowing* is heavily metaphysical and theoretical. There are enough references to the Humanity of Jesus to dissipate this uneasiness. In fact meditations and considerations on the Humanity and the Passion of our Lord are pre-requisites for the higher form of prayer which "This Work" involves. These meditations form part of the whole process, though in the earlier stages before the "special call". The author uses very strong images to stress this condition. But always realizing the *Absolute Freedom* of God, the author stresses the fact that God can dispense with this pre-requisite and grant the *special grace* even without this condition, in the same way that He remains free to withold the *special grace* even when all these conditions have been verified.

In the context of "This Work" the author makes a distinction as regards those called to "salvation" and those called to "perfection". The meditations on the Humanity and Passion of our Lord are for those who are called to "salvation", while "This Work" is for those called to "perfection". In the light of the Universal Call to Perfection, having in mind the teaching of the Constitution of the Second Vatican Council *On The Church, Lumen Gentium,* we see the author making the distinction between the life of prayer and the higher reaches of the mystical life. "Perfection" in the sense of *The Cloud of Unknowing* is limited to the perfection of "This Work", and therefore has to do with the higher reaches of the mystical life. But for all his desires to equate "This Work" with the mystical life, nowhere does he say that it is *the only way* to perfection.

God is the Object and End of "This Work". Because of His Transcendence as well as the Nature of "This Work", we can expect that the only initiative to the undertaking of an ascent to Him must be made by God Himself. One cannot presume to make the start. It is God who issues the call and invitation, and this *Divine Initiative* the author calls "a special grace", "the privy teaching of the Spirit of God". We have noted the different distinctions in terms that later theologians have made. However, without using the terms of latterday theology, distinctions actually existed in the mind of the author when he described this intervention of God as involving a "special grace". But for all his insistence on the need of a "special grace", the author likewise teaches that this, too, may be lawfully petitioned in prayer. The solutions that the author gives as regards the problem of the *Omnipotence of God* and the *freedom of the Will* are more practical than theoretical, and we think that if he were asked precisely to explain his side, he might have answered in his characteristic fashion, "I wot not". From the nature of "This Work" and the special intervention of God, we see that the author teaches complete "passivity" in the Hand of God although he does not lessen or discount the part of man involved in the pain and the travail of the ascent.

Since the initiative must first come from God, we can expect that God can make known his desires and wishes. And so we have the "Tests" for the presence of this "special grace". This "call to perfection" is needed right at the start of "This Work", not only at the later stages. We shall see later on that at the perfection of the state in "the cloud of unknowing", God will come through with a still more special intervention to "pierce this cloud of unknowing".

The tests given by the author are quite objective and exhaustive. The catalogue of indications may seem ponderous, indeed, but we think that once the "special call" is there, the tests will somehow be verifiable. Like "This Work" which grows in intensity, so it is not necessary that all these tests be verified right at the beginning. It is enough if one or two of the signs be experienced. But there is one test on which he insists, namely, that the internal and external evidences must concur. The presence of one without the other is not enough.

Finally, the author is true to his message of heroic hope and encouragement. While he teaches that the *Divine Choice* can fall on anyone at all, the author teaches that sinners, too, could be called to do "This Work" and could even reach perfection sooner than those who never sinned grievously. For this, the author gives the example of Mary Magdalene. And from her the sinner turned contemplative must take heart and courage. In these passages, full of hope and encouragement, the author literally means those who had actually sinned whom God had chosen to pick up and raise to intimate friendship with Him. The author does not mean just that very acute sense of sin which mystics have of their own sinfulness and those of others. He makes very clear contrasts to stress this point. In the light of this claim we see the value of Sacramental Confession. This is the only Sacrament that the author deals with in *The Cloud* and other treatises. But the author minces no words to remind his disciple that such a *Divine Choice* cannot be an occasion for pride. Rather, it should be an incentive for courage and humility, and for effort to accomplish his part ir "This Work".

CHAPTER V

The Cloud of Forgetting

A.   "FORGETTING ALL"

We have been moving gradually towards the matter most intimately connected with "This Work". Considering the matters and problems that put *The Cloud* in its proper setting we have discussed the nature of "This Work", and seen in the last chapter that the *Divine Initiative* can only come from God, Who gives "special grace" to whomever He wishes. With this grace comes a corresponding *ableness* to do "This Work".

In this chapter we shall see the part that most properly belongs to man. Indeed, the "privy teaching of the Spirit of God" is needed even to start "This Work". But the soul so chosen cannot entertain the thought that he can be idle. The author uses expressions denoting strength and vigour to describe the part of man, to "stand stiffly . . . against all the subtle assailing of thy bodily and ghostly enemies . . ."[1] "to lift up the foot of thy love"[2] "and keep thou the windows and the door, for flies and enemies assailing . . . Press on then, let see how thou bearest thee"[3]. With the Divine Call which the author says is present in the disciple, "He is full ready and doth abideth thee"[4]. In this chapter we see the response of the disciple to this call, "But what shalt thou do, and how shalt thou press?"[5]. Even with this more general description of the part of the soul, we can see that we can rule out any form of idleness or "quietism"[6].

1 *The Cloud*, Prologue, Underhill, p. 58; Hodgson, 13: 4-6.
2 Ibid. Ch. 1, Underhill, p. 60; Hodgson, 14: 13-14.
3 Ibid. Ch. 2, Underhill, p. 62; Hodgson, 15: 19-21, 16: 1.
4 Ibid. Ch. 2, Underhill, p. 62; Hodgson, 16: 1.
5 Ibid. Ch. 2, Underhill, p. 62; Hodgson, 16: 1-2.
6 Walter Hilton has a similar passage to show that his particular teaching on contemplation cannot be called "idleness". "This restful travail is full far from fleshly idleness and from blind security. It is full of ghostly work; but it is called rest, for grace looseth the heavy yoke of fleshly love from the soul, and maketh it mighty and free through the gift of the Holy Ghostly love, for to work gladly, softly and delectably in all things that grace stirreth it for to work in. And therefore it is called an holy idleness and a rest most busy; and so is it, *in stillness* from the great crying and the beastly noise of fleshly desires and unclean thoughts". *Scale II*, Ch. 40, Underhill, p. 418.

The author uses the expression "the cloud of forgetting" to describe the part of the soul, and the perfection of this state is a complete emptiness of the mind as regards everything except the "naked thought of God only for Himself". This part involves labour and can be accomplished progressively. However, the complete obliteration can be done only by God Himself when He makes the soul attain to this perfection, even if it be only for a brief moment. This state, represented by the figure of "the cloud of forgetting", marks the *sixth character* of the mystical life, namely "that the contemplation of God is not produced by reasonings, or by the consideration of created things, or by interior images of the sensible order"[7].

Considering the part that most properly belongs to the soul, the author enumerates successively the things that must be hidden under "the cloud of forgetting". The author makes no exceptions. Everything must be covered by the "cloud of forgetting".

"As oft I say, all the creatures that ever be made, as oft I mean not only the creatures themselves, but also all the works and the conditions of the same creatures. I take out not one creature, whether they be bodily creatures or ghostly, nor yet any condition or work of any creature, whether they be good or evil: but shortly to say, all should be hid under the cloud of forgetting in this case"[8].

The meaning of the author cannot be mistaken. He goes to great lengths to explain his assertion and enumerates what must be covered by the "cloud of forgetting". The author's bare statement is sufficient in itself, but he would not be misunderstood and enumerates the things to be completely "forgotten". Even the *Attributes of God* must be hidden by this "cloud of forgetting".

". . . and therefore, although it be good sometime to think of the kindness and the worthiness of God in special, and although it be a light and a part of contemplation: nevertheless yet in this work it shall be cast down and covered with a cloud of forgetting. And thou shalt step above it stalwartly, but listily, with a devout and a pleasing stirring of love, and try for to pierce that darkness above thee"[9].

[7] A. Poulain, *The Graces of Interior Prayer*, p. 122.
[8] *The Cloud*, Ch. 5, Underhill, pp. 74-75; Hodgson, 24: 9-14.
[9] Ibid. Ch. 6, Underhill, pp. 77-78; Hodgson, 26: 5-11.

If the *Attributes of God* must be "forgotten", so must any lesser thing, including thoughts then of Our Lady, the saints and the angels.

"Yea! and, if it be courteous and seemly to say, in this work it profiteth little or nought to think of the kindness or the worthiness of God, nor on our Lady, nor on the saints or angels in heaven, nor yet on the joys in heaven: that is to say, with a special beholding to them, as thou wouldest by that beholding feed and increase thy purpose. I trow that on nowise it should help in this case and in this work. For although it be good to think upon the kindness of God, and to love Him and praise Him for it, yet it is far better to think upon the naked being of Him, and to love Him and praise Him for Himself"[10].

In *Privy Counsel* the author makes the disciple offer *his own being* as an act of love to God, and what could be considered in *The Cloud* as simply an act of *forgetting* is here translated into a spiritual exercise. And in the same way that the *Attributes of God* must be hidden, so also must all the attributes of man. Only the thought of *one's own being* must remain.

"But it sufficeth now unto thee to do whole worship unto God with thy substance, and for to offer up the naked being, the which is the first of thy fruits, in continued sacrifice of praising of God, both for thyself and for all others, as charity asketh; not clothed with any quality or special beholding that on any manner pertaineth or may pertain to the being of thyself or of any other. . . ."[11].

In *Privy Counsel,* too, we see a progression and a greater unification of the consideration of the "naked Being of God". As the author develops his message in *Privy Counsel* he comes to a point where he tells the disciple that even his "naked feeling of your own being" must be "forgotten", and only "the naked Being of God" remain.

"For although I bid theee in the beginning, because of thy boisterousness and thy ghostly rudeness, lap and clothe the feeling of thy God in the feeling of thyself, yet shalt thou after, when thou art made by continuance more subtle in cleanness of spirit, strip, spoil, and utterly unclothe thyself of all manner of feeling of thyself, that thou mayest be able to be clothed with the gracious feeling of God himself"[12].

10 Ibid. Ch. 5, Underhill, pp. 75-76; Hodgson, 25 : 4-12.
11 *Privy Counsel*, McCann, pp. 111-112; Hodgson, 142 : 1-6.
12 Ibid. McCann, p. 126; Hodgson, 156 : 9-15.

Since "the naked Being of God" is the only Object of "This Work", we can see the reason for the complete "forgetting" of all other things. Not only are they not the objects of "This Work" but the thought of any of them can hinder the progress of the soul.

> "And as unlawful a thing as it is, and as much as it would let a man that sat in his meditations, to have regard then to his outward bodily works, the which he had done, or else should do, although they were never so holy works in themselves: surely as unlikely a thing it is, and as much would it let a man that should work in this darkness and in this cloud of unknowing with an affectuous stirring of love to God for Himself, for to let any thought or any meditation of God's wonderful gifts, kindness, and works in any of His creatures bodily or ghostly, rise upon him to press betwixt him and his God; although they be never so holy thoughts, nor so profound, nor so comfortable"[13].

To think of anything other than the "naked Being of God" would result in a successive lowering of the attention of the mind away from the principal consideration of "This Work".

> "And there will he let thee see the wonderful kindness of God, and if thou hear him, he careth for nought better. For soon after he will let thee see thine old wretched living, and peradventure in seeing and thinking thereof, he will bring to thy mind some place that thou hast dwelt in before this time. So that at the last, or ever thou wit, thou shalt be scattered thou wottest not where. The cause of this scattering is, that thou heardest him first wilfully, then answeredest him, receivedest him, and lettest him alone"[14].

In his characteristic fashion the author does not deprecate these other things. He merely says that in "This Work" they do not help.

> "For although it be full profitable sometime to think of certain conditions and deeds of some certain special creatures, nevertheless yet in this work it profiteth little or nought. For why? . . . for the eye of thy soul is opened on it and even fixed thereupon, as the eye of a shooter is upon the prick that he shooteth to. And one thing I tell thee, that all thing that thou thinketh upon, it is above thee for the time, and betwixt thee and thy God: and insomuch thou art the further from God, that aught is in thy mind but only God"[15].

---

13 *The Cloud*, Ch. 8, Underhill, pp. 87-88; Hodgson, 32: 21-24, 33: 1-7.
14 Ibid. Ch. 7, Underhill, p. 80; Hodgson, 27: 3-14.
15 Ibid. Ch. 5, Underhill, p. 75; Hodgson, 24: 15-21, 25: 1-3.

The author finally gives a fundamental reason for this extreme "forgetting", in the context now of the Love of God:

> "Surely he that seeketh God perfectly, he will not rest him finally in the remembrance of any angel or saint that is in heaven"[16].

He gives the merits of the considerations other than the "naked Being of God".

> "And where thou asketh me thereof whether it be good or evil, I say that it behoveth always be good in its nature. For why, it is a beam of the likeness of God. But the use thereof may be both good and evil. Good, when it is opened by grace for to see thy wretchedness, the passion, the kindness, and the wonderful works of God in His creatures bodily and ghostly. And then it is no wonder though it increase thy devotion full much, as thou sayest. But then is the use evil, when it is swollen with pride and with curiosity of much clergy and letterly cunning as in clerks . . ."[17].

It will be seen that the work involved here is at the level of mind, and is described by the author as "the cloud of forgetting". This is just one phase. There is another, involving both pain and labour, which the author calls "travail".

B.   "TRAVAIL" IN "THIS WORK"

In the previous section we have seen that the "worker of This Work" is actively engaged in the act of "forgetting". Here, however, we shall see that the soul is more a sufferer than an active doer, although we shall see that in this part, too, he has some work to do. This will be his attempt to alleviate the painful condition. The author gives us a glimpse of the intensity of *travail* involved in "This Work". In these passages we are struck by the *experimental quality* of "This Work".

The author does not lessen the fact of the *travail* but puts it squarely before his disciple. He encourages him, however, by assuring him that it is God Who has called him even to this intense suffering.

> "Do on then, and travail fast awhile, I pray thee, and suffer meekly the pain if thou mayest not soon win to these arts. For truly it is thy pugatory, and then when thy pain is all passed and thy devices be given of God, and graciously gotten in

16 Ibid. Ch. 9, Underhill, p. 91; Hodgson, 35: 15-17.
17 Ibid. Ch. 8, Underhill, p. 84; Hodgson, 30: 5-13.

custom; then it is no doubt to me that thou art cleansed not only of sin, but also of the pain of sin"[18].

In the section on "the mights of the soul" we noted that while the will and its act of love have the primacy in "This Work", all the other "mights" have a part to play in the matter of the *pain* and *travail*. This comes about when the Memory brings to mind all the sins that the person had committed in his past life. And in addition to the *pain* brought about by the remembrance of past sins, there will always be the *pain* of Original Sin that will provide constant provocation and temptation.

"I mean, of the pain of thy special foredone sins, and not of the pain of the original sin. For that pain shall always last on thee to thy death day, be thou never so busy. Nevertheless, it shall but little provoke thee, in comparison of this pain of thy special sins; and yet shalt thou not be without great travail. For out of this original sin will all day spring new and fresh stirrings of sin: the which thee behoveth all day to smite down, and be busy to shear away with a sharp double-edged dreadful sword of discretion"[19].

The author distinguishes between the *pain* brought about by the memory of personal sins and Original Sin. The intensity of the *pain* occasioned by personal sin can lessen progressively as the soul gains perfection, but the *pain* of Original Sin will always be present to try the soul.

"And hereby mayest thou see and learn, that there is no soothfast security, nor yet no true rest in this life"[20].

This *pain* can be so intense that it can serve to induce the soul to turn back and abandon "This Work".

"For at the first time that a soul looketh thereupon, it shall find all the special deeds of sin that ever he did since he was born, bodily or ghostly, privily or darkly painted thereupon. And however that he turneth about, evermore they will appear before his eyes; until the time be, that with much hard travail, many sore sighings, and many bitter weepings, he have in great part washed them away. Sometime in this travail him think that it is to look thereupon as on hell; for him think that he despaireth to win to perfection of ghostly rest out of that pain.

---

18 Ibid. Ch. 33, Underhill, p. 151; Hodgson, 67: 20-22, 68: 1-3. Cf. Walter Hilton, *Qui Habitat*, Jones, p. 140.
19 *The Cloud*, Ch. 33, Underhill, pp. 151-152; Hodgson, 68: 3-11.
20 Ibid. Ch. 33, Underhill, p. 152; Hodgson, 68: 11-12.

Thus far inwards come many, but for greatness of pain that they feel and for lacking of comfort, they go back in beholding of bodily things: seeking fleshly comforts without, for lacking of ghostly they have not yet deserved, as they should if they had abided"[21].

As in "the cloud of forgetting" the complete obliteration of the memory of all creatures can be brought about only by God, so in this *travail* it is only God who can completely alleviate the *pain* involved.

There is still another form of *pain* and *travail* and this is in the consideration of one's being. This seems surprising that the consciousness of one's being and existence can be a matter of intense *pain* and *travail*. But that is what it is and, before the perfection of "This Work" can be reached, even the thought of one's own being must be "forgotten".

"For, an thou wilt busily set thee to the proof, thou shalt find when thou hast forgotten all other creatures and all their works —yea, and thereto all thine own works—that there shall live yet after, betwixt thee and thy God, a naked witting and a feeling of thine own being: the which witting and feeling behoveth always be destroyed, ere the time be that thou feel soothfastly the perfection of this work"[22].

It is characteristic of the author that he explains in such detail to his disciple the reason for the *pain* and *travail*. When one sins the right order of nature is reversed, so that when the soul finally wishes to take the road to perfection these past misdeeds stand in the way.

"And not only that, but in pain of the original sin it shall evermore see and feel that some of all the creatures that ever God made, or some of their works, will evermore press in remembrance betwixt it and God. And this is the right wisdom of God, that man, when he had sovereignty and lordship of all other creatures, because that he wilfully made him underling to the stirring of his subjects, leaving the bidding of God and his Maker; that right so after, when he would fulfil the bidding of God, he saw and felt all the creatures that should be beneath him, proudly press above him, betwixt him and his God"[23].

21 Ibid. Ch. 69, Underhill, pp. 252-253; Hodgson, 122: 19-23, 123: 1-9. Cf. Walter Hilton, *Scale II*, Ch. 28, Underhill, p. 348: *Scale II, Ch.* 23, Underhill, p. 316.
22 *The Cloud*, Ch. 43, Underhill, p. 179; Hodgson, 82: 22-23, 83: 1-5.
23 Ibid. Ch. 28, Underhill, p. 143; Hodgson, 63: 22-64: 1-9, Cf. Hilton, *Scale II*, Ch. 28, Underhill, pp. 348-349.

And he puts courage into his disciple's heart, bidding him not to give up but persevere even in this pain.

"Nevertheless, herefore shalt thou not go back, nor yet be over-feared of thy failing. For an it so be that thou mayest have grace to destroy the pain of thine foredone special deeds, in the manner before said—or better if thou better mayest—sure be thou, that the pain of the original sin, or else the new stirrings of sin that be to come, shall but right little be able to provoke thee"[24].

This *travail* is likewise a step towards the perfection of "This Work".

"And therefore, whoso coveteth to come to cleanness that he lost for sin, and to win to that well-being where all woe wanteth, him behoveth bidingly to travail in this work, and suffer the pain thereof, whatsoever that he be: whether he have been an accustomed sinner or none"[25].

Hence it is not just past sinfulness that is the cause of the *pain* and *travail*. The way of perfection likewise demands much sacrifice.

In *Privy Counsel* this *pain* and *travail* are more graphically described. He has a passage which for its descriptive detail can be taken to be autobiographical.

"And be not astonied with any unrestful dread, though the fiend (as he will) come with a sudden fearsomeness, pushing and beating on the walls of thy house where thou sittest; or though he stir any of his mighty limbs to rise and to run in upon thee suddenly as it is without any warning. . . . And all is done for to draw thee down from the height of this precious working"[26].

This is a very noteworthy passage for we have seen that the author is very chary of anything that smacks of the sensational in the spiritual life. We have seen how he insists that "This Work" is concerned with the "substance" of the spiritual life, in contrast to those phenomena involving the senses which pertain to the "accidents" of the spiritual life.

The author uses the image of a storm-tossed boat to express the state of the soul undergoing this terrible purgation.

"Many great storms and temptations, peradventure, shall rise

24 Ibid. Ch. 33, Underhill, p. 152; Hodgson, 68: 13-18.
25 Ibid. Ch. 29, Underhill, p. 144; Hodgson, 64: 10-13.
26 *Privy Counsel*, McCann, p. 118; Hodgson, 148: 13-22.

in this time, and thou knowest never whither to run for sorrow. All is away from thy feeling, common grace and special. Be not overmuch afraid, then, although thou have matter, as thou thinkest; but have a lovely trust in our Lord, so little as thou mayest get for the time, for he is not far. He shall look up, peradventure, right soon and touch thee again with a more fervent stirring of that same grace than ever thou feltest any before. Then art thou all whole and all is good enough, as thou thinkest, last while it last may. For suddenly, or ever thou knowest, all is away and thou left barren in the boat, blown with blundering blasts now hither and now thither, thou knowest never where nor whither"[27].

He keeps returning to his theme of heroic trust and hope. And we notice how tenderly he elicits this attitude from his disciple, not bludgeoning him into acceptance. For he reveals a thorough knowledge of the condition of the disciple, and while he suffers with him he makes very clear the reason for it.

"Yet be not abashed; for he shall come, I promise thee, full soon, when he liketh, to relieve thee and doughtily deliver thee of all thy dole, far more worthily than ever he did before. Yea! and if he after go, after will he come again; and each time, if thou wilt bear thee by meek suffering, will he come more worthlier and merrylier than other. And all this he doth because he will have thee made as pliant to his will ghostly as a roan glove to thine hand bodily"[28].

One is struck by the author's deep assurance, revealing his personal knowledge and experience. He even speaks for the Lord Himself which he could not do had he not experienced these comings and goings. His teaching on complete *passivity* in the Hands of the Lord could not be clearer.

With descriptions such as these to show the intensity of the *pain* and *travail* involved in "This Work", the thought that comes to mind is whether these refer to what St. John of the Cross calls "the dark nights of the soul". It seems natural to use St. John of the Cross as the reference for experiences of the spiritual life. Certainly in the narrations of St. John and *The Cloud* author on the trials of the soul there is great similarity of description. However, whilst it seems safe to say that what St. John of the Cross calls "nights of the soul" is des-

27 Ibid. McCann, p. 136; Hodgson, 167: 17-25, 168: 1-2.
28 Ibid. McCann, pp. 136-137; Hodgson, 168: 3-9.

cribed by *The Cloud* author as *pain* and *travail*, yet there is an obvious danger in relating the terms of one author to another. Similarly, as every mystic stands alone before God, it is not our intention to fit the narration of *The Cloud* author to the ascent described by St. John.

Even in such a specialized lesson as "This Work" the author gives his disciple simple and down-to-earth directions. Thus he teaches him how to act in the presence of the intense pain brought about by the *travail*. First of all there is the strategy of a counter-offensive.

"And if they oft rise, oft put them down: and shortly to say, as oft as they rise, as oft put them down. And if thee think that the travail be great, thou mayest seek arts and wiles and privy subtleties of ghostly devices to put them away: the which subtleties be better learned of God by the proof than of any man in this life"[29].

The author suggests another simple device. He counsels his disciple to disregard the enemy in all these buffetings, and turn the attention of the mind away from them. But it is not merely a turning away. There is a corresponding action, which is to fill the mind with something else while turning away from these troublesome thoughts. And this other thing is ONLY GOD. For, indeed, with God in the centre of the attention, all other things must necessarily be in the periphery.

"Nevertheless, somewhat of this subtlety shall I tell thee as me think. Prove thou and do better, if thou better mayest. Do that in thee is, to let be as thou wist not that they press so fast upon thee betwixt thee and thy God. And try to look as it were over their shoulders, seeking another thing: the which thing is God, enclosed in a cloud of unknowing. And if thou do thus, I trow that within short time thou shalt be eased of thy travail. I trow that an this device be well and truly conceived. it is nought else but a longing desire unto God, to feel Him and see Him as it may be here: and such a desire is charity, and it obtaineth always to be eased"[30].

There is still another device to overcome these temptations. The author uses an image from military life. When the odds are definitely against one, there is no point in continuing the battle alone. The course that lies open is to ask for reinforce-

29 *The Cloud*, Ch. 31, Underhill, pp. 147-148; Hodgson, 66: 7-12.
30 Ibid. Ch. 32, Underhill, p. 149; Hodgson, 66: 13-22.

ments, and so the author tells the disciple to call on the strength of his ally. With the strength of God, is there need for any other?

"Another device there is: prove thou if thou wilt. When thou feelest that thou mayest on nowise put them down, cower thou down under them as a caitiff and a coward overcome in battle, and think that it is but a folly to thee to strive any longer with them, and therefore thou yieldest thee to God in the hands of thine enemies. And feel then thyself as thou wert foredone for ever. Take good heed of this device I pray thee, for me think in the proof of this device thou shouldest melt all to water"[31].

Taken by itself, this passage could give rise to misunderstanding and uneasiness[32], but this is not a message of despair. The author is most insistent on hope. Rather, this passage should be taken in the light of the whole "Work", and its insistent demands for perfection[33]. The author himself gives an interpretation of this passage based on the nature of "This Work".

"And surely me think an this device be truly conceived it is nought else but a true knowing and a feeling of thyself as thou art, a wretch and a filthy, far worse than nought: the which knowing and feeling is meekness"[34].

There are other devices to help one in this difficult part of the *travail*. The presence of the grace for "This Work" gives the assurance that the Lord will teach the disciple just what to do. The author points out certain things, but it is always God Who is the better teacher. There is a gap between teaching and practice, and this is the part that God can fill.

"More devices tell I thee not at this time; for an thou have grace to feel the proof of these, I trow that thou shalt know better to learn me than I thee. For although it should be thus, truly yet me think that I am full far therefrom. And therefore I pray thee help me, and do thou for thee and for me"[35].

Finally, the author repeats his message of hope.

"And yet in all this sorrow he desireth not to unbe: for that were devil's madness and despite unto God. But him listeth

---

31 Ibid. Ch. 32, Underhill, pp. 149-150; Hodgson, 66: 23, 67: 1-7.
32 C. Wolters, *The Cloud of Unknowing*, p. 35.
33 See C. Pepler, *The English Religious Heritage*, pp. 256-257.
34 *The Cloud*, Ch. 32, Underhill, p. 150; Hodgson, 67: 7-10.
35 Ibid. Ch. 33, Underhill, p. 151; Hodgson, 67: 15-19.

right well to be; and he intendeth full heartily thanking to God,
for the worthiness and the gift of his being, for all that he
desire unceasingly for to lack the witting and the feeling of his
being"[36].

Even in the midst of this "travail" the comfort of God is
not lacking. This is proof of the presence of this "special
grace".

"For he that abideth feeleth sometime some comfort, and hath
some hope of perfection; for he feeleth and seeth that many of
his fordone special sins be in great part by help of grace rubbed
away. Nevertheless yet ever among he feeleth pain, but he
thinketh that it shall have an end, for it waxeth ever less and
less. And therefore he calleth it nought else but purgatory.
Sometimes he can find no special sin written thereupon, but
yet him think that sin is a lump, he wot never what, none other
thing than himself; and then it may be called the base and the
pain of the original sin. Sometime him think that it is paradise
or heaven, for diverse wonderful sweetness and comforts, joys
and blessed virtues that he findeth therein. Sometime him think
it God, for peace and rest that he findeth therein"[37].

These then are the things that make up the *pain* and *travail*
of "This Work". All this teaching is enough to dispel any
trace of uneasiness as regards "quietism" in any form. The
whole ascent to God is a mixture compounded of very hard
work and reward. And all these take place in that state of
soul which the author describes by the figure of the "cloud
of forgetting". We shall see in the next section that the author
uses a special vocabulary to describe this state of "the cloud
of forgetting", distinctly different from the state preceding

---

[36] Ibid. Ch. 44, Underhill, p. 182; Hodgson, 84: 20-23, 85: 1-2.
[37] Ibid. Ch. 69, Underhill, p. 253; Hodgson, 123: 10-21. St. John of the
Cross has a similar passage wherein he describes the purgation as
"purgatory". "This severe purgation comes to pass in few souls—in those
alone whom He desires to raise to some degree of union by means of
contemplation; and those who are to be raised to the highest degree
of all are the most severely purged. This happens as follows. When God
desires to bring the soul forth from its ordinary state—that is, from its
natural way and operation—to a spiritual life, and to lead it from
meditation to contemplation, which is a state rather heavenly than
earthly, wherein He communicates Himself through union of love, He
begins at once to communicate Himself to the spirit, which is still im-
pure and imperfect, and has evil habits, so that each soul suffers
according to the degree of its imperfection; and at times this purgation
is in some ways as grievous to the soul whom it is preparing for the
reception of perfect union here below as is that of purgatory, wherein
we are purged in order to see God in the life to come" (*Living Flame*,
Allison-Peers, p. 28).

the "special call", and different likewise from the state that follows, "the cloud of unknowing".

C. THE AUTHOR'S VOCABULARY
FOR "THE CLOUD OF FORGETTING"

In the state which the author describes by the figure of "the cloud of forgetting", a downward movement which looks towards creatures is principally involved. The upward movement that gazes up towards GOD ALONE will be discussed in great detail by the author in the state which he describes by the figure of "the cloud of unknowing".

While the complete obliteration of the remembrance of all creatures can be brought about only by the grace of God, there is a part for man involving much effort and vigour. And so we hear the crisp order of the author to "put a cloud of forgetting beneath thee; betwixt thee and all the creatures that ever be made"[38]. The result is the obstruction from view of all manner of creatures so that they are not visible. For when one "forgets" it is as good as if the thing "forgotten" is not there at all. The disciple should be above all creatures ". . . nevertheless yet in this work it shall be cast down and covered with a cloud of forgetting. And thou shalt step above it stalwartly, but listily, with a devout and a pleasing stirring of love, and try for to pierce that darkness above thee"[39]. This part of the work is definitely within the disciple's own power. And once again we see the primacy of love permeating "This Work" in "the cloud of forgetting." ". . . tread him fast down with a stirring of love"[40]. There is that element of perseverance and continuity in the work of concealing all creatures under "the cloud of forgetting". ". . . and put them and hold them far down under the cloud of forgetting, if ever he shall pierce the cloud of unknowing betwixt him and his God"[41]. There is then this intimate connection between the two "clouds" in "This Work" in the manner of "the cloud of forgetting" being a condition for the "cloud of unknowing". The phrase, ". . . put him down and away so far under the

---

[38] *The Cloud,* Ch. 5, Underhill, p. 74; Hodgson, 24: 3-4.
[39] Ibid. Ch. 6, Underhill, p. 78; Hodgson, 26: 7-11; also Ch. 9, p. 89; Ch. 31, p. 147.
[40] Ibid. Ch. 7, Underhill, p. 79; Hodgson, 26: 19-27: 1; also Ch. 26, p. 139.
[41] Ibid. Ch. 7, Underhill, p. 81; Hodgson, 27: 22, 28: 1-2.

cloud of forgetting",[42] suggests distance and exile and when one is far away "forgetting" is easier. There has to be the positive act of banishing thoughts from the mind. The author uses a figure taken from the field of battle. "This word shall be thy shield and thy spear, whether thou ridest on peace or on war. . . . With this word, thou shalt smite down all manner of thought under the cloud of forgetting"[43].

With this note on the language of the author describing the state of "the cloud of forgetting" we pass to the description of a subsequent and a higher state in "This Work". In "the cloud of forgetting" the soul is preoccupied with the obliteration of all manner of thought of creatures, reaching up even to the very Attributes of God.

Set in the context of Mystical Theology we see that this teaching of *The Cloud* author is echoed in that of the masters of the spiritual life.

"For Augustine, for Gregory, for Bernard, the beginnings of contemplation, the getting under way, is a striving and a struggle of mind and soul to transcend earthly things and fix its gaze on heavenly; and the first step is the stripping the mind of all images and the 'hushing' of the faculties"[44].

CONCLUSIONS

There is in "This Work" a seemingly endless stream of effort and labour on the part of one chosen by God. A "special call" is needed to start "This Work" but there is required of the one chosen great vigour and strength.

In his particular ascent to God, the author uses the double figure of a "cloud" downwards for creatures and upwards for GOD ALONE. In this chapter we noted this downward movement, and "the cloud of forgetting" must stand between the "worker" and all creatures. The result is a complete emptying of the mind of every thought, even the Attributes of God, save only the "naked Being of God". And in this

---

[42] Ibid. Ch. 8, Underhill, p. 84; Hodgson, 29: 17-18.
[43] Ibid. Ch. 7, Underhill, p. 82; Hodgson, 28: 17-20.
[44] C. Butler, *Western Mysticism*, p. 19.

action the "worker" is the master of the task, and this is one thing he can do by his own powers. He is pictured as being *above* the memory of all creatures which he must *tread down* and *cover* with "the cloud of forgetting".

Another aspect of the part of man in this state the author describes as "travail" which involves actual pain and suffering for the "worker". This *pain* and *travail* is brought about by the memory of one's personal sins and of Original Sin. The author distinguishes the pain and suffering brought about by these two kinds of sins. That brought about by the remembrance of one's personal sins is more intense, but the pain gradually diminishes. That brought about by Original Sin may not be so intense, but it will always be present to provide constant provocation and trial for the soul. In trying to alleviate this pain, the author gives both ascetical and natural means for overcoming these troublesome thoughts. These passages reveal the *experimental quality* of "This Work".

While St. John of the Cross describes a state similar to one described by *The Cloud* author, we prefer to limit the use of terms to the author who uses them. It seems very natural to try to put the narrations of *The Cloud* author in the context of the categories of St. John of the Cross. However, this we will not do as it is our intention to allow *The Cloud* author to speak for himself; the passages from St. John are cited only to point out the similarity between the states they describe. And while the particular ascent to God which the author describes as "This Work" is proper to him, his way is not completely new, but echoes of it being found in the teachings of the masters of the spiritual life, to whom *The Cloud* author makes references.

This then is the state described by the author with the figure of "the cloud of forgetting". The next chapter will be devoted to a discussion of a still higher state, which the author describes by the figure of "the cloud of unknowing". Even when this state is reached we shall see that there is a still higher perfection, depending solely on the Divine Pleasure when God chooses to invade the soul and "pierce the cloud of unknowing with a beam of His everlasting light".

CHAPTER VI

The Cloud of Unknowing

A. A RECAPITULATION

The unknown English writer of the 14th century entitled his major work *A Book Of Contemplation The Which Is Called The Cloud Of Unknowing, In The Which A Soul Is Oned With God*. Right at this point the author intimates that the culmination of his writing is "Union with God". The 14th-century English writer had a sound knowledge of the different degrees of prayer, and unlike 17th-century and later writers used the word "contemplation" to describe a very high state.

With this chapter we reach the very heart of the author's teaching. The gradual development we have slowly made from the beginning up to the state of "the cloud of forgetting" reveals the author's intention to show this progression and ascent. We see this from the development of the "states of life", which is equated with the life of the disciple. We see the progress from one state to another, but always from a lower to a higher one. So we see the progress of the disciple from the *Common*, through the *Special*, to the *Singular* in which he finds himself at this stage, and within which "degree and form of Christian men's living", he "mayest learn to lift up the foot of thy love and step towards the state and degree of living that is *perfect*, and the last state of all"[1]. And within this "singular form of living" which is the life of a "solitary," there is a further subdivision and progression of state in the form of "manners of living", which the author describes by his terms of "good, better, best" after the story of Mary and Martha. And within this context "This Work" is described as "the best".

The disciple, then, is not yet in the "perfect" state, but still in the "singular degree of living". Within this state the author teaches him a particular way and ascent to God which he describes as "This Work", which is "the best part which Mary chose", on the achievement of which he would find himself

[1] *The Cloud*, Ch. 1, Underhill, p. 60; Hodgson, 14: 13-15.

in the "perfect degree" which is the fourth and last and which "may by grace be begun here, but it shall ever last without end in the bliss of Heaven"[2].

The reason for this whole treatise is that the disciple had received the "special grace to do This Work" while in this "singular degree". So the author teaches him what he knows of "This Work" in order that the disciple may set out in peace towards union with God.

In concluding Chapter V we made the statement that the state of "the cloud of unknowing" is a state higher than "the cloud of forgetting". In saying this, we did not mean that either of the two states is separate from "This Work". For "This Work" comprises the whole process from the time the disciple received the "privy teaching of the Spirit of God" through the "cloud of forgetting" and into "the cloud of unknowing". In this state, if God should so choose, He would "send out a beam of ghostly light, piercing this cloud of unknowing that is betwixt thee and Him . . ."[3]. There is then gradual progress in intensity and perfection of "This Work". On the other hand, there is a clear break between the state before "the special grace" and that which comes after "the call to perfection". What makes the difference is the *Divine Choice*.

We have so far described the different elements involved in "This Work" up to the "cloud of forgetting". In this final chapter we shall see the characteristic elements of the perfection of "This Work", which the author describes as that of "the cloud of unknowing".

The author recognizes degrees of perfection in "This Work". It is worth remembering that we are now within the "Singular Degree of Living" and, within this, in the highest part of the three "Manners of Living" which the author identifies as "strictly contemplative". And this "contemplative life", which is "the best part which Mary chose", the author further subdivides, according to the differing grades of perfection, into "beginners, profiters and perfects".

"Nevertheless, means there be in the which a contemplative prentice should be occupied, the which be these—Lesson,

2 Ibid. Ch. 1, Underhill, p. 59; Hodgson, 13: 12-13.
3 Ibid. Ch. 26, Underhill, p. 140; Hodgson, 62: 14-15.

Meditation, and Orison: or else to thine understanding they may be called—Reading, Thinking, and Praying . . . these three be so coupled together, that unto them that be beginners and profiters—but not to them that be perfect, yea, as it may be here—thinking may not goodly be gotten, without reading or hearing coming before"[4].

The enumeration of the spiritual exercises for "beginners and profiters" might create some confusion since they are not the proper acts of "This Work". But we see the clear intention of the author as regards this fact when he makes short shrift of these exercises by a mere reference to another work, revealing his desire to show the transitory nature of this stage.

"Of these three thou shalt find written in another book of another man's work, much better than I can tell thee; and therefore it needeth not here to tell thee of the qualities of them"[5].

The author realizes that at the transition stage, even with the presence of this "special grace", there has to be some adjustment made in the prayer life of the "worker of This Work". Things are not done by leaps and bounds even with the spiritual life.

Having recognized this need for a period of transition, he passes immediately to the "perfection" of "This Work", which is the heart of the matter of "The Cloud", stressing the progression of the successive states[6]. And he emphasizes this fact in his characteristic way.

"But it is not so with them that continually work in the work of this book"[7].

And in this stage of "the cloud of unknowing" it is with "them that continually work in the work of this book" that we shall be dealing and not with the "beginner" or "profiter".

With this note we continue to consider the characteristic elements of "the cloud of unknowing" which the author describes in different ways.

---

[4] Ibid. Ch. 35, Underhill, p. 157; Hodgson, 71: 11-20.

[5] Ibid. Ch. 35, Underhill, p. 157; Hodgson, 71: 14-17. See C. Pepler, *The English Religious Heritage*, p. 243: "*The Cloud* apparently refers the reader to the Carthusian prior Guigo II's *Scala Claustralium* in which the beginners are principally concerned with 'Lesson' (or Reading), the profiters with 'Meditation' (or Thinking), the devout with 'Orison' (or Praying) and they 'that be holy and blessed with God' with Contemplation".

[6] *The Cloud*, Ch. 35, Underhill, p. 157; Hodgson, 71: 17-20.

[7] Ibid. Ch. 36, Underhill, p. 160; Hodgson, 72: 23-73: 1.

B.   THE VOCABULARY FOR "THE CLOUD OF UNKNOWING"

We have said before that while "the cloud of forgetting" looks downward towards creatures, "the cloud of unknowing" looks upward towards GOD ONLY. For, merely to cover all creatures with "the cloud of forgetting" with nothing to take their place, would leave only a void and an emptiness. A void is not meant to be the end of "This Work". The emptiness created by this "covering down of all creatures" must be filled with God, and "the naked Being of God alone".

There is nothing negative about "This Work", for it can be negative only in the sense of a preliminary stripping away or forgetting. But the part of man does not end there; there is the "filling up" of that which has been left empty by "the cloud of forgetting".

There is then that upward movement which looks towards God.

> "Lift up thine heart unto God with a meek stirring of love; and mean Himself, and none of His goods"[8].

There is that sense of darkness and obscurity which the author terms more specifically "unknowing" when it comes to having a clear knowledge of God in this life.

> "For at the first time when thou dost it, thou findest but a darkness; and as it were a cloud of unknowing, thou knowest not what, saving that thou feelest in thy will a naked intent unto God"[9].

Because of our intellectual background we find it difficult to understand this "unknowing". For the role of knowledge presupposes objects that are known and perceived. But in the context of *The Cloud* the "unknowing" that is involved does not mean an intellectual vacuum, but a higher perception. In this case the soul is completely full of the experience of "the naked Being of God" and all the other perfections of "This Work". Having had no previous experience of this "feeling" the mystics had difficulty in expressing themselves, and frequently resorted to figures. This darkness has been aptly described as that ". . . in which the soul is lost before the Great Unknown"[10].

8 Ibid. Ch. 3, Underhill, p. 63; Hodgson, 16: 3-4.
9 Ibid. Ch. 3, Underhill, 6. 64; Hodgson, 16: 19-20, 17: 1-2.
10 J. V. Bainvel, Introduction to A. Poulain, *The Graces of Interior Prayer*, p. lxi, note 2.

This "cloud" must necessarily be between God and the soul as long as this life lasts.

> "This darkness and this cloud is, howsoever thou dost, betwixt thee and thy God, and letteth thee that thou mayest neither see Him clearly by light of understanding in thy reason, nor feel Him in sweetness of love in thine affection"[11].

But however dark this "cloud" may be, it is here that God may be found. The "worker" must remain in this "cloud" if he is to "see" the place where God "IS".

> "And therefore shape thee to bide in this darkness as long as thou mayest, evermore crying after Him that thou lovest. For if ever thou shalt feel Him or see Him, as it may be here, it behoveth always to be in this cloud in this darkness"[12].

The Cloud author teaches very clearly that the sight of God in this life is not the same as in the next. He qualifies the sight of God in "the cloud of unknowing" with the phrase "as it may be here". There is a very intimate relation between the two "clouds", even in the sense of one being a condition for the other.

> "And yet, nevertheless, it behoveth a man or a woman that hath long time been used in these meditations, nevertheless to leave them, and put them and hold them far down under the cloud of forgetting, if ever he shall pierce the cloud of unknowing betwixt him and His God"[13].

Despite the distinctions there is only one reality in "This Work", and the whole process, for all its varying intensity, involves only one upward motion towards God[14].

In his characteristic manner the author says explicitly what this "cloud" is not.

> "And ween not, for I call it a darkness or a cloud, that it be any cloud congealed of the humours that flee in the air, nor yet any darkness such as is in thine house on nights when the candle is out. For such a darkness and such a cloud mayest thou imagine with curiosity of wit, for to bear before thine eyes in the lightest day of summer: and also contrariwise in the darkest night of winter, thou mayest imagine a clear shining light. Let be such falsehood. I mean not thus. For when I say darkness, I mean

11 *The Cloud*, Ch. 3, Underhill, p. 64; Hodgson, 17: 2-5.
12 Ibid. Ch. 3, Underhill, p. 64; Hodgson, 17: 5-9.
13 Ibid. Ch. 7, Underhill, pp. 80-81; Hodgson, 27: 20-22, 28: 1-2.
14 Ibid. Ch. 7, Underhill, p. 82; Hodgson, 28: 17-20.

a lacking of knowing: as all that thing that thou knowest not, or else that thou hast forgotten, it is dark to thee; for thou seest it not with thy ghostly eye. And for this reason it is not called a cloud of the air, but a cloud of unknowing, that is betwixt thee and thy God"[15].

Here is stressed the psychological element, for it is with the spiritual faculties of man that union with God is to be achieved. And the primacy of will and love is at once intimated by this psychological emphasis.

While this life lasts, no matter how high the degree of perfection one may attain, there will always be this "cloud of unknowing" between the soul and God.

"For one thing I tell thee, that there was never yet pure creature in this life, nor never yet shall be, so high ravished in contemplation and love of the Godhead, that there is not evermore a high and a wonderful cloud of unknowing betwixt him and his God"[16].

And even in this "cloud", which involves high perfection, there is work to be done. The characteristic labour for this stage is graphically described by the author.

". . . and try for to pierce that darkness above thee. And smite upon that thick cloud of unknowing with a sharp dart of longing love; and go not thence for thing that befalleth"[17].

The author insists that it is love that can pierce this "cloud of unknowing".

". . . such a blind stirring of love unto God for Himself, and such a privy pressing upon this cloud of unknowing . . ."[18].

While in "the cloud of forgetting" the intellect is involved in a negative way, in "the cloud of unknowing" it is the will and love that is involved. We notice that the activity of the will and love is described by the words "piercing", "beating", "pressing". All these denote vigour and strength. There is no trace of laziness in "This Work" even at this height. And while in "the cloud of forgetting" the worker is so much the master in the sense that it is within his power to "forget" all creatures, here in "the cloud of unknowing", despite all his

15 Ibid. Ch. 4, Underhill, pp. 72-73; Hodgson, 23 : 13-24.
16 Ibid. Ch. 17, Underhill, p. 114; Hodgson, 47 : 17-20.
17 Ibid. Ch. 6, Underhill, p. 78; Hodgson, 26 : 10-12.
18 Ibid. Ch. 9, Underhill, p. 90; Hodgson, 34 : 8-10.

labour and exertions, he is pictured as a suppliant, waiting for the *Divine Response*.

But we must not underestimate this state. That is one of high perfection, the highest that man can go by his own powers, aided always by "special grace". When the soul reaches this state, although there is still much work to be done, he must "abide" and "wait". The author describes this state of the "cloud of unknowing" in terms easier to understand.

"Sometime him think that it is paradise or heaven, for diverse wonderful sweetness and comforts, joys and blessed virtues that he findeth therein. Sometime him think it God, for peace and rest that he findest therein. Yea! think what he think will; for ever more he shall find it *a cloud of unknowing*, that is betwixt him and his God"[19].

This sense of obstruction and separation has been aptly described by Fr. Poulain.

"An illustration will make this clear. If one of my friends is hidden behind a wall, I can always *think* of him when I wish to do so. But if I wish *really* to enter into relation with him, my will is no longer sufficient. The wall must disappear. In like manner God is hidden. With the aid of grace it is always within the power of my will to *think* of Him, which is ordinary prayer. But it is clear that if I wish really to enter into communication with Him, this will is no longer sufficient. *An obstacle must be removed;* and the Divine Hand alone is powerful to accomplish this"[20].

Notwithstanding the *Divine Choice* there is labour to be done from the beginning of "the call" to the state of "the cloud of unknowing". For that matter, the "special grace" presupposes that the one so chosen "hath done long time before, for to able him to contemplative living by the virtuous means of active living . . . to be a perfect follower of Christ . . . the which is possible by grace . . ."[21].

Some of these passages have been quoted alongside comparable passages of Hadewijch the Beguine, Blessed Angela of Foligno, Ruysbroeck, and St. John of the Cross, and described as *mystical* and *transconceptual* wisdom, as knowledge that is *nescience*[22].

[19] Ibid. Ch. 69, Underhill, p. 253; Hodgson, 123: 18-23.
[20] A. Poulain, *The Graces of Interior Prayer*, p. 116.
[21] *The Cloud*, Prologue, Underhill, pp. 39, 40; Hodgson, 1: 14-2: 1-8.
[22] C. Journet, *The Dark Knowledge of God*, pp. 81-88.

Having noted the author's special vocabulary and descriptions of "the cloud of unknowing", we shall see in the next section that he compares this state with similar descriptions in the works of other authors.

C. COMPARISON WITH OTHER AUTHORS AND WRITINGS

For all his hesitation in speaking of the high things of God, the author is in no way self-effacing when the occasion demands. He displays keen perception in appreciating the relative value of things, but whilst he is quick to identify the higher things of God he does not deprecate the lesser. For, to the author, humility is truth. We have seen from his choice of expressions that he means exactly what he says, and this is illustrated by the clearly marked progression of ideas, from lower to higher, in which he points out the breaks between states. We shall see in this part that he identifies "This Work" in yet another way—by comparing the state he describes with states described by other authors. All these writings belong to the highest realms of spirit, and are commonly described now as "mystical".

> "For this same work, if it be verily conceived, is that reverent affection and the fruit separated from the tree that I speak of in the little *Epistle of Prayer*. This is *the cloud of unknowing;* this is that privy love put in purity of spirit; this is the ark of the testament. This is Denis' divinity, his wisdom and his treasure, his lightsome darkness and his unknown knowing"[23].

The author then identifies "this same work" of *Privy Counsel* with the perfection of the prayer in *Epistle of Prayer,* with "the cloud of unknowing", with the Mystical Theology of Dionysius, and with the *Ark of the Testament,* which has always been interpreted as meaning the "Presence of God". The Ark has been used by Richard of St. Victor to mean a state of a mystical character. It would seem that the author anticipated the objection that his avowals regarding the character of "This Work" in "The Cloud" are mere words signifying nothing. And so, while he uses his own words to describe the high state of "This Work", he puts in as confirmation the descriptions of comparable states in other writers' works, which have already been accepted as belonging to the highest

---

[23] *Privy Counsel*, McCann, p. 124; Hodgson, 154: 13-18.

rung of the spiritual life. "The fruit taken from the tree" in
the *Epistle of Prayer* is the end and perfection of the particular
exercise which the author teaches in that letter. He describes
this more specifically.

"In this time it is that this reverent affection is so meedful as
I said. And, therefore, shape thee for to depart this fruit from
the tree, and for to offer it up by itself to the high King of
heaven; and then shalt thou be cleped God's own child loving
Him with a chaste love for Himself, and not for His goods. . . .
And therefore, following the rule of mine ensample, shape thee
to depart the fruit from the tree, and for to offer it up by itself
unto the King of heaven, that thy love be chaste; for evermore
as long as thou offrest Him this fruit green and hanging on the
tree, thou mayest well be likened to a woman that is not chaste,
for she loveth a man for his goods more than for himself"[24].

The "work" of the *Epistle of Prayer* is likewise the "chaste
love of God only for Himself". This in turn is the perfection
of "This Work" in *The Cloud*. It is significant to note that
this perfection is attained when the person is, as it were, ready
to appear before God. For the soul engaged in the "work" of
the *Epistle of Prayer* cannot even be sure that he will be alive
at the end of this short prayer.

While the author insists in *The Cloud* on the two virtues of
meekness and *charity* in their *perfect* form, in the *Epistle of
Prayer* he puts much stress on *the fear of God* and *hope in His
mercy*. If we were to look for differences in usage and temper
of mind in *The Cloud* group, here is one example that reveals
a great difference. Had the author not identified the work as
his own, the present writer believes that common authorship
would have been very difficult to prove.

The author likewise compares "This Work" of *Privy Counsel*
with the *Ark of the Testament*. The *Ark* was built on instructions from Moses, after the vision shown to him by God on
the mountain, and it contained the tablets of the Command-
ments. The *Ark* was the Visible Presence of God among His
Chosen People. It was to the *Ark* that the High Priests
repaired when there was a special problem confronting the
Chosen People, and the Divine Presence was revealed by the
overshadowing cloud which filled the Tent, or hovered over
the marching Israelites.

24 *Epistle of Prayer*, Gardner, pp. 83-86; Hodgson, 53: 4-55: 1.

The encounter of Moses with God on the Holy Mountain is used by mystical writers to signify mystical encounters, although it is not God as HE IS in Himself that Moses saw, but the Place where He was[25]. The Pseudo-Dionysius uses the story of Moses in the sense of a mystical encounter of the soul with God, and "in the following passage we get the three stages tabulated by later Mystical Theology: (1) Purgation, (2) Illumination, (3) Union"[26].

"For not without reason is the blessed Moses bidden first to undergo purification himself and then to separate himself from those who have not undergone it; and after all purification hears the many-voiced trumpets and see many lights flash forth with pure and diverse-streaming rays, and then stands separate from the multitudes and with the chosen priests presses forward to the topmost pinnacle of the Divine Ascent. Nevertheless he meets not with God Himself, yet he beholds—not Him indeed (for He is invisible)—but the place wherein He dwells"[27].

Richard of St. Victor, in *Benjamin Major*, sees the mystical element of the story of Moses.

"If we may have leave, by the gift of his inspiration who has the key of knowledge, we should like, by our small commentary, to unlock the mystical ark of Moses, at least to some extent.... For I think there is something precious enclosed in that ark.... When the Lord was about to teach Moses how to construct the tabernacle, he first instructed him about building the ark so that he might understand thereby that all other things were to be constructed in relation to the ark. I am sure that no one would hestitate to say that the ark was the chief and principal shrine among all those objects which the tabernacle of the covenant contained"[28].

In his classic work, Dom Cuthbert Butler, O.S.B., makes the following observation:

"It will therein be seen that the two cases relied on by St. Augustine for his affirmative answer, the two cases in which he holds that the essential vision of God has certainly been given, are Moses and St. Paul. St. Paul figures much more largely with St. Thomas; but it will be seen that for St. Augustine the real strength of the case lies in Moses"[29].

25 L. Reypens, "Connaissance Mystique De Dieu", *Dictionnaire De Spiritualité*, III, Cols. 911-912.
26 C. Rolt, *Dionysius the Areopagite*, p. 193, note 4.
27 Pseudo-Dionysius, *Mystical Theology*, Ed. Rolt, pp. 193-194.
28 Richard of St. Victor, *Benjamin Major*, Ed. Kirchberger, pp. 131, 132, 133.
29 C. Butler, *Western Mysticism*, p. 52.

Like St. Augustine *The Cloud* author uses the story of Moses to describe the encounter with God. It is true that the author gives an exegesis of passages from St. Paul, but for the intimate encounter with the Godhead it is the story of Moses that is the controlling one.

We have pointed out that the other authors which *The Cloud* author uses for reference were considered by him to be mystical. In doing so, the author intended that his own works be similarly considered. In this section, then, we have limited our work to indicating the mystical character of the author's works.

D.   THE PERFECTION OF "THIS WORK"

After this oblique way of identifying the mystical character of "This Work" by comparing it with other mystical writings, we have the express declaration of the author as regards its perfection. This perfection consists in "union with God".

> "At the first I ask of thee, what is perfection of man's soul and which be the properties that pertain to this perfection? I answer in thy person and I say, that perfection of man's soul is nought else but a onehead made betwixt God and it in perfect charity. This perfection is so high and so pure in itself above the understanding of man, that it may not be known nor perceived in itself. But there where the properties that pertain to this perfection be verily seen and perceived, there it is likely that the substance is abounding. And therefore we must know here which be the qualities that pertain to perfection, in declaring of the nobleness of this ghostly exercise before all others"[30].

It is good to remember that the author has a predilection for synthesizing everything that has to do with "This Work". Hence, *nature* and *perfection* blend with one another, and with all other properties of "This Work".

In this section, we shall see "the qualities that pertain to perfection". The author connects this idea with the *virtues*. But we shall see that he equates the *virtues* with the different "qualities that pertain to perfection" which in the end will be nothing else but ONLY GOD.

1.   *THE SYNTHESIS OF THE VIRTUES*

"The properties that pertain to perfection, the which each perfect soul ought to have, be virtue. And then, if thou wilt verily

30 *Privy Counsel*, McCann, p. 123; Hodgson, 153: 24-29, 154: 1-4.

behold to this work in thy soul and to the property and the condition of each virtue diversely, thou shalt find that all virtues be clearly and perfectly comprehended in it, without any crooking or corruption of the intent"[31].

The author gives the explanation for this synthesis.

"For virtue is nought else but an ordained and a measured affection, plainly directed unto God for himself. For why? He in Himself is the pure cause of all virtues: insomuch, that if any man be stirred to any one virtue by any other cause mingled with Him, yea, although he be the chief, yet that virtue is then imperfect"[32].

The only object of "This Work" is the "naked Being of God for Himself Alone", and this is what the perfection of the virtues achieves.

The author did not reach this point at one leap. He is careful to draw the steps of the ascent. Even though the perfection of the virtues is God Himself, he insists on only two virtues, meekness and charity.

We have seen how careful the author is to point out that there are many things that lead to the perfection of "This Work". While they are not intimately connected with "This Work" at the state of perfection, they have done their part by leading up to it and their value should not be depreciated. The virtues, too, come at different levels, and so, in his insistence on the two virtues of meekness and charity, he describes their lower forms, that of *imperfect meekness* and *imperfect charity*. The reason for the distinction is the *Object* Itself.

". . . how that it is imperfect when it is caused of any other thing mingled with God although He be the chief; and how that it is perfect when it is caused of God by Himself"[33].

Imperfect meekness is thus described by the author:

". . . one is the filth, the wretchedness, and the frailty of man, into the which he is fallen by sin; and the which always him behoveth to feel in some part the while he liveth in this life, be he never so holy"[34].

And for *imperfect charity,* the object is the same consideration that looks to man himself.

---

31 Ibid. McCann, pp. 123-124; Hodgson, 154: 5-10.
32 *The Cloud,* Ch. 12, Underhill, p. 98; Hodgson, 39: 17-21.
33 Ibid. Ch. 13, Underhill, p. 100; Hodgson, 40: 1-4.
34 Ibid. Ch. 13, Underhill, pp. 100-101; Hodgson, 40: 11-14.

"And that in this work the second and the lower branch of charity unto thine even-christian is verily and perfectly fulfilled, it seemeth by the proof"[35].

On the other hand, the object of *perfect meekness* is God Himself, which is the same as that for "This Work".

"Another is the over-abundant love and the worthiness of God in Himself; in beholding of the which all nature quaketh, all clerks be fools, and all saints and angels be blind"[36].

In the same manner is it with *perfect charity*.

"For charity is nought else to bemean to thine understanding, but love of God for Himself above all creatures, and of man for God even as thyself. . . . And thus it seemeth that in this work God is perfectly loved for Himself, and that above all creatures"[37].

And, again, we see the telescoping of these two virtues into one, that of "This Work".

". . . and in this time it is perfectly meeked, for it knoweth and feeleth no cause but the Chief. . . . And that in this work God is loved for Himself, and above all creatures, it seemeth right well. For it is said before, that the substance of this work is nought else but a naked intent directed unto God for Himself"[38].

All the virtues, synthesized in two, finally come in the end to be just one: only God.

"For all virtues they find and feel in God; for in Him is all thing, both by cause and by being. For they think that an they had God they had all good, and therefore they covet nothing with special beholding, but only good God. Do thou on the same manner as far forth as thou mayest by grace: and mean God all, and all God, so that nought work in thy wit and in thy will, but only God"[39].

2.   *"CHASTE LOVE"*

The perfect love of God, which is another characteristic of the state of "the cloud of unknowing", the author calls "chaste love". This is a high state of abandonment to the

---

35 Ibid. Ch. 24, Underhill, p. 134; Hodgson, 59: 5-6.
36 Ibid. Ch. 13, Underhill, p. 101; Hodgson, 40: 14-17.
37 Ibid. Ch. 24, Underhill, pp. 133, 134; Hodgson, 58: 11-20, 59: 1-2.
38 Ibid. Ch. 13, Underhill, p. 101, Ch. 24, p. 133; Hodgson, 41: 8-9, 58: 13-16.
39 Ibid. Ch. 40, Underhill, p. 172; Hodgson, 79: 7-12.

love of God in which nothing else, good or evil, has importance. It is *God Alone* that matters.

We see again this gathering of everything into One. Now
the author identifies this "chaste love" with the "naked intent"
which is also "This Work", and which in turn is the "perfect
prayer", the "perfection of the Virtues".

> "A naked intent I call it. For why, in this work a perfect pren-
> tice asketh neither releasing of pain, nor increasing of meed, nor
> shortly to say, nought but Himself. Insomuch, that neither he
> recketh nor looketh after whether that he be in pain or in
> bliss, else that His will be fulfilled that he loveth. And thus it
> seemeth that in this work God is perfectly loved for Himself,
> and that above all creatures. For in this work, a perfect worker
> may not suffer the memory of the holiest creature that ever
> God made to commune with him"[40].

In *Epistle of Prayer*, the author describes this "chaste love".

> "Chaste love is that when thou askest of God neither releas-
> ing of pain, nor increasing of meed, nor yet sweetness in His
> love in this life; but if it be any certain time that thou covetest
> sweetness as for a refreshing of thy ghostly mights, that they fail
> not in the way; but thou askest of God nought but Himself,
> and neither thou reckest nor lookest after whether thou shall
> be in pain or in bliss, so that thou have Him that thou lovest—
> this is chaste love, this is perfect love"[41].

This "chaste love" is likewise the "reverent affection", the
"fruit from the tree", which in turn is "the cloud of unknowing", the "Ark of the Covenant", the "Mystical Theology"
and, of course, "the naked intent" and "This Work".

> "And therefore shape thee for to depart the fruit from the
> tree; that is to say, this reverent affection from the thoughts of
> dread and of hope coming before; so that thou mayest offer
> it ripe and chaste unto God by itself, not caused of any thing
> beneath Him, or meddled with Him (yea, though all it be the
> chief), but only of Him, by Himself; and then it is so meedful
> as I say that it is"[42].

The significance of this "chaste love" of God is seen in
greater relief when the author describes the most intense pain
as "deep ghostly sorrow".

[40] Ibid. Ch. 24, Underhill, pp. 133-134; Hodgson, 58: 16-20, 59: 1-4.
[41] *Epistle of Prayer*, Gardner, p. 86; Hodgson, 55: 7-13. Cf. Hilton's passage
on what he describes as "clean love". *Scale II*, Ch. 35, Underhill, pp.
388-389.
[42] *Epistle of Prayer*, Gardner, pp. 86-87; Hodgson, 55: 13-19.

3. THE PRAYER OF "THE PERFECT WORKER"

We saw earlier in this chapter that the author distinguishes between the prayers of "beginners and profiters", for whom the exercises may be "Reading, Thinking and Praying", and those of "the perfect worker". "This short prayer" is one of the qualities of the perfection of "This Work".

The author compares the prayer of the "beginners and profiters", with that of "the perfect worker".

"But it is not so with them that continually work in the work of this book. For their meditations be but as they were sudden conceits and blind feelings of their own wretchedness, or of the goodness of God; without any means of reading or hearing coming before, and without any special beholding of any thing under God. These sudden conceits and these blind feelings be sooner learned of God than of man"[43].

Like the "special grace" for "This Work" the source of this prayer is God Himself. He distinguishes between this prayer and the liturgical prayers of the Church, explicitly describing the *suddenness* and *unforseeableness* of the former.

"And right as the meditations of them that continually work in this grace and in this work rise suddenly without any means, right so do their prayers. I mean of their special prayers, not of those prayers that be ordained of Holy Church"[44].

With these passages we understand the *eighth* mark of the mystical life, namely, "that it demands less effort than meditation"[45]. Prayers and meditations are one and the same thing for the "perfect worker" of "This Work". We shall see that at this state "All is one". This character of "sudden conceits" rising "suddenly without any means" is characteristic of mystical prayer. The prayer of "the cloud of unknowing" is characterized also by its wordless character which, with utmost simplicity, contains a world of meaning in one or two syllables.

"But their special prayers rise evermore suddenly unto God, without any means or any premeditation in special coming before, or going therewith. And if they be in words, as they be seldom, then be they but in full few words: yea, and in ever the fewer the better. Yea, and if it be but a little word of one

---

[43] *The Cloud*, Ch. 36, Underhill, p. 160; Hodgson, 72: 23, 73: 1-6.
[44] Ibid. Ch. 37, Underhill, p. 162; Hodgson, 73: 24-25, 75: 1-2.
[45] A. Poulain, *The Graces of Interior Prayer*, p. 114.

syllable, me think it better than of two: and more, too, according to the work of the spirit, since it so is that a ghostly worker in this work should evermore be in the highest and the sovereignest point of the spirit"[46].

This *short* and *wordless* prayer is summed up by the author in *Privy Counsel*.

"When thou comest by thyself think not before what thou shalt do after, but forsake as well good thoughts as evil thoughts. And pray not with thy mouth, unless thou likest right well. And then, if thou aught shall say, look not how much more nor how little that it be, nor weigh not what it is, nor what it meaneth, be it orison, be it psalm, hymn, or anthem, or any other prayer, general or special, mental within endited by thought, or vocal without by pronouncing of word. And look that nothing remain in thy working mind but a naked intent stretching unto God, not clothed in any special thought of God, in himself, how he is in himself, or in any of his works, but only that he is as he is"[47].

So "This Work" and the "short prayer" of *The Cloud* are one and the same thing, and are similarly described by the author in *Epistle of Prayer* as taking less than "a twinkling of an eye".

"And I say that me thinketh that it should be full speedful unto thee at the first beginning of thy prayer, what prayer so ever it be, long or short, for to make it full known unto thine heart, without any feigning, that thou shalt die at the end of thy prayer. . . . For why, the soothfastness of this thing is only in God, and in thee is but a blind abiding of His will, without certainty of one moment, the which is as little or less than a twinkling of an eye . . . this short prayer, so little as it is, shall be accepted of thee unto God for thy full salvation, if thou then didst die, and to the great increase of thy perfection, if thou didst live longer"[48].

We see again this desire of the author not to be inflexible in his behests. The best prayer is wordless, but if there have to be words, then, he says what words would be best.

"I care not though thou haddest nowadays none other meditations of thine own wretchedness, nor of the goodness of God (I mean if thou feel thee thus stirred by grace and by counsel),

---

[46] *The Cloud*, Ch. 37, Underhill, pp. 162-163; Hodgson, 74: 5-13.
[47] *Privy Counsel*, McCann, p. 105; Hodgson, 135: 13-22. Hilton has a similar passage: see Letter to a Hermit, translated by J. D. Russell-Smith, *The Way*, July, 1966, p. 237.
[48] *Epistle of Prayer*, Gardner, pp. 77-79; Hodgson, 48: 1-50: 1.

but such as thou mayest have in this word SIN and in this word GOD; or in such other, which as thee list. Not breaking nor expounding these words with curiosity of wit in beholding after the qualities of these words, as thou wouldest by that beholding increase thy devotion. I trow it should never be so in this case and in this work. But hold them all whole these words . . ."[49].

The author specifically excludes the considerations which have to do with "imperfect meekness and imperfect charity".

The author gives another word, LOVE. He also intimates in the following passage why a prayer of one syllable is better than of two.

"And if thee list have this intent lapped and folden in one word, for thou shouldest have better hold thereupon, take thee but a little word of one syllable: for so it is better than of two, for ever the shorter it is the better it accordeth with the work of the Spirit. And such a word is this word GOD or this word LOVE. Choose thee whether thou wilt, or another; as thee list, which that thee liketh best of one syllable. And fasten this word to thine heart, so that it never go thence for thing that befalleth"[50].

With this description of the prayer of one syllable we see the unity and synthesis of "This Work". The state of "the cloud of forgetting", for all our analysis of it, is not separate from "the cloud of unknowing", for the two are but one "Work". We see that everything involved in "This Work" is being synthesized and united as ONE, for with "This Work" ALL is ONE. Whereas for us it is necessary slowly to study each part, considering the stages separately, the "worker", through experience, sees everything as one.

The author gives his reason why he chose these two short words SIN and GOD.

"And then, since it so is that all evil be comprehended in sin, either by cause or by being, let us therefore when we will intentively pray for removing of evil either say, or think, or mean, nought else nor no more words, but this little word 'sin'. And if we will intentively pray for getting of good, let us cry, either with word or with thought or with desire, nought else nor no more words, but this word 'God'. For why, in God be all good, both by cause and by being. Have no marvel why I set these words forby all other"[51].

49 *The Cloud*, Ch. 36, Underhill, pp. 160-161; Hodgson, 73: 7-15.
50 Ibid. Ch. 7, Underhill, pp. 81-82; Hodgson, 28: 10-16.
51 Ibid. Ch. 39, Underhill, pp. 168-169; Hodgson, 77: 6-14.

And there is always that summing up.

"Prayer in itself properly is not else, but a devout intent direct unto God, for getting of good and removing of evil"[52].

The author means that this prayer is nothing else but the "naked intent unto God", which is "This Work". He gives further meaning to the word SIN.

". . . and mean by sin, a *lump*, thou wottest never what, none other thing but thyself. Me think that in this blind beholding of sin, thus congealed in a lump, none other thing than thyself, it should be no need to bind a madder thing, than thou shouldest be in this time"[53].

We shall see how this idea of SIN being a lump, identified with "the worker" himself, will have greater and deeper significance when the "being" of man is considered in relation to the "Being of God". And then we shall see how this "being of man" is the cause of deep "ghostly sorrow" for the "worker" himself. We see, too, how the author now identifies the perfection of this prayer with the "worker" himself. For this "short prayer" the author uses the figures of "shield" and "spear" to describe the *downward* and *upward* movements of the two clouds[54]. The urgency of the prayer in *Epistle of Prayer*, likewise *wordless* and *silent*, is caused by the sense of impending death, even before the short prayer is finished. But this fear is balanced with *hope*, which is always a dominant theme of *The Cloud*.

"For what reaveth from a soul more readily the affection of sinning, than doth a true working of dread of death? And what moveth a soul more fervently to working of good, than doth a certain hope in the mercy and the goodness of God, the which is brought in by this second thought? For why, the ghostly feeling of this second thought, when it is thus truly joined to the first, shall be to thee, a sure staff of hope to hold thee by all thy good doing"[55].

In the *Epistle of Prayer*, too, the object of the prayer is God only for Himself.

". . . yet this soul, seeing the loveliness of God in Himself, and the abundance thereof, should be ravished over his might for

52 Ibid. Ch. 39, Underhill, p. 168; Hodgson, 77: 4-5.
53 Ibid. Ch. 36, Underhill, p. 161; Hodgson, 73: 15-19.
54 Ibid. Ch. 7, Underhill, p. 82; Hodgson, 28: 17-20.
55 *Epistle of Prayer*, Gardner, pp. 79-80; Hodgson, 50: 5-12.

to love God, till the heart brast; so lovely and so liking, so good and so glorious He is in Himself"[56].

The thing that naturally comes to mind is the origin of this prayer. The author anticipates this question and gives the answer. It is from God that he learned this prayer. In the same way the disciple could learn a similar prayer from God Himself[57]. And this is the best way. One is struck by the consuming desire of the author always to put God in the foreground. Whatever he teaches his disciple, he most carefully points out the source as being God. He would not deflect any trace of honour to himself. This overriding humility and charity is one of the stamps of authenticity of *The Cloud*. The author then explains the value of this "short prayer". He shows that he is full of ordinary good sense and can use homely examples as well as very sublime ones.

"That this be sooth, see by ensample in the course of nature. A man or a woman, afraid with any sudden chance of fire or of man's death or what else that it be, suddenly in the height of his spirit, he is driven upon haste and upon need for to cry or for to pray after help. Yea, how? Surely, not in many words, nor yet in one word of two syllables. And why is that? For him thinketh it over long tarrying for to declare the need and the work of his great spirit. And therefore he bursteth up hideously with a great spirit, and cryeth a little word, but of one syllable: as is this word 'fire' or this word 'out' "[58].

And he describes the similar effects they produce.

"And right as this little word 'fire' stirreth rather and pierceth more hastily the ears of the hearers, so doth a little word of one syllable when it is not only spoken or thought, but privily meant in the deepness of spirit; the which is the height, for in ghostliness all is one, height and deepness, length and breadth. And rather it pierceth the ears of Almighty God than doth any long psalter unmindfully mumbled in the teeth"[59].

So the prayer of *The Cloud* becomes identified now with the loss of distinction as to space, or rather as to the ALLNESS of it. And with this he describes the value of this "short prayer" on the basis of an exegesis of a passage from St. Paul.

56 Ibid. Gardner, p. 84; Hodgson, 53: 17-21.
57 *The Cloud*, Ch. 39, Underhill, p. 169; Hodgson, 77: 14-22.
58 Ibid. Ch. 37, Underhill, p. 163; Hodgson, 74: 13-22.
59 Ibid. Ch. 37, Underhill, pp. 163-164; Hodgson, 74: 23-75: 1-4.

"In this time it is that a soul hath comprehended after the lesson of Saint Paul with all saints—not fully, but in manner and in part, as it is according unto this work—which is the length and the breadth, the height and the deepness of everlasting and all-lovely, almighty, and all-witting God. The everlastingness of God is His length. His love is His breadth. His might is His height. And His wisdom is His deepness. No wonder though a soul that is thus nigh conformed by grace to the image and the likeness of God his maker, be soon heard of God!"[60].

And there is a wonderful effect of this "short prayer" on the sinner-now-turned-contemplative, and he brings in most tellingly his insistence on the virtue of heroic hope.

"Yea, though it be a full sinful soul, the which is to God as it were an enemy; an he might through grace come for to cry such a little syllable in the height and the deepness, the length and the breadth of his spirit, yet he should for the hideous noise of his cry be always heard and helped of God"[61].

His summing-up is more of a punch line.

"And herefore it is written, that short prayer pierceth heaven"[62]. Immediately he explains why this is so by his favourite device of an anticipated question and answer.

"And why pierceth it heaven, this little short prayer of one little syllable? Surely because it is prayed with a full spirit, in the height and in the deepness, in the length and in the breadth of his spirit that prayeth it. In the height it is, for it is with all the might of the spirit. In the deepness it is, for in this little syllable be contained all the wits of the spirit. In the length it is, for might it ever feel as it feeleth, ever would it cry as it cryeth. In the breadth it is, for it willeth the same to all other that it willeth to itself"[63].

The author emphasizes the psychological importance of this

---

60 Ibid. Ch. 38, Underhill, pp. 165-166; Hodgson, 75: 13-21. Walter Hilton has a similar application of this exegesis of St. Paul " ... but that ye might know and feel with all holy, which is the length of the endless being of God, the breadth of the wonderful charity and the goodness of God, the height of the almighty majesty of Him, and the groundless deepness of the wisdom of God". (*Scale I*, Ch. 12, Underhill, p. 26.)
61 *The Cloud*, Ch. 38, Underhill, p. 166; Hodgson, 75: 21-76: 1-3.
62 Ibid. Ch. 37, Underhill, p. 164; Hodgson, 75: 4-5.
63 Ibid. Ch. 38, Underhill, p. 165; Hodgson, 75: 6-13. St. John of the Cross has a passage explaining why the "short prayer penetrates the Heavens". "For this cause the Wise Man said: 'Better is the end of a prayer than the beginning'. But those that so succeed instantly become acts in God, for which reason it is said that the short prayer penetrates the Heavens. Wherefore the soul that is prepared can perform more acts, and acts of greater intensity, in a short time than the soul that is not prepared can perform in a long time ... " *Living Flame*, Allison-Peers, p. 33.)

"short prayer" in which "all the wits of the spirit" are drawn and synthesized.

This then is the "short prayer" of the "perfect worker of This Work".

4. "HOLY DESIRE" AND "GOOD WILL"

The author identifies "This Work" which is the "meek stirring of love" with "good will".

> "And therefore I pray thee, lean listily to this meek stirring of love in thine heart, and follow thereafter: for it will be thy guide in this life and bring thee to bliss in the tother. It is the substance of all good living, and without it no good work may be begun nor ended. It is nought else but a good and an according will unto God, and a manner of well-pleasedness and a gladness that thou feelest in thy will of all that he doth".[64].

In this passage, too, we see the excellence of "This Work". And the "chaste love", discussed earlier in this chapter, is also here contained.

We should not consider the terms "good will' and "holy desire" out of context of the whole discussion, as to do so gives the impression that the author intends the ordinary states before the "special call". "Good will" and "desire" are identified with the "ghostly nature of This Work".

> "Insomuch, that whoso had a true desire for to be at heaven, then that same time he were in heaven ghostly. For the high and the next way thither is run by desires, and not by paces of feet. . . . And surely as verily is a soul there where it loveth, as in the body that liveth by it and to the which it giveth life"[65].

In the test by which one may know the presence of "the privy teaching of the Spirit of God", the author insists that the continuing presence of "true desire", despite the many absences of the Lord, is the truest means of identifying "grace". This habitual, dominant, intransigent quality of the "desire" is a mark of the mystical life. This is so only because the "desire" itself is caused by God and signifies a "Presence of God".

> "And Saint Gregory to witness, that all holy desires grow by

---

[64] *The Cloud*, Ch. 49, Underhill, p. 197; Hodgson; 92: 14-20.
[65] Ibid. Ch. 60, Underhill, p. 232; Hodgson 112: 12-19. Cf. Hilton's passages on "great desire to Jhesu". *Scale I*, Ch. 46, Underhill, p. 112.

delays: and if they wane by delays, then were they never holy desires. . . . Of this holy desire speaketh Saint Austin and saith, that all the life of a good Christian man is nought else but holy desire"[66].

Spiritual writers love to speak of the darkest part of the night just before the breaking of the dawn. Surely, the descriptions which the author gives of "chaste love" and "deep ghostly sorrow" as well as the *pain* and the *travail* involved in "the cloud of forgetting" indicate a depth of state below which the soul cannot be brought. And we see that even with the "special grace" these difficulties make the less courageous turn back. We hear from St. John of the Cross that there are few who attain to the lofty state, not because God desires that this be so, but because only a small number are strong enough to endure the rigours of the ascent[67]. To recapitulate, we see that the author intended his various descriptions of "the cloud of unknowing" to be taken as one.

The "work" of *Privy Counsel*, the short prayer of the *Epistle of Prayer*, which is also described as "the fruit for the King", the Mystical Theology of Dionysius, the Ark of the Covenant, "the short prayer of the perfect worker of The Cloud", the synthesis of the Virtues, "chaste love", "deep ghostly sorrow", "Holy Desire" and "Good Will"—all these are but one, which is "This Work" and "the cloud of unknowing". And in all these the author means a certain presence of

---

[66] *The Cloud*, Ch. 75, Underhill, pp. 269-270; Hodgson, 132: 20-133: 1-3. Walter Hilton has a similar passage on "desire" which was noted by Miss Dorothy Jones. "St. Austin saith that the life of each good Christian man is a continual desire to God; and that is of great virtue, for it is a great crying in the ears of God. The more thou desirest, the higher thou criest, the better thou prayest, the wiselier thou thinkest. And what is this desire? Soothly, but a loathing of all this world's bliss, of this fleshly liking in thine heart, and a wonderful longing with a trustful yearning for endless bliss and heavenly desire and joy. This thinkest me may be called a desire to God for Himself" (*Mixed Life*, Jones, p. 44; also *Qui Habitat*, Ch. xiv, Jones, p. 163). Notice that in this short paragraph, three important ideas of *The Cloud* are contained: desire, St. Austin, and the desire of God for Himself.

[67] St. John of the Cross, *Living Flame*, Allison-Peers, p. 46. Note also another description of this state. "By means of these trials whereinto God leads the soul and the senses, the soul gradually acquires virtues and strength and perfection, together with bitterness, for virtue is made perfect in weakness, and is wrought by the experience of sufferings. For iron cannot be subservient to the intelligence of the artificer, unless he use fire and a hammer, which do harm to the iron if it be compared with what it was in its former state. . . . He that is not tried, what does he know and whereof has he knowledge?" (*Living Flame*, p. 46.)

God. All this is also "nought", as it is also "The ALL". This identification reaches its peak when the "perfect stirring of love" that comes successively with each moment of time, is equated with that eternal state of heaven when time shall be no more.

> "For why, that perfect stirring of love that beginneth here is even in number with that that shall last without end in the bliss of heaven, for all it is but one"[68].

Despite the *travail* and *deep ghostly sorrow* that the disciple has to undergo, the author says that it is a "rest". and he insists on the need for "great restfulness and peace" in "This Work".

> "But now mayest thou say: What rest is this that thou speakest of? For methinketh it is travail painful and no rest. For when I set me to do as thou sayest, I find therein no rest, but pain and battle on all sides. For on that one part my wits would have me away, and I will not; and on that other part I would feel God and lack the feeling of myself, and I may not. So that battle is on all sides and pain, and this seemeth to me a quaint rest that thou speakest of. To this I answer and say: that thou art not yet used in this work, and therefore it is more painful to thee. But if thou wert wont thereto and knewest by experience what profit were therein, thou wouldst not willingly come out thereof to have all the bodily rest and joy of this world. And yet it is great pain and travail also. But in that I call it a rest, for the soul is not in doubt what it shall do; and also for a soul is assured—I mean in the time of this doing, that it shall not much err"[69].

This state of rest and peace sums up all the various descriptions that the author had been giving.

It is into this state that the *personal invasion* by God of the soul takes place. And while prior to this the author's expressions and phrases tended to be abstract, indicating a certain presence of God, in this direct *invasion* by God the author is much more precise in his descriptions. What the author describes as "rest" the disciple sees as nothing but "affliction and strife", and we see again the problems of expressing the higher, mystical state.

The author reconciles his view with the difficulty of the disciple when he says that it "is an affliction, and a labour, too.

---

[68] *The Cloud*, Ch. 20, Underhill, p. 123; Hodgson, 52: 21-23.
[69] *Privy Counsel*, McCann, p. 140; Hodgson, 172: 4-18. Cf. Walter Hilton's description of "This restful dravail", *Scale II*, Ch. 40; Underhill, p. 418.

But still I call it rest". This reconciliation is possible only in the higher reaches of the mystical life when everything becomes synthesized, unified and concentrated into extreme simplicity. We touch here a problem posed by a spiritual writer.

"It remains, you say, that the further one advances the easier virtue becomes, and consequently progress is less difficult. Then there is no need of the grace of contemplation to finish the course in the case of the man who has completed the first and the most difficult stages. Is there not a misunderstanding here? . . . It would then, to be logical, be necessary to maintain that the first polishing of a soul which has but just returned from a state of mortal sin, and is raising itself to a certain degree of spiritual life and inward comeliness (that very commonplace thing which we see every day) represents a greater moral effort, the overcoming of a greater difficulty, than those last and sublime purifications from self-love whereby the soul is prepared for final and perfect union with God in Heaven. Who will believe this? Why then are there so many souls who afford us the spectacle of a beginning in virtue, and so few that of its consummation? Why that feeling of powerlessness, which affects us in quite another way after years of effort, before the task in prospect, than in the first steps by which we journeyed up to the foot of that so rugged and steep mountain?"[70].

The answer is the "special grace" which makes all difficulties light.

"What may sometimes cause illusion in the observer is that the help of God is poured into souls with such abundance and superabundance that for a time it takes away the feeling of a difficulty to be overcome. But this does not mean that the difficulty is not there, and that it is not great relatively to the agent considered in himself; but rather that the divine succour is so strong that in comparison the difficulty is a bagatelle. Let this profuse succour come in more sparing measure, and you would see the soul panting, sinking under its burden, beseeching for grace. Let us not say, then, that the difficulty was smaller, and therefore required less aid: but rather that if the difficulty were relatively smaller, it is because the help was more abundant"[71].

This passage is a lovely commentary on *Passivity,* the absolute powerlessness of the soul in the presence of the *mystic touch. The Cloud* author attests also to the power of

[70] M. De La Taille, *Letter,* included in Introduction to A. Poulain, *The Graces of Interior Prayer,* pp. c-ci.
[71] Ibid. p. ci.

I

this *special* grace. Without it, no one could endure the *pain* and *travail* involved in "This Work". This passage is only one of several in *The Cloud* and *Privy Counsel* in which is verified the *ninth character* of the *mystic union,* namely, "that it is accompanied by sentiments of love, of repose, of pleasure and often of suffering"[72]. The author claims that there is a feeling produced in the soul "that it shall not much err". St. John of the Cross and St. Teresa of Avila say the same. Fr. Poulain makes his concluding observation on this matter:

> "Whatever opinion may be adopted, this, at least, is the case, that it *seems* to the soul that she can no longer sin, so fully does she feel herself to be participating in the life of God. This does not prevent her seeing very clearly at the same time that of herself she is capable of all kinds of sins. She sees the abyss into which she may fall, and the powerful Hand that sustains her"[73].

One who was writing a treatise on *Mystical Theology* would be very careful to refer to authorities on whom he relied. *The Cloud* author makes this daring claim in such a straightforward manner and stresses the fact that it is God who is the source of his teaching.

5. *"DEEP GHOSTLY SORROW" FOR ONE'S OWN BEING*

We have seen that the more abstract and philosophical aspect of "This Work" in *The Cloud* is translated into a concrete and practical spiritual exercise in *Privy Counsel.* And so we hear the author telling his disciple what to do.

> "But it sufficeth now unto thee to do whole worship unto God with thy substance, and for to offer up thy naked being, the which is the first of thy fruits, in continual sacrifice of praising of God, both for thyself and for all others, as charity asketh . . ."[74].

This complete forgetting of one's being goes far beyond the ordinary act of forgetting (which may be merely a matter of convenience), and is intimately connected with the essence of "This Work".

> "For, an thou wilt busily set thee to the proof, thou shalt find when thou has forgotten all other creatures and all their works —yea, and thereto all thine own works—that there shall live

---

[72] A. Poulain, *The Graces of Interior Prayer*, p. 114.
[73] Ibid. p. 292.
[74] *Privy Counsel*, McCann, pp. 111-112; Hodgson, 142: 1-4.

yet after, betwixt thee and thy God, a naked witting and a feeling of thine own being: the which witting and feeling behoveth always be destroyed, ere the time be that thou feel soothfastly the perfection of this work"[75].

The "destroying" of the feeling of one's being is identified with the perfection of "This Work". And this is possible only by "a full special grace" and in the complete obliteration of all creatures in "the cloud of forgetting".

"But now thou askest me, how thou mayest destroy this naked witting and feeling of thine own being. For peradventure thou thinkest that an it were destroyed, all other lettings were destroyed: and if thou thinkest thus, thou thinkest right truly. But to this I answer thee and I say, that without a full special grace full freely given of God, and thereto a full according ableness to receive this grace on thy part, this naked witting and feeling of thy being may on nowise be destroyed. And this ableness is nought else but a strong and a deep ghostly sorrow"[76].

This "deep ghostly sorrow" is "this special grace", "This Work" and the "perfect prayer" of *The Cloud*, and is seen in terms of deep physical suffering of *pain* and *travail*.

"This is true sorrow; this is perfect sorow; and well were him that might win to this sorrow. All men have matter of sorrow; but most specially he feeleth matter of sorrow, that wottest and feeleth that he is. All other sorrows be unto this in comparison but as it were game to earnest. For he may make sorrow earnestly, that wottest and feeleth not only what he is, but that he is"[77].

This sorrow then has to do with the consideration of one's being. One reason for the sorrow is comparing the soul with God. There is that contrast between the "stinking lump of himself" and the Perfection of God. And in this is sorrow.

"For as oft as he would have a true witting and a feeling of his God in purity of spirit, as it may be here, and sithen feeleth that he may not—for he findeth evermore his witting and his feeling as it were occupied and filled with a foul stinking lump of himself, the which behoveth always be hated and be despised and forsaken, if he shall be God's perfect disciple learned of Himself in the mount of perfection—so oft he goeth nigh mad for sorrow. Insomuch, that he weepeth and waileth, striveth,

[75] *The Cloud*, Ch. 43, Underhill, p. 179; Hodgson, 82: 22-83: 1-5.
[76] Ibid. Ch. 44, Underhill, p. 180; Hodgson, 83: 6-13.
[77] Ibid. Ch. 44, Underhill, p. 181; Hodgson, 83: 17-84: 1.

curseth, and banneth; and shortly to say, him thinketh that he beareth so heavy a burden of himself that he careth never what betides him, so that God were pleased"[78].

Surely in this consideration there is matter enough for sorrow. The author speaks in terms of an experience, not something abstract in which he has not been involved. Perhaps another reason for this sorrow is that God had made the disciple "taste and see the Lord", and thereafter he could never be the same again. And the disciple is acutely aware that it is his "being" that stands in the way. There is that intense longing for the Lord which has been awakened by the Lord Himself. The condition that the author here describes seems similar to that related by St. John of the Cross, when the soul asks the "living flame of love . . . break the web of this sweet encounter"[79].

The author has physical life clearly in mind. And the "being of man" has to do with his physical existence, which is the "first of his fruits" on which all his other perfections depend.

"And yet in all this sorrow he desireth not to unbe: for that were devil's madness and despite unto God. But him listeth right well to be; and he intendeth full heartily thanking to God, for the worthiness and the gift of his being, for all that he desire unceasingly for to lack the witting and the feeling of his being"[80].

We then arrive at the point when it is the "being of man" that is in direct confrontation with the "Being of God". And the full perfection is reached when the "being of man" is, as it were, "drowned in the Being of God", so that the "Being of God" alone remains without any confusion of nature, their respective identities always preserved distinct and separate.

[78] Ibid. Ch. 44, Underhill, pp. 181-182; Hodgson, 84: 11-20. Cf. Walter Hilton, *Qui Habitat*, Jones, p. 164. *Bonum Est*, Jones, pp. 180-181.

[79] "And when it sees that it has only now to break the frail web of this human condition of natural life wherein it feels itself to be enmeshed and imprisoned, and its liberty to be impeded, it desires to be loosed and to see itself with Christ, and to burst these bonds of spirit and of flesh, which are of very different kinds, so that each may receive its deserts, the flesh remaining upon the earth and the spirit returning to God that gave it". (St. John of the Cross, *Living Flame*, Allison-Peers, p. 32.) Saints have spoken of this homesickness for God, the classic example being St. Augustine's exclamation, "Thou hast made us for thyself, O Lord, and our hearts are restless till they rest in Thee". (*Confessions*, Book I, Ch. I.)

[80] *The Cloud*, Ch. 44, Underhill, p. 182; Hodgson, 84: 20-85:-1-2.

"Let that meekness be thy mirror and thy mind wholly. Think no further of thyself than I bid thee do of thy God, so that thou be one with him in spirit as thus, without any separating and scattering of mind"[81].

The author may give the impression of being tame. But we have to bear in mind that he is giving to his passages much deeper and profounder meaning than the words suggest, even when used to express their fullest meaning. It is in relation to the context of "This Work" that these words must be seen. This union between the "being of man" and the "Being of God" is described in more concrete terms as a "noble denial of itself", as the "full and final forsaking of itself". This is also the condition of "chaste love".

"So that for this noble noughting of itself in very meekness, and this high alling of God in perfect charity, it deserveth to have God—in whose love it is deeply drenched in full and final forsaking of itself as nought and less, if less might be—mightily, wisely and goodly succouring it, keeping it, and defending it from all adversities bodily and ghostly without business or travail, regard or care of itself"[82].

The passage suggests the desire of the author to carry the force of words to greater depths and yield the meaning he desires of them, "as nought and less, if less might be . . .".

Finally we see that the author continues to identify his descriptions one with another. This "deep ghostly sorrow" is now also "holy desire", which is also "This Work".

"This sorrow, if it be truly conceived, is full of holy desire: and else might never man in this life abide it nor bear it. For were it not that a soul were somewhat fed with a manner of comfort of his working, else should he not be able to bear the pain that he hath of the witting and feeling of his being"[83].

E.   "THE BEING OF MAN"

The concept of "being" is a key and dominant theme in the teaching of the author of *The Cloud*. We shall see that the highest experience in the ascent to God is accomplished when the "being of man" is drowned in the "Being of God". The author's treatment of the "being of man" runs parallel to the development of "the naked Being of God".

[81] *Privy Counsel*, McCann, p. 106; Hodgson, 136: 7-9.
[82] Ibid. McCann, p. 119; Hodgson, 149; 13-19.
[83] *The Cloud*, Ch. 44, Underhill, p. 181; Hodgson, 84: 6-11.

There is, however, this difference as regards the person himself. While he must concentrate only on the "naked Being of God for himself only", to the exclusion of everything else, he must also "completely forget" his own "being". The two aspects are inseparable. While the "being of man" is completely forgotten, it is done only so that the "Being of God" can completely occupy the attention of "This Work". This supporting role of the "being of man" in the ascent to God is a particular and personal nuance of the tradition of the *Mystics of the Divine Essence,* proper to *The Cloud* author. The inseparable character of these two concepts is best seen in the passage on "the short prayer", which is a perfection of "This Work".

> "This word shall be thy shield and thy spear, whether thou ridest on peace or on war. With this word, thou shalt beat on this cloud and this darkness above thee. With this word, thou shall smite down all manner of thought under the cloud of forgetting . . ."[84].

Like "the naked Being of God" the "being of man" is more heavily philosophical in its treatment in *The Cloud*. It is in *Privy Counsel* that the development takes the form of an *offering,* and where it is given full development. It seems that this is one of the questions posed by the disciple. Right in the opening passages of *Privy Counsel,* the author concentrates his attention on "the naked intent stretching unto God . . . only that he is as he is"[85], and this is joined to the concept of the "being of man" which is "nought else . . . but a naked thought and a blind feeling of thine own being"[86]. And this in the form of an offering: "That that I am, Lord, I offer unto thee, without any looking to any quality of thy being, but only that thou art as thou art, without any more"[87]. This is one of the arguments in favour of *The Cloud* and *Privy Counsel* having been written by the same author to the same disciple. The author speaks of a "special grace" which he and his disciple had received for "This Work" and it would not be easy to find two people so favoured.

In developing this theme we shall follow its course through

---

[84] Ibid. Ch. 7, Underhill, p. 82; Hodgson, 28: 17-20.
[85] *Privy Counsel,* McCann, p. 105; Hodgson, 135: 20-22.
[86] Ibid. McCann, p. 106; Hodgson, 136: 2-3.
[87] Ibid. McCann, p. 106; Hodgson, 136: 4-6.

The Cloud to *Privy Counsel*. We see a definite progression of ideas, not so much on the part of the author as on the understanding that the disciple has of the theme. The author testifies to this gradual growth of understanding on the part of the disciple.

> "But for methought that thou wert not yet able suddenly to be lifted up to the ghostly feeling of the being of God, for rudeness in thy ghostly feeling, therefore, to let thee climb thereto by degrees, I bade thee first gnaw on the naked feeling of thine own being, unto the time that thou mightest be made able to the high feeling of God by ghostly continuance in this privy work"[88].

The author describes the "being of man" in relation to the perfections of "This Work". In the passages he stresses the *experimental* quality in so far as the "being of man" is concerned, and this he describes by "witting and feeling" in connection with the "deep ghostly sorrow" which is a perfection of "This Work". This *feeling*, too, is that intense habitual sense of one's sinfulness that mystics so commonly attest to, in the presence of the Infinite Holiness of God. And in relation to the ascent, it is this unworthiness that stands in the way and makes the disciple see what he is in the sight of God. There is always a parallel development between "the naked Being of God" and the "being of man" in relation to "This Work".

> "And thou shalt understand, that thou shalt not only in this work forget all other creatures than thyself, or their deeds or thine, but also thou shalt in this work forget both thyself and also thy deeds for God, as well as other creatures and their deeds"[89].

And just as the IS of God contains all the perfections and attributes of God, so the being of man is the first of his gifts on which all his other qualities depend. This fundamental awareness of one's existence will always be present. This, too, must be forgotten in "This Work".

> "For, an thou wilt busily set thee to the proof, thou shalt find when thou hast forgotten all other creatures and all their works —yea, and thereto all thine own works—that there shall live after, betwixt thee and thy God, a naked witting and a feeling of thine own being: the which witting and feeling behoveth

88 Ibid. McCann, pp. 125-126; Hodgson, 156: 3-8.
89 *The Cloud*, Ch. 43, Underhill, p. 178; Hodgson, 82: 2-6.

always be destroyed, ere the time be that thou feel soothfastly the perfection of this work"[90].

The complete forgetting of one's "being" is also the perfection of "This Work". The author will also equate this with "chaste love".

Since the *feeling* of one's "being" is the fundamental awareness and experience of one's existence, it will always be present as long as one lives. In the context of "This Work" this complete forgetfulness of even one's fundamental awareness can be accomplished only by God's special grace. Does this mean ecstasy as is commonly understood in the context of mystical experiences? "I wot not", as the author would say, so we simply leave him to speak for himself. The passages on the "being of man" and "deep ghostly sorrow" could have been fully understood only by the author and the disciple.

We have said before that in *Privy Counsel* the "being of man" receives more practical treatment than in *The Cloud*, the spiritual exercise taking the form of an offering. He gives an exegesis of a passage from Scripture to describe the manner of this offering: *"Si tetigero vel fimbriam vestimenti ejus, salva ero* . . . Bear up thy sick self as thou art unto gracious God as he is, without any curious or special beholding to any of all the qualities that belong to the being of thyself or of God, whether they be clean or wretched, gracious or natural, godly or manly . . . "[91].

In this close correspondence of "the naked Being of God" and the "being of man", the perfection of "This Work" is reached. The author uses the expressions commonly employed by mystical writers to describe the union between God and the soul.

"It mattereth not now to thee, but that thy blind beholding of thy naked being be gladly borne up in listiness of love, to be knitted and oned in grace and in spirit to the precious being of God in himself only as he is, without more"[92].

The end of "This Work" is reached in this "oneing" of the soul with God. And this in a union of *Love* and *Spirit*. It is tempting to analyse these claims of the author, but it is better

90 Ibid. Ch. 43, Underhill, p. 179; Hodgson, 82; 22-23, 83: 1-5.
91 *Privy Counsel*, McCann, p. 109; Hodgson, 139: 3-11.
92 Ibid. McCann, p. 109; Hodgson, 139: 11-14.

that we should not probe too deeply. The claims are there, that is enough, and if one doubts that the author means what he says then passages in *The Cloud* and *Privy Counsel* making lesser claims must similarly be discounted. The claim concerning "union" is also made elsewhere by the author, and in these passages he uses "union" in the sense of other mystical writers.

F. EXPRESSIONS OF UNION

In order to keep our sights properly trained on the purpose of this study, it may be helpful at this stage to recapitulate. The study has set out to show that the author of *The Cloud* was a mystic, that at least *The Cloud* and *Privy Counsel* are writings of a mystical character, and that the author belongs to the tradition of the *Mystics of the Divine Essence. Nemo dat quod non habet* is a common saying. In writing *The Cloud* the author does not draw on any one particular author, but says that God is the Source of his teaching. The personal experiences described by the author confirm the statement that he was a mystic, and he draws on these experiences rather than on other writers, in his teachings.

As if to anticipate the objection that he may not be serious in his claim to a mystical experience in his writing, he compares "This Work" with other writings which have already been accepted as *mystical*. But this is not enough. He describes "This Work" in such a way that its mystical character comes to the fore. He explicitly uses expressions which are commonly accepted to describe experiences as mystical. One of these is his use of the expression "union", which in *Mystical Theology* is the *union* that can be achieved in this life between God and the soul. He insists on his credentials to encourage his disciple. We see that the author makes bold and startling claims, but although it was never the intention of the present writer to decide, independently of the texts, for or against these claims, their importance cannot be denied. In this regard we are guided by an excellent comment from Professor David Knowles.

"The mystical life must always remain indescribable and incomprehensible to those who stand without. We are confronted by a double danger, that of ignoring or distrusting what we do not understand, and that of exalting the smallest appearance of what is unfamiliar—*omne ignotum pro magnifico*. We may

err by regarding as marvellous what is in fact of little or no
significance, or we may on the other hand regard as ordinary
or negligible what is in fact most precious and most holy. Or
we may in a kind of desperation regard all of which we have no
experience as equally insignificant. If we would do the barest
justice to the importance of the matter we must be prepared
to use the most searching criticism and at the same time to
recognize the true sublime. While we must not be deceived
by words, or by every account of signs and wonders, we must
recognize real worth wherever it is found"[93].

It is at this juncture that we wish to make another observation. On the basis of this study the present writer cannot
wholly agree with the following conclusion of Professor
Knowles concerning Walter Hilton and *The Cloud* author.

"Of the two writers, the author of *The Cloud* excels in clear
instructions and fine analysis of the initial stages of contemplative prayer, while Hilton's strength lies in his distinction of the
active and contemplative lives and his fuller description of the
stages. Neither dwells in any detail on the highest degrees of the
contemplative life as given by Ruysbroeck, St. Teresa, St. John
of the Cross and others, and whereas with the writers just
mentioned there is abundant evidence, external and internal,
that they themselves have directly experienced the sublime
states they describe, there is no external and little internal
evidence in the case of the two Englishmen. Most readers will
feel assured that they were in fact contemplatives, but they will
probably feel also that their range was far smaller than that of
Ruysbroeck and the great Spaniards"[94].

This whole study answers the observation as regards *The
Cloud* author, but the present writer agrees with Professor
Knowles' comments concerning Walter Hilton.

At this stage, too, the present writer wishes to take a stand
as regards the Hilton claim to the authorship of *The Cloud*.
We have mentioned before that on the basis alone of the
published writings of Walter Hilton it would be safe to say that
he was not a mystic. At no place in his writings does he admit
the presence of a "special grace" for himself to do any spiritual
exercise comparable to "This Work" of *The Cloud*. He does
not say that God is the Source for his teachings. A perusal
of *Scale I* and *II* yields the impression that he is writing something like a treatise in spiritual direction, with a practical and

93 D. Knowles, *The English Mystical Tradition*, p. 19.
94 Ibid. pp. 191-192.

immediate need in view. The impression of a personal experience faithfully narrated does not even cross the mind of the present writer. Their respective destinations would preclude discussions comparable to *The Cloud* and *Privy Counsel*. On the basis of these theological arguments drawn from the texts of both groups of writings, it would seem that Walter Hilton cannot be the author of *The Cloud* and *Privy Counsel*. If the arguments drawn from a study of the texts are kept separate from those drawn from Spiritual Theology, it may help to clarify the problem. Philologists would, for example, find some difficulty in seeing clearly the implications drawn from the field of Spiritual Theology. This is different from saying that the meanings of the words are not spiritual. They are "ghostly", as the author says, for they work purely on "ghostly things".

When we limit our observations to *Scale I* and *II*, we do not belittle the other writings of Walter Hilton. We simply wish to point out that the high water mark of Walter Hilton has been reached in the *Scale of Perfection*, which actually is not outstanding for originality or brilliance.

However, notwithstanding these considerations, the present author admits a preference for Walter Hilton as the author of *The Cloud*. This is not unreasonable. The question is still open, and the present writer desires only to clarify the position and suggest fresh avenues for research.

At this juncture we recall the statement of the case made by Professor Helen Gardner quoted earlier in this study:

"Perhaps we ought to put our question the other way round, and ask, not whether Hilton could possibly have written *The Cloud*, but whether the author of *The Cloud* could possibly have written the works of Hilton"[95].

This is not hair-splitting. It is not unreasonable to think that *The Cloud* author could have produced the writings included in the Hilton canon, for they are not so utterly different as to preclude this possibility.

[95] H. Gardner, "The Cloud of Unknowing", *Medium Aevum*, Vol. XVI (1947), p. 42.
"From the evidence available at present it is not possible to decide definitely whether Hilton wrote *The Cloud* or not, but the question may still be regarded as open, so that a comparison of the mystical teaching of *The Scale of Perfection* and *The Cloud* has a further interest from the light it may throw on this problem". (G. Sitwell, "Contemplation in the Scale of Perfection", *Downside Review*, Summer 1949, p. 278.) Hilton's *Scale II*, Chs. 40-44 deserve special attention.

To sum up, it is the opinion of the present writer that on the strength of arguments drawn purely from Spiritual Theology Walter Hilton cannot be the author of *The Cloud* and *Privy Counsel*. But whether or not *The Cloud* author could have been the author of the writings included in the Hilton canon is an entirely different matter. Whilst we have touched upon this point it is really outside the scope of our study.

As *The Cloud* author would say, "but forth of our matter".

The author calls his principal work "A Book of Contemplation The Which Is Called The Cloud Of Unknowing, In The Which A Soul Is Oned With God". Right at the beginning, the author has set the sights on *Union with God*. This *union* is not achieved straight away, but is the culmination of "This Work". Whether the ascent be long or short depends on God alone. The author describes this union always with the saving clause "such as may be had here".

> ". . . as God vouchsafeth for to learn to His ghostly disciples after His well willing and their according ableness in body and in soul, in degree and disposition, ere the time be that they may perfectly be oned unto God in perfect charity—such as may be had here—if God vouchsafeth"[96].

In this passage, too, we see the primacy of love, here described as "charity". It is not, therefore, an act of a faculty of the soul as such, but a whole and total response of man as a person.

God is Spirit, and the union with Him must therefore be achieved through the spiritual faculty of man.

> "Thou wottest well this, that God is a Spirit; and whoso should be oned unto Him, it behoveth to be in soothfastness and deepness of spirit, full far from any feigned bodily thing"[97].

In this passage is verified the *Sixth mark* of the mystical life that Fr. Poulain gives, namely "The union is produced neither by reasoning, nor by the consideration of creatures, nor by sensible images . . ."[98].

To the qualification of this union being *in spirit* and *in love,* the author gives a further qualification which looks to the dynamic response of man. In this we hear the echo of the

---

96 *The Cloud,* Ch. 44, Underhill, pp. 182-183; Hodgson, 85: 4-8.
97 Ibid. Ch. 47, Underhill, p. 190; Hodgson, 88: 19-21.
98 A. Poulain, *The Graces of Interior Prayer,* p. 114.

end for which God tries the soul, to make the soul as pliant to God's will "as a roan glove to thine hand bodily". There is never a confusion of *natures* in *union*. The author takes great pains to make the distinction clear. He gives a further description of union which is *by grace*. Because of this, there is a continuity of union, begun here, till heaven is reached.

"For why, He is God by nature without beginning; and thou, that sometime wert nought in substance, and thereto after when thou wert by His might and His love made ought, wilfully with sin madest thyself worse than nought, only by His mercy without thy desert are made a God in grace, oned with Him in spirit without departing, both here and in bliss of heaven without any end"[99].

In *Privy Counsel* the author describes the same qualities with varying nuances more in relation to "This Work". Thus, there is that extreme concentration that accompanies the thought of the "naked Being of God alone".

"Think no further of thyself than I bid thee do of thy God, so that thou be one with Him in spirit as thus, without any separating and scattering of mind"[100].

In an exegesis of a passage from Solomon, the author describes this union between God and the Soul:

"In great commendation of this sweet subtle working, the which in itself is the high wisdom of the Godhead graciously descending into man's soul, knitting it and oneing it unto himself in ghostly subtlety and prudence of spirit, the wise man Solomon bursteth up and saith: *Beatus homo qui invenit sapientiam, et qui affluit prudentia . . .*"[101].

He describes the *union* in the sense of the *perfection of the virtues,* which is a perfection of "This Work" also.

"I answer in thy person and I say, that perfection of man's soul is nought else but a onehead made betwixt God and it in perfect charity. This perfection is so high and so pure in itself above the understanding of man, that it may not be known nor perceived in itself"[102].

Like two converging streams, the principal ideas of "the naked Being of God" and the "being of man" come together

99 *The Cloud*, Ch. 67, Underhill, pp. 247-248; Hodgson, 120: 13-19.
100 *Privy Counsel*, McCann, p. 106; Hodgson, 136: 7-9.
101 Ibid. McCann, p. 115; Hodgson, 145: 3-7.
102 Ibid. McCann, p. 123; Hodgson, 153: 25-29.

towards the middle of *Privy Counsel*. The streams meander through various byways because the author wishes to explain the different elements of "This Work". Now "the naked Being of God" and the "being of man" unite in the perfection of "This Work". Each is explained in relation to the other. For the highest perfection of "This Work" is reached when the "being of man" is merged with "the naked Being of God". Only "the naked Being of God" remains in the end.

> "For know thou for certain, that although I bid thee forget all things but the blind feeling of thy naked being, yet nevertheless my will is—and that was mine intent in the beginning—that thou forget the feeling of the being of thyself as for the feeling of the being of God. And for this reason I proved thee in the beginning that God is thy being"[103].

We see the author describing this "forgetting" in another way, this time in the context of what he calls "chaste love". This takes place when the disciple removes, as it were, the clothing of his own being to put on "God's livery". Here the author uses the figures of *utterly spoiling, clothing,* and *enwrapping*.

> "And this is the true condition of a perfect lover, only and utterly to spoil himself of himself for that thing that he loveth, and not admit nor suffer to be clothed but only in that thing that he loveth; and that not only for a time, but endlessly to be enwrapped therein in full and final forgetting of himself"[104].

The author then takes up this theme of "chaste love" and explains it in terms of the scriptural passage of "Whoso will love me, let him forsake himself". He then gives an exegesis of this passage in relation to "This Work".

> "As who should say: Let him spoil himself of himself, if he will be verily clothed in me that am the full garment of love and of lasting that never shall have end. And therefore, ever when thou beholdest to thy working, and seest and feelest that it is thyself that thou feelest and not God, then shalt thou make sorrow earnestly and heartily long after the feeling of God, evermore desiring without ceasing for to forgo the woeful witting and the foul feeling of thy blind being; and covet to flee from thyself as from venom"[105].

In the perfection of "This Work" when the "final forgetting"

---

103 Ibid. McCann, p. 125; Hodgson, 155: 27-29, 156: 1-3.
104 Ibid. McCann, p. 126; Hodgson, 156: 16-20.
105 Ibid. McCann, p. 126; Hodgson, 156: 22-29, 157: 1-2.

of one's "being" is reached, the Lord gives a glimpse, as it were, of Himself, to the soul striving to reach Him in love.

> ". . . for there will always follow and go with thy doing a naked feeling of thy blind being, be thou never so busy, except it be some seldom short time when God will let thee feel Himself in abundance of love . . ."[106].

This is the reason for the "deep ghostly sorrow", for the Lord has allowed the soul "to taste and see the Lord", and the soul can never return to its former state. The different *feelings* that one has as regards one's "own being" and that of "God's Being" is summed up by the author.

> "Lo! here mayest thou see that thou must sorrowfully desire to forgo the feeling of thyself, and painfully bear the burthen of thyself as a cross, ere thou mayest be oned to God in ghostly feeling of Himself, the which is perfect charity. And here mayest thou see somewhat and in part feel—according as thou art touched and ghostly marked with this grace—the worthiness of this work before all other"[107].

In these passages the importance of allowing the author to speak for himself is most felt. Because they had the "special grace" for "This Work" there is a whole field of understanding between the author and the disciple about which we can only speculate. And at such a level speculation is not rewarding. The passages were intended for the disciple, so that even a man blessed with a like "grace" would be unable to gain the full meaning. The disciple had only the letter to guide him, the rest had to be supplied by the "privy teaching of the Spirit of God".

Once this point is reached the development stops and the author goes back to explaining the various elements that go to make "This Work". We shall not follow the author but will continue the development to that still further intervention of God, when the *invasion* and *breakthrough* is by God alone. The author states that this intervention is actually capable of being "seen".

G. "A BEAM OF GHOSTLY LIGHT PIERCING THIS CLOUD OF UNKNOWING"

We have seen how clearly and carefully the author

---

[106] Ibid. McCann, p. 126; Hodgson, 157: 7-10.
[107] Ibid. McCann, p. 127; Hodgson, 157: 20-26.

delineates the various stages in the ascent to God. We have seen, too, the great care that he takes to describe the "otherness" of God and "His Own Work". And while he follows the thought of the Pseudo-Dionysius as regards the *Divine Transcendence,* he has his own particular description of the *Divine Transcendence,* acknowledging that God can do what He wills, in whatever manner He wills, to whom He wills. It is more the acceptance that *God acts* in the soul without misunderstanding His mind. A point is reached in the ascent beyond which the soul cannot go on his own. From this point on God can carry the soul wherever He desires, but there will always be this "cloud of unknowing" between the soul and God. This "cloud" signifies a "Presence" of God, something like the "burning bush" in the story of Moses, which was the "Place Where God Was".

And so from out of this cloud, comes the *direct invasion* of the soul by God.

"Then will He sometimes peradventure send out a beam of ghostly light, piercing this cloud of unknowing that is betwixt thee and Him . . ."[108].

This *breakthrough* by God reveals a state distinct from the one immediately preceding it. The author emphasizes that the *invasion* by God is unmistakable, and his words reveal a personal experience. He insists on the proper understanding of the workings of "the mights of the soul" to avoid delusions and deceits. He is wary of comforts and consolations although for that matter he does not condemn them. His temperament is not one that would easily accept as an experience any exceptional phenomena. So when we notice the economy and almost reluctance with which he narrates his experiences, then we can say that these experiences are genuine.

In this passage too is described the clarity of the interior vision of the "presence of God". This is what is called *The Mystic Claim.* The author does not speak of a vision of God as in the *beatific vision.* It is rather "an intellectual knowledge of God, generally regarded as distinct from the beatific vision, not only in *degree,* but in *kind;* and on the other hand,

---

[108] *The Cloud,* Ch. 26, Underhill, pp. 139-140; Hodgson; 62: 14-15.
Cf. Hilton *Scale II,* Ch. 27, Underhill, p. 345.

no less distinct from all abstract knowledge"[109]. There is verified in this image of a "beam" the *fifth* mark of the mystical life, namely that "the mode of communication is partially incomprehensible"[110].

When he uses the expression "sometimes peradventure", it is not a denial of the reality of his experience. He attests rather to it being sudden and unexpected. He would not speak for God, and having described the experience, he does not promise the same for the disciple.

This "beam of ghostly light" should not be taken in the material sense but rather as brilliance "in the sovereignest point of the spirit", something *seen* by "the inner eyes" in the emptiness and void left by the "cloud of forgetting". Mystics attest to this spiritual sense. We find in this passage the *second fundamental* mark of the mystical life, namely that "this knowledge is the result of an impression, a spiritual *sensation* of a special kind"[111]. This experience is in the "intentional order" following the teaching of the author on "the cloud of unknowing" as "a lacking of knowing: as all that thing that thou knowest not, or else thou hast forgotten, it is dark to thee; for thou seest it not with thy ghostly eye"[112]. This "beam of ghostly light" is what was seen by the author with his "ghostly eye", and is the response of God to his work to "try for to pierce that darkness above thee. And smite upon that thick cloud of unknowing with a sharp dart of longing love . . ."[113]. There is a coincidence of "piercing" between the soul and God. And in this "piercing" is a brief coincidence with the "Essence of God", not as God IS in the Beatific Vision but "as may be in this life". It is then the "cloud of unknowing" that was pierced by God, and which the soul keeps on piercing with "This Work". The author gives specific meaning to this figure in *The Epistle of Prayer*: ". . . The clear beam of everlasting light, the which is God"[114]. The symbolism of "the cloud" in Holy Scripture, both in the Old

[109] J. V. Bainvel, Introduction to A. Poulain, *The Graces of Interior Prayer*, p. lxi.
[110] A. Poulain, *The Graces of Interior Prayer*, p. 114.
[111] Ibid p. 88.
[112] *The Cloud*, Ch. 4, Underhill, p. 73; Hodgson, 23 : 20-22.
[113] Ibid. Ch. 6, Underhill, p. 78; Hodgson, 26 : 10-12.
[114] *Epistle of Prayer*, Hodgson, 54 : 7-8.

and the New Testament, has been that of a "Presence of God", accompanying always the "Theophanies" of Jahweh[115].

Other mystical writers have made similar descriptions. Guige de Pont says that "the *via affirmationis* of the speculative contemplation leads to the exceptional favour of a vision of the Divine Light"[116]. And this narration by *The Cloud* author finds close resemblance to that which Jean van Leeuen describes as an *"unus simplex aspectus . . . which dissipates and reduces to nothing by the force of his look . . ."*[117]. St. John of the Cross uses the figure of "piercing"[118], and St. Teresa was pierced with a lance by the angel she saw in her vision. The figure of "piercing" then is one that mystical writers have used to describe a mystical experience. Ruysbroeck uses the expression "ibi est oculus contra oculum", while Gerlac describes such an encounter as "facies contra faciem"[119].

This *breakthrough* and *invasion* by God is not done for nothing. Such a rare intervention must have a great effect on the soul, and to this the author attests.

". . . and shew thee some of His privity, the which man may not, nor cannot speak. Then shalt thou feel thine affection inflamed with the fire of His love, far more than I can tell thee, or may or will at this time. For of that work, that falleth to only God, dare I not take upon me to speak with my blabbering fleshly tongue: and shortly to say, although I durst I would do not. But of that work that falleth to man when he feeleth him stirred and helped by grace, list me well tell thee: for therein is the less peril of the two"[120].

The effect that we are most interested in is the tremendous love of God that is aroused in the soul by this encounter with the Divine Presence. This is a safe guide as to the authenticity of the experience narrated by the author, for any other effect than this tremendous love of God would make the experience suspect. And it is this tremendous love that arouses the "deep ghostly sorrow" in the soul of the seer, but then such a

---

[115] *Encyclopedic Dictionary of the Bible*, (1963), Cols. 399-400; McKenzie. *Dictionary of the Bible*, (1966), p. 145; *Interpreter's Dictionary of the Bible*, Vol. I, p. 655.

[116] L. Reypens, "Connaissance Mystique de Dieu", *Dictionnaire De Spiritualité*, III, Col. 899.

[117] Ibid. III, Col. 910.

[118] St. John of the Cross, *Living Flame*, Allison-Peers, p. 39.

[119] L. Reypens, "Connaissance Mystique de Dieu", *Dictionnaire De Spiritualité*, III, Col. 911.

[120] *The Cloud*, Ch. 26, Underhill, p. 140; Hodgson, 62: 16-23.

revelation of "His Privity" cannot but have the effect of longing to be with Him.

We see the reticence and hesitation to speak of "His Privity" so characteristic of mystical writers. This is not sham modesty or humility, neither is it a denial of the reality of the experience. Rather, we see in this hesitation the inadequacy of language, as well as perfection of humility that would not speak of intimacies that others could not understand. God chose this particular soul, and it is to him alone that He revealed some of His secrets.

We have already noted the hesitation exhibited by St. John of the Cross. In another passage he tells us of the tremendous love for God produced by the experience[121]. And there is the lovely description by St. Paul of his encounter with the God-head, and his admission that he "heard things which must not and cannot be put into human language"[122].

We see the significance of this reticence as regards "His Privity" in greater relief when he contrasts it with "that work that fallest to man". To the end of helping his disciple in his ascent to God and Union in Love, the author wrote *The Cloud* and *Privy Counsel;* and it is our opinion that the *Epistle of Prayer, Knowing of Spirits* and *Discretion of Stirrings* were also written to the same disciple.

H. THE EXCELLENCE OF "THIS WORK"

After all that has been said about *The Cloud* and other treatises, it might seem unnecessary again to mention the excellence of "This Work". But we do so just the same, for the author went to great lengths to describe to his disciple the excellence of "This Work", seen in relation to the "worker" himself, to the rest of the world, and to God. The author's intention in stressing this excellence was to give courage and strength to the disciple, and when we consider that it is God

---

[121] "Of that breathing of God I should not wish to speak, neither do I desire now to speak; for I see clearly that I cannot say aught concerning it, and that, were I to speak of it, it would seem less than it is . . . the Holy Spirit has filled it with goodness and glory, wherein He has inspired it with a love for Himself which transcends all description and all sense, in the deep things of God. And for that reason I leave speaking of it here" (*Living Flame*, Allison-Peers, pp. 101-102). Cf. Walter Hilton, *Scale II*, Ch. 40, Underhill, p. 416.

[122] II Cor. 12: 4.

alone who initiates, sustains and perfects "This Work", we must expect it to have excellence without comparison.

This ascent and way to God has to do with the doing away of sin and the putting on of God. And so we see the excellence in relation to the "worker" himself as regards this aspect of the spiritual life. "This Work" has a devastating effect on sin.

"For this is only by itself that work that destroyeth the ground and the root of sin"[123].

And the purification of the soul is already accomplished in this life.

"For truly it is thy purgatory, and then when thy pain is all passed and thy devices be given of God, and graciously gotten in custom; then it is no doubt to me that thou art cleansed not only of sin, but also of the pain of sin"[124].

Now and again the author makes daring claims that would be considered presumptuous in one who did not profess to be blessed with the "special grace". And yet throughout, we see his abject humility and reticence to speak of the high things of God, and his consuming desire to attribute everything to Him.

"This Work" will have effects on both spirit and body.

"Whoso had this work, it should govern them full seemly, as well in body as in soul: and make them full favourable unto each man or woman that looked upon them. Insomuch, that the worst favoured man or woman that liveth in this life, an they might come by grace to work in this work, their favour should suddenly and graciously be changed: that each good man that them saw, should be fain and joyful to have them in company, and full much they should think that they were pleased in spirit and holpen by grace unto God in their presence"[125].

It is interesting to note this transforming quality of "This Work". The natural gifts of one so blessed are in a strange way transformed, so that those poorly endowed by nature become blessed by even more gifts than those richly endowed. And the effects of these gifts will be seen by others as a subtle change in the "worker".

"And yet peradventure, whoso looked upon thee should think

123 *The Cloud*, Ch. 12, Underhill, p. 97; Hodgson, 38: 15-16.
124 Ibid. Ch. 33, Underhill, p. 151; Hodgson, 67: 21-68: 1-3.
125 Ibid. Ch. 54, Underhill, p. 211; Hodgson, 100: 5-13.

thee full soberly disposed in thy body, without any changing of countenance; but sitting or going or lying or leaning or standing or kneeling, whether thou wert, in a full sober restfulness"[126].

One quality of "This Work" is that of "peace and great restfulness". And this quality is revealed to others with whom the worker comes into contact. This overflowing of interior graces is also noted by St. John of the Cross.

"For God bestows no favours upon the body without bestowing them first and principally upon the soul"[127].

A certain instinct results from this grace, which governs the soul in its various acts, spiritual and secular.

"Choose thee Him, and thou art silently speaking, and speakingly silent, fastingly eating, and eatingly fasting, and so forth of all the remenant"[128].

And the grace for "This Work" bears fruit for other people. The author employs the image of the human body, which later theologians describe as "The Mystical Body of Christ".

"For right as if a limb of our body feeleth sore, all the tother limbs be pained and diseased therefore, or if a limb fare well, all the remnant be gladded therewith-right so is it ghostly of all the limbs of Holy Church. For Christ is our head, and we be the limbs if we be in charity: and whoso will be a perfect disciple of Our Lord's, him behoveth strain up his spirit in this work ghostly, for the salvation of all his brethren and sisters in nature, as our Lord did His body on the Cross. And how? Not only for His friends and His kin and His homely lovers, but generally for all mankind, without any special beholding more to one than to another"[129].

And with the grace of "This Work" comes also an instinct for universal charity.

"But I say that he shall be made so virtuous and so charitable by the virtue of this work, that his will shall be afterwards, when he condescendeth to commune or to pray for his even—Christian—not from all this work, for that may not be without great sin, but from the height of this work, the which is speedful and needful to do some time as charity asketh—as specially

---

126 Ibid. Ch. 36, Underhill, p. 161; Hodgson, 73: 19-23.
127 *Living Flame*, Allison-Peers, p. 41.
128 *Discretion of Stirrings*, Gardner, pp. 107-108; Hodgson, 71: 26-72: 1-2.
129 *The Cloud*, Ch. 25, Underhill, pp. 136-137; Hodgson, 60: 22-61: 1-6.

then directed to his foe as to his friend, his stranger as his kin. Yea, and some time more to his foe than to his friend"[130].

The author finally summarizes the excellence of "This Work" in relation to heaven and earth, to time and eternity. It is easier to understand the feelings of those who object to the contemplative life when we consider its excellence only in relation to the perfection of the person himself, for indeed this is a matter that is "hidden with Christ in God". But when we see the effects of the contemplative life overflowing to the external world and the benefits, even materially, that accrue to other people because of the contemplative's intimacy with the Lord, then we appreciate the significance of the remark of the author that it is ignorance on the part of those who find fault with the contemplative that is the reason for their criticisms. And so we have a grand summing-up.

> "For one thing I tell thee, it is more profitable to the health of thy soul, more worthy in itself, and more pleasing to God and to all the saints and angels in heaven—yea, and more helpful to all thy friends, bodily and ghostly, quick and dead—such a blind stirring of love unto God for Himself, and such a privy pressing upon this cloud of unknowing, and better thee were for to have it and for to feel it in thine affection ghostly, than it is for to have the eyes of thy soul opened in contemplation or beholding of all the angels or saints in heaven or in hearing of all the mirth and the melody that is amongst them in bliss"[131].

There is one thing more to note as regards the excellence of "This Work". This is the effect of abject humility and profound charity that it produces in the person. Some may find it difficult to understand an effect at this level, but we can all recognize its manifestations of charity and humility of such depth that the soul looks more to its own failings than to those of others. We see the soul of the author revealed in the lovely lines, worth quoting again.

> "And also when I think on mine innumerable defaults, the which I have made myself before this time in words and deeds for default of knowing, me thinketh then if I would be had excused of God for mine ignorant defaults, that I should charitably and piteously have other men's ignorant words and deeds always excused. And surely else, do I not to others as I would they did to me"[132].

130 Ibid. Ch. 25, Underhill, p. 135; Hodgson, 59: 19-60: 1-6.
131 Ibid. Ch. 9, Underhill, pp. 89-90; Hodgson, 34: 5-14.
132 Ibid. Ch. 19, Underhill, pp. 119-120; Hodgson, 51: 2-8.

But the depth of this profound charity and humility does not stop there. He looks into himself and recognizes the faults, but does not become involved with them. For to be concerned only with oneself may result in pride or self-pity. So a glance is enough, then the gaze is lifted up to God, his Strength. We see the significance of his message of heroic hope.

"For not what thou art, nor what thou hast been, beholdeth God with His merciful eyes; but that thou wouldest be"[133].

GENERAL CONCLUSIONS

In Chapter VI of this dissertation we reached the state of "the cloud of unknowing", the end and term of "This Work" which the unknown author of the 14th century teaches. "This Work" is an ascent and a way to God, a union in love, which includes the whole process from the time God chooses a soul. The author uses the figure of "the cloud" in two ways, as a covering or "forgetting" of all creatures, and as an obstruction which must always be present between God and the soul. For in this life there must always be this veil to hide God from the soul, and the author qualifies his union with God by the expression "as may be in this life". He calls the "cloud" that covers creatures "the cloud of forgetting" and the "cloud" that hides God, "the cloud of unknowing". Although he gives detailed descriptions of these "two clouds", there is actually a desire to arrive at extreme unity, simplicity, intensity and concentration of the perfection of "This Work". So the author identifies the various terms "the cloud of unknowing", "the short prayer of the perfect worker", "deep ghostly sorrow", "chaste love", and "desire" with the perfection of "This Work", all of which mean a certain "Presence of God". He means by this the "Place where God was", as in the story of Moses and his encounter with Jahweh. All these descriptive terms are summed up in the word "IS", which is the Name most proper to God and which also sums up the Divine Essence. It is this consideration which puts *The Cloud* author within the tradition of the *Mystics of the Divine Essence*.

133 Ibid. Ch. 75, Underhill, p. 269; Hodgson, 132: 19-20.

Seen in its historical context we noted that *The Cloud* was written when the rumblings of dissent seemed distant, although it is possible that the passages on the pride of the intellect refer to Wycliffe and his followers. We noted that the terms "ordinary and extraordinary" prayer were not known at the time of *The Cloud* although, in fact, the distinctions between them where known and used by the author.

In relation to his contemporaries in the field of English spiritual writings, we noted that the author of *The Cloud* was a mystic, and that his teaching reaches the heights of the mystical life, right up to the *direct and personal intervention* and *invasion* of the soul by God. In this connection, judged only by his writings, we do not believe that Walter Hilton was a mystic. On the other hand Mother Julian of Norwich and John Whiterig, the Monk of Farne, were mystics. Richard Rolle did not reach this level.

Having considered many parallel passages from *The Cloud* group and writings included in the Hilton canon, we have shown our preference for Walter Hilton as the author of *The Cloud*. However, the present writer does not claim to be a mediaevalist, the considerations having been made from a theological viewpoint, which has not been done so extensively before. It is our hope that this study will throw some light on the authorship question of *The Cloud*, and pave the way for future detailed studies.

We have compared the teaching of *The Cloud* author with similar passages from St. John of the Cross and other mystical writers, but this has been done only to show the orthodoxy of the teaching of "This Work". We have preferred not to judge *The Cloud* by the categories of St. John of the Cross, for who can appreciate the realities contained in their intimate experiences of the Godhead?

No one author exclusively influenced the author of *The Cloud*. We have noted that the Pseudo-Dionysius, St. Augustine, St. Bernard, Richard of St. Victor and Thomas Gallus have been the principal figures regarding the primacy of the will and love in the teaching of "This Work". And whilst we acknowledge that the inspiration of *The Cloud* is Dionysian, it is not specifically so in the sense that "This Work" is the "Via Negativa" of the Pseudo-Dionysius.

It has been said that the mystics were products of their age. But their influence reaches far beyond that period; the timeless element of their lives and teaching comes down to us, and has a relevance for all time and for all peoples. We have noted the exclusiveness of "This Work", as well as the necessity of a "special call" from God, but *The Cloud* has great value for its general edification of the spirit. The message of *The Cloud* that has universal relevance is one of courage and perseverance once God has made known a particular way. That He should call one in preference to another is not for us to question.

The God Who gave His Name as "IS" to Moses is likewise the God of Abraham, of Isaac and of Jacob. He is therefore a Living God and this is the relevance of *The Cloud* teaching to the world of the 20th century.

And in this age of Ecumenism and Dialogue we can perhaps learn from the way the author approaches problems in the spiritual life. His flexibility of character in those things where vital issues are not concerned, and his overriding and profound humility and charity, will help us to devote our attention to things that unite, rather than to those which irritate or destroy. Certainly the two virtues on which he places such store, humility and charity, could help us solve many problems of the modern world.

It is clear from the texts of *The Cloud* and other treatises that the author was narrating a personal experience. It is the reality of this experience that has relevance for us, especially in these times of widespread disbelief and doubt.

It was in the 14th century that the author of *The Cloud* described his encounter with God. Like our own, this was a century of transition, uncertainty and fear, which in a sense gives the teaching a particular relevance for us. Not that we must expect similar experiences to those recounted by the author but a fuller understanding of *The Cloud* may awaken in our minds and hearts a faith and trust in *This Transcending God*, Who remains the Master of our own times as He was six hundred years ago.

BIBLIOGRAPHY

Editions of *The Cloud of Unknowing* and Minor Treatises attributable to the same Author

Colledge, E. *The Mediaeval Mystics of England*. Edited with an Introduction. Contains *The Book of Privy Counsel*, New York, 1961, London, 1962. (A modernized version).

Collins, H. *The Divine Cloud* (with notes and a preface by Father Augustine Baker), London, 1871. (A modernized version).

Gardner, J. E. G. *The Cell of Self-Knowledge*, Edited with an Introduction and Notes. (contains *Benjamin Minor, Epistle of Prayer, Epistle of Discretion in Stirrings, Of Discerning of Spirits*, modernized from Pepwell's edition of 1521), London, 1910. (A good and reliable translation of the above Treatises).

Hodgson, P. *The Cloud of Unknowing* (contains also *The Book of Privy Counselling*), E.E.T.S. No. 218, London 1958. (A middle English text).

Hodgson, P. *Deonise Hid Diuinite,* (contains also *A Tretyse of The Stodye of Wysdome That Men Clepen Beniamyn, A Pistle of Preier, A Pistle of Discrecioun of Stirrings, A Tretis of Discrescyon of Spirites*), E.E.T.S. No. 231, London, 1958. (A middle English text).

Horstman, C. *Yorkshire Writers, Richard Rolle of Hampole and His Followers* (contains *Benjamin Minor*, vol. i, pp. 162 ff.), London, 1895. (A middle English text).

Ivanka, E. von *Die Wolke Des Nichtwissens*, Einsiedeln, 1958. (A modernized version).

McCann, Abbot J. *The Cloud of Unknowing* (contains also *The Epistle of Privy Counsel, Denis Hid Divinity*, and a commentary on *The Cloud* by Father Augustine Baker), London, 1924, 1936, Fifth Edition, 1947, Sixth and Revised edition, 1952). (A good and reliable translation).
The Cloud of Unknowing (contains *The Epistle of Privy Counsel*), London, Golden Library Edition, 1964. (A good and reliable translation).

Noetinger, Dom M. *Le Nuage de l'Inconnaissance* (contains also *Epître sur la Prière, Epître sur la Discretion, Traité sur le Discernement des Esprits, Epître de la Direction Intime*), Tours 1925.

Pepwell, H. *Benjamin Minor, The Epistle of Prayer, The Epistle of Discretion in Stirrings, Of Discerning of Spirits* are contained in a quarto printed by Pepwell in 1521.

Progoff, I. *The Cloud of Unknowing,* London, 1959. (A very free translation).

Underhill, E. *The Cloud of Unknowing,* London, 1912, 1922, 1934, 1946, 1950, 1956, 1960. (A good and reliable translation).

Walsh, J. *A Letter of Private Direction,* London, 1965.
"A Letter on Prayer", *The Way,* Spring, 1967, pp. 156-162.
"A Letter on the Discernment of Spiritual Impulses", *The Way,* Summer 1967, pp. 240-248. (Modernized versions).

Wolters, C. *The Cloud of Unknowing,* London, 1961. (A very free translation).

Anon. *The Cloud of Unknowing* (an interpretation written at Pendle Hill, Wallingford, Pennsylvania), published by Harper & Bros., New York and London, 1948. (A free modernized version).

The Works of Walter Hilton

Colledge, E. *The Mediaeval Mystics of England.* Edited with an Introduction. Contains excerpts from Books I and II of *The Scale of Perfection,* New York, 1961. London, 1962.

Gardner, J. E. G. *The Cell of Self-Knowledge.* Edited with an Introduction and Notes (contains *The Song of Angels*), London, 1910.

Jones, D. *Minor Works of Walter Hilton,* London, 1929.

Kirchberger, C. *The Goad of Love,* edited from manuscripts with an Introduction, London, 1951.

Russell-Smith, J. *"A Letter to a Hermit",* *The Way,* July, 1966, pp. 230-241.

Sitwell, Dom G. *The Scale of Perfection,* London, 1953.

Underhill, E. *The Scale of Perfection,* London, 1923, 1948.

Works on *The Cloud of Unknowing* and other spiritual writers of the fourteenth century in England

Allen, H. E. *Writings Ascribed to Richard Rolle,* The Modern Language Association of America, Monograph Series, III, New York, 1927.
English Writings of Richard Rolle, Oxford, 1931.

Bullett, G. *The English Mystics,* London, 1950.

Coleman, T. W. *English Mystics of the Fourteenth Century,* London, 1938.

Colledge, E. *The Mediaeval Mystics of England,* New York, 1961, London, 1962.
"Recent Work on Walter Hilton", *Blackfriars,* June, 1956.
Review of "The Mysticism of The Cloud of Unknowing", in *Clergy Review,* September 1968.

Davis, C. *English Spiritual Writers,* London, 1961.

Elwin, H. V. H. *Christian Dhyana: or Prayer of Loving Regard. A Study of the Cloud of Unknowing,* London, 1930.

Fairweather, W., *Among the Mystics,* Edinburgh 1936.

Gardner, H. "Walter Hilton and the Authorship of the Cloud of Unknowing", *Review of English Studies,* Vol. IX, No. 23, April, 1933, pp. 129-147.
"Review of the Cloud of Unknowing". *Medium Aevum,* Vol. XVI, 1947, pp. 36-42.

"The Text of the Scale", *Medium Aevum,* V, 1936.

"Walter Hilton and the Mystical Tradition in England", *Essays and Studies,* XXII, 1937.

Graef, H. C. *Mystics of our Times,* London, 1962.
The Light and the Rainbow, London, 1959.

Hodgson, P. "Walter Hilton and the Cloud of Unknowing. A Problem of Authorship Reconsidered", *Modern Language Review,* Vol. No. 4, October, 1955, pp. 395-406.
Three 14th-Century English Mystics, London, 1967.
Review of *The Mediaeval Mystics of England,* in *Modern Language Review,* Vol. 58 (1963), pp. 88-89.

Hort, G. *Sense and Thought,* A Study in Mysticism, London, 1936.

Hughes, A. C. *Walter Hilton's Direction to Contemplatives,* Rome: Gregorian University Press, 1962.

Inge, W. R. *Studies of English Mystics,* London, 1906.

Johnston, W. *The Mysticism of the Cloud of Unknowing,* New York, Rome, Tournai, Paris, 1967.

Journet, C. *The Dark Knowledge of God,* Translated by James F. Anderson, London, 1948.

Kirchberger, C. *The Coasts of the Country,* Chicago, London, 1952.

Knowles, Dom D. "The Excellence of the Cloud", *The Down-*

side Review, Vol. LII, January, 1934, pp. 71-92.

The English Mystical Tradition, New York, 1961, London, 1964.

The English Mystics, London, 1927.

"Prayer of Great Simplicity", A review of "The Mysticism of The Cloud of Unknowing" by William Johnston, *The Tablet*, Jan. 20, 1968.

What Is Mysticism? London, 1967.

Lawlor, J. Review of *"The English Mystical Tradition"* in *Modern Language Review*, Vol. 56 (1961), pp. 574-575.

McCann, Abbot J. "The Cloud of Unknowing", *Ampleforth Journal*, Summer, 1924, pp. 192-197.

M'Intyre, D. M. "The Cloud of Unknowing", *Expositor*, 7th Series, No. 22, IV, October, 1907, pp. 373-384.

McLaughlin, B. "The Cloud of Unknowing", *Ampleforth Journal*, Spring, 1925, pp. 88-94.

Milosh, J. *The Scale of Perfection and the English Mystical Tradition*, Madison, Milwaukee, London, 1966.

Molinari, P. *Julian of Norwich*, London, 1958.

Noetinger, D. M. "The Authorship of the Cloud of Unknowing", *Blackfriars*, March, 1924, pp. 1457-1464.

Pepler, C. "On Reading the Mystics", *The Life of the Spirit*, Supplement II (July 1945) to *Blackfriars*, Vol. XXVI, 1947, pp. 88-92. (An article review of *The Cloud*). Articles on "The Way of Perfection" in the English Mystics appeared in *The Life of the Spirit*, Oxford, 1946-56: Vols. I, II, III, IV, V, X.

The English Religious Heritage, London, 1958.

Renaudin, P. *Mystiques Anglais*, Aubier, Editions Montaigne, 1954.

Robbins, R. H. Article-review of "Deonise Hid Diuinite", *Speculum*, Vol. XXXII, 1957, pp. 406-410.

Russell-Smith, J. "Walter Hilton", *The Month*, September, 1959, New Series, Vol. 22, No. 3, pp. 133-148.

"Decline of Mysticism", *The Catholic Herald*, No. 3746, Friday, January 17, 1958, p. 2.

Review of "The English Mystical Tradition", *Blackfriars*, September, 1961, pp. 386-389.

Review of *"Deonise Hid Diuinite* and Other Treatises on Contemplative Prayer related to *The Cloud of Unknowing"*, in *English Studies*, Vol. 41 (1960), pp. 261-267.

Sitwell, Dom G. "Contemplation in The Scale of Perfection",

The Downside Review, Summer, 1949, pp. 276-290. Winter, 1949/50, pp. 21-34, Summer, 1950, pp. 271-289.

Review of *"The Mediaeval Mystics of England"* in *Medium Aevum*, Vol. 32 (1963) pp. 145-146.

Review of "Deonise Hid Diuinite", in *Medium Aevum*, Vol. 25 (1956) pp. 110-112.

Sudbrack, J. Review of "The Mysticism of the Cloud of Unknowing" by W. Johnston, in *Geist und Leben*, October, 1968, pp. 396-397.

Review of "Glaube und Erfahrung" (The Scale of Perfection) Translated into German by Hans Urs V. Balthasar, in *Geist und Leben*, October, 1968, p. 397.

Underhill, E. *The Mystics of the Church*, London, 1925.

Mixed Pasture, London, 1933.

Walsh, J. "The Cloud of Unknowing", *The Month*, December, 1963, pp. 325-336.

Pre-Reformation English Spirituality, (Ed.) London, 1966.

White, H. V. *Review of the "English Mystical Tradition"*, and *"The Mediaeval Mystics of England"*. New York in *Speculum*, Vol. 37, (1962) pp. 447-448.

Woolf, R. Review of "The Mediaeval Mystics of England", in *Review of English Studies*, N.S. 15 (1964) pp. 64-65.

Works Used and Consulted

Abbott, W. *The Documents of Vatican II*, London, 1967.

Adolfs, R. *The Graves of God*, London, 1967.

Aquinas, St. Thomas, *On Prayer and the Contemplative Life*, Edited by Rev. Hugh Pope, London, 1914.

Baker, A. *Holy Wisdom*, London, 1964.

Benigar, A. *Compendium Theologiae Spiritualis*, Rome, 1959.

Bonhoeffer, D. *Letters and Papers From Prison*, London, 1964.

Butler, C. *Western Mysticism*, London, Gray Arrow Edition, 1960. The 1967 Edition contains a new Introduction by Professor Dom David Knowles, O.S.B.

Mystical Books and Books on Mysticism, 1911. Reprinted from *Downside Review* for March 21, 1911.

Buttrick, G. A. *The Interpreter's Dictionary of the Bible*, Vol. I and III, New York, 1962.

Callus, D. A. "An Unknown Commentary of Thomas Gallus on the Pseudo-Dionysian Letters", *Dominican Studies*, 1948, pp. 58-67.

The Condemnation of St. Thomas at Oxford, Blackfriars, 1955.

Chapman, Dom J. "Mysticism" *Encyclopedia of Religion and Ethics,* Edinburgh and New York, 1917.
The Spiritual Letters, London, 1935.

Clay, R. M. *Hermits and Anchorites of England,* London, 1914.
"Further Studies on Mediaeval Recluses", *Journal of the British Archaeological Association,* 3rd Series, Vol. XVI, 1953.

Congar, Y. M. *The Mystery of the Temple,* London, 1962.

Cunliffe, C. R. A. "The Divine Name of Yahweh", *Scripture,* April, 1954, No. 4.

Darwin, F. D. S. *The English Mediaeval Recluse,* London, 1944.

Dawson, C. H. *Mediaeval Essays,* London, 1953.

Deanesly, M. *A History of the Mediaeval Church,* London, 1954.
"Vernacular Books in the Fourteenth and Fifteenth Centuries", *Modern Language Review,* Vol. XV, No. 4, October, 1920, pp. 349-358.

Dumeige, G. *Notae de Historia Spiritualitatis in Aetate Patristica,* Romae, 1963.

Emden, A. E. *A Biographical Register of the University of Oxford to A.D.* 1500, Oxford, 1957.
A Biographical Register of the University of Cambridge to 1500, Cambridge, 1963.

Enciclopedia Cattolica, Citta Del Vaticano, 1949, Vol. 3.

Gilson, E. *God and Philosophy,* Yale 1966.
The Spirit of Mediaeval Philosophy, London, 1950.

Farmer, H. "Meditationes" *Studia Anselmiana,* Fasc. 41, Rome, 1957;
The Monk of Farne, London, 1961.

Häring, B. *The Law of Christ,* Translated by Edwin G. Kaiser, Cork, 1962.

Hartman, L. F. *Encyclopedic Dictionary of the Bible,* New York, 1963.

Hodgson, G. E. *The Form of Perfect Living,* London, 1910.
English Mystics, London, 1922.

Hodgson, P. "Dionysius the Areopagite and the Christian

Mystical Tradition", *Contemporary Review,* Nov. 1949, pp. 281-285.

Horstman, C. *Library of Early English Writers,* London, 1895.

Inge, W. R. *Christian Mysticism,* London: Anglican Evangelical Group Movement Pamphlet, No. 20, 1924.
Christian Mysticism, Seventh Edition, London, 1933.
The Awakening of the Soul, London, 1959.
Personal Idealism and Mysticism, London, New York, Toronto, Bombay, Calcutta and Madras, 1924.
Mysticism in Religion, London, New York, Melbourne, Sydney, Cape Town, 1947.

James, W. *The Varieties of Religious Experience,* New York, 1963.

St. John of the Cross, *Complete Works.* Edited by E. Allison Peers, Three-Vols.-in-One, London, 1964.

Kirchberger, R. *Richard of Saint Victor. Selected Writings on Contemplation,* London, 1957.

Langland, W. *Piers the Plowman,* Edited by Rev. W. Skeat, Oxford, 10th Edition, 1965.

Marechal, J. *Studies in the Psychology of the Mystics,* Translated by A. Thorold, London, 1927.

McFarlane, K. B. *John Wycliffe and the Beginnings of English Non-Conformity,* London, 1952.

McKenzie, J. L. *Dictionary of the Bible,* London-Dublin, 1965.

McKisack, M. *The Fourteenth Century,* 1307-1399, Oxford, 1963.

Migne, J. P. *Patrologiae Cursus Completus,* Tomus CXCVI, Series Latina Prior, Paris, 1880.
Patrologiae Cursus Completus, Series Graeca, Tom. 44. S. Gregorius Nyssenus, Paris, 1858.

Noth, M. *Exodus,* London, 1962.

O'Rourke, W. "Moses and The Prophetic Vocation", *Scripture,* April, 1963, No. 30.

Pantin, W. A. *The English Church in the Fourteenth Century,* Cambridge, 1955.

Pepler, C. *The Three Degrees, A Study of Christian Mysticism,* London, 1957.

Plastaras, J. *The God of Exodus,* Milwaukee, 1966.

Poulain, A. *The Graces of Interior Prayer,* Revised and

Corrected to accord with the Tenth French Edition, London, 1957.

Reypens, L. "Connaissance Mystique De Dieu", in *Dictionnaire de Spiritualité*, Tome III, Paris, 1967.

Robinson, J. *Honest to God*, London, 1967.
The Honest to God Debate, London, 1963.

Rolt, C. E. *Dionysius the Areopagite on the Divine Names and the Mystical Theology*, London, 1957.

Royo-Marín, A. Teología de la Perfección Christiana, Madrid, 1962.

Tanquerey, A. *The Spiritual Life*, Translated by Herman Branderis, 2nd Rev. Edition, Tournai, 1930.

St. Teresa of Avila, *Complete Works*, Translated and Edited by E. Allison Peers, London, 1963.

Thils, G. *Christian Holiness*, Tielt, Belgium, 1961.

Underhill, E. *Mysticism*, London, 1962.
Medieval Mysticism, The Cambridge Medieval History, Vol. VIII, 1932.

Vandenbroucke, F. *The Spirituality of the Middle Ages*, London, 1968.

INDEX

References to "This Work" are so numerous that only particular ideas
and phrases are given page numbers. The *Saints* are grouped under *ST*.
Characteristic words and phrases which may be considered personal to
The Cloud author are placed in quotation marks.

DATE DUE